From

The Women's Press Ltd
34 Great Sutton Street, London EC1V 0DX

Cheryl Buckley was born in Havercroft, a small mining village in West Yorkshire in 1956. She studied art history at the University of East Anglia during 1974–77, followed by post-graduate research at the University of Newcastle upon Tyne. Since 1980 she has worked as a full-time lecturer at Newcastle Polytechnic teaching both practical design students and art and design history students. She is now Course Leader of the BA (Hons) degree in History of Modern Art, Design and Film in the Department of Historical and Critical Studies. Her doctoral thesis, 'Women Pottery Designers 1914–40', is nearing completion from the University of East Anglia.

CHERYL BUCKLEY

■

Potters and Paintresses

Women designers in the pottery industry
1870–1955

The Women's Press

To my parents and to Allan

First published by The Women's Press 1990
A member of the Namara Group
34 Great Sutton Street, London EC1 0DX

British Library Cataloguing in Publication Data
Buckley, Cheryl
Potters and paintresses: women designers in the pottery industry,
1870–1955.
1. Pottery industries. Women personnel, 1870–1955
I. Title
738.3'092'2

ISBN 0–7043–4211–1

Typeset by Input Typesetting Ltd, London
Printed and bound in Great Britain by
BPCC Hazell Books
Aylesbury, Bucks, England, Member of BPCC Ltd.

Contents

Picture Sources

Figures 1, 2, 3, 5, 6, 7, 28, 32, 34, 38, 39, 46, 51, 68, 90 copyright: Trustees of the Wedgwood Museum, Barlaston, Staffordshire.

Figures 4, 62, 63, 64, 66, 67, 87, 88, 89 copyright: private collections.

Figures 8, 9, 10, 11, 12, 13, 14, 15, 17, 20, 21, 22, 23, 24, 25, 26, 27, 77, 78, 79, 80, 81, 82, 83, 84, 85, 86 copyright: Royal Doulton Ltd.

Figure 16 copyright: Phillips Fine Art Auctioneers.

Figures 18, 19 copyright: Richard Dennis, *Doulton Catalogue Parts I and II.*

Figures 29, 31, 33, 35, 36, 45, 48 copyright: Richard Dennis, *Wedgwood Ceramics 1846–1959.*

Figures 30, 37, 43, 44, 47, 49, 50, 60, 61, 65, 69, 75, 76, 91, 92, 93, 94 copyright: the author.

Figure 40 copyright: used with the permission of the Trustees of the Victoria and Albert Museum, London.

Figures 41, 42, 70, 71, 72, 73, 74 copyright: Stoke-on-Trent City Museum and Art Gallery.

Figures 52, 53, 54, 55, 56, 57, 58, 59 copyright: B. Bumpus.

Acknowledgments

Many individuals and organisations have helped in the research and preparation of this book. These include Lynn Miller, Sharon Gater and Gaye Blake Roberts at The Wedgwood Museum; Pat Halfpenny and Kathy Niblett at the City Museum and Art Gallery, Stoke-on-Trent; the Gladstone Pottery Museum, Longton; Susie Cooper, Star Wright, Joan Crossley-Holland, Jessie Hazlehurst, Anita Hoy, Freda Hulme, Peggy Davies, Moira Forsyth, Tony Van Hallen, Grete and Harold Marks, May Lindsay, Ken and Doris Gleaves, Ada Haynes, the paintresses from A. E. Gray, Jacqui Sarsby, Marguerite Dupree, Frank Burchill, Richard Whipp, the Ceramic and Allied Trade Union, Hilda Salt, Ethel Hood, Desmond Eyles, Louise Irvine, Maureen Batkin, Isabelle Anscombe, John Houston, Barley Roscoe, Anne Eatwell and Jennifer Opie at the Victoria and Albert Museum. I especially want to thank my friends and colleagues for their help, particularly Jane Beckett, Deborah Cherry, Lynne Walker, Allan Cassidy and, finally, Heather Stewart for reading and commenting on my manuscript.

INTRODUCTION

▪

Women, Design History and the Pottery Industry

Between 1870 and 1955 women made a substantial contribution to the British pottery industry. Representing half the workforce, they occupied a variety of skilled and unskilled jobs. Most laboured as unskilled assistants to skilled men, while a few, such as the women designers and paintresses,[1] – the 'noblesse of the potbanks' – enjoyed relative autonomy from men and the enhanced working conditions and pay attached to skilled work. At all levels they confronted and challenged patriarchal working practices to secure their jobs. This book is an account of the role of women designers in the pottery industry during that period. While the history of pottery design and manufacture is now well documented, the history of this group of women is not. In fact, it is only in the last few years that some of their names have gained greater currency, mainly through pottery collectors who have not been deterred by the gender of the designer.

My own starting point was different from theirs in that my priority was not to date and categorise pottery. Instead, I wanted to demonstrate that women worked successfully as designers in the pottery industry but were often constrained by a narrow definition of appropriate gender roles. My aim, then, has been to explain *why* and *how* women designed rather than to provide a detailed description of *what* they designed.[2] I have traced the lives and work of little-known women in order to construct a history of design which shows how women's opportunities in the industry and their designs for pottery were formulated within specific cultural, political, social and economic conditions in this period. At the same time, I have highlighted the difficulties encountered by historians who attempt to slot these women into design history as it now stands.

1

As we shall see, this relatively recent academic discipline is underpinned by patriarchal assumptions that serve to devalue, marginalise and exclude women's contribution to design.

Historically, women have been involved with design in a variety of ways. They have worked as designers of fashion, textiles, furniture, buildings, graphics, industrial products, as well as pottery. They have been involved with design not only as designers, but also as consumers of design; they have selected, bought and used design products. Advertising has represented and reinforced their role as consumers. Their needs and desires have been articulated and contructed through a plethora of advertising images. But what has been written about this?

With a few notable exceptions, not much![3] Historians of design, like their counterparts in other disciplines, have not paid particular attention to women. This is no accident. Women have been marginalised and devalued in history in the same way that they have been in society at large. This has been so systematic, and the occasional acknowledgment of their achievements so partial, that an inherent bias in the definition of what constitutes history and what is important in society must be assumed.[4] The ground-rules of history which define the criteria for the selection, classification and prioritisation of types of design, categories of designers, distinct styles and periods and different modes of production are shaped within patriarchy.[5] While acting as barriers to women, these qualifying rules maintain and enhance the power and status of men. Even the few women who are deemed worthy of inclusion in the design history books are described within a patriarchal framework. They are 'token' men, they are adjuncts to their husbands, lovers, brothers or fathers, or they are defined by their gender as designers or consumers of 'feminine' products.[6]

Patriarchy historically has defined women's relationship to design in the same way that it has circumscribed their roles in society at large.[7] This has been achieved through a combination of psychological, economic, social and political means. Specific social roles and occupations, as well as a physical and intellectual ideal, have been laid down for women: these were modified according to class position, but they still represented an attempt to locate women firmly in the home, in a separate sphere from that of men whose activities were public and professional.[8]

Ideas about the appropriateness of certain types of design for women were delineated within patriarchy, although these changed as women challenged and redefined their positions within society. Women's design abilities were described as 'natural' or innate, a product of their biological sex. Consequently, they were considered to possess gender-specific skills, to be dextrous, decorative, delicate and meticulous. Between 1870 and 1955 these perceptions underwent some modification, although it was still firmly believed that women were inherently suited to certain areas of design.[9] These were the so-called 'minor', 'applied' or 'decorative' arts whose title betrays their inferior status in the artistic hierarchy.[10]

The decorative arts included design activities such as jewellery, embroidery, graphic illustration, printed, woven and knitted textiles, fashion and pottery. Linking all these activities together was the notion that they were inherently female; either the resultant design products were decorative and worn or used by women, or they were produced by them for an essentially domestic purpose. Pottery design fell into both categories. Ornamental wares were primarily decorative and often bought for display within the home, while a substantial amount of tableware production was for the domestic market with decoration applied to add prestige and value. Women's relationship to pottery design was articulated within this context. In the 1870s their involvement in pottery design was explained by their apparent facility as women to produce beautiful objects for the home. In the 1930s it was agreed that women designers were well suited to the design of domestic tableware because they had an intuitive understanding of domestic matters. In both the nineteenth and twentieth centuries, nurseryware design was thought more appropriate for women as a result of a crude form of biological determinism that connected them to children. Both Mabel Lucie Atwell at the Shelley Potteries and Barbara Vernon Bailey, who was responsible for the 'Bunnykin' range at Royal Doulton, were noted for nurseryware.

Men were not excluded from these areas of design production, although their products required re-evaluation. Dressmaking, for example, was traditionally women's work. It was thought to be quintessentially 'feminine' as it catered for what was supposed to be an intrinsic desire to decorate and a preoccupation with appearance. Fashion design, however, was appropriated by male designers who assumed the persona of genius. It is claimed that the first *haut couturier* was Charles Frederick Worth under whose influence the fashion design process transcended the sex-specific skills of dexterity, patience and decorativeness associated with dressmaking. Instead, it was elevated to the status of high art and required the aggressive business and marketing skills which were, and still are, embodied in the male stereotype.[11]

The definition of women's design skills in terms of biology was reinforced by socially constructed notions of 'masculine' and 'feminine' which assigned different characteristics to men and women. Sonia Delaunay, the designer and painter, is noted by historians for her *instinctive feeling for colour*, whereas her husband, Robert, is attributed with having *formulated a colour theory*. Robert Delaunay embodies the male stereotype as logical and intellectual, while Sonia embodies the female stereotype as instinctive and emotional. In pottery design, certain types of pattern, the intricate and those that used soft, subtle colour combinations, were thought to be 'feminine', and ultimately an expression of women's nature.[12]

In the pottery industry, opportunities for women designers have been circumscribed by this process of tying design skills to gender. Women have been cast primarily in the role of designers of decorative surface pattern rather than designers of pottery shapes.[13] Dominant perceptions of women's artistic abilities persuaded pottery manufacturers that women were best suited to the design of two-dimensional decoration. Detailed and complex patterns for the beautification and embellishment of domestic products were thought to accord with women's innate sensibilities. In contrast it was assumed that men were better able to conceptualise the three-dimensional form of pottery shapes than women.

This gender distinction in pottery design was reinforced by a sexual division of labour in the production process. Such a division of labour has been defined as 'the underpinning of sexual subcultures in which men and women experience life differently: it is the material base of male power'.[14] In the pottery industry, the sexual division of labour was carried out on the basis of perceived 'masculine' and 'feminine' skills. Women workers predominated in the decorating stages of the production process, while men predominated in the forming stages of production. Overlying this sexual division was a demarcation of jobs based on craft which distinguished skilled from unskilled work. Men monopolised skilled jobs and controlled access to these through the apprenticeship system. The net result of these labour divisions was a hierarchical industrial structure with skilled men at the top and unskilled women at the bottom.

The majority of women in the pottery industry worked in

4

unskilled jobs and as assistants to skilled men. Most semi-skilled and skilled women's work was found in the decorating stages of the production process, although by the end of the nineteenth century women were beginning to find work as semi-skilled makers of ware in the forming sections. Decorating included enamelling, groundlaying, tube-lining, gilding, banding, aerographing and free-hand painting. Design was the most prestigious form of skilled work for women, while free-hand painting could lead to promotion as a designer. Women's access to skilled decorating work was primarily determined by class position and educational background. Most women designers in the pottery industry between 1870 and 1955 were from middle-class families and benefited from art school training. Even the paintresses usually had the advantages of some type of formal design education, if only from evening classes.[15]

Powerful trade unions maintained and reinforced the craft and gender-based labour divisions between 1870 and 1955. However, these were not static but in a state of flux for a number of reasons. First, women's struggles for social and economic freedom served to highlight the issue of their labour rights and claims for better opportunities. New technology began to undermine the traditional craft power-base of the pottery trade unions, whose role had to change. The disruption to labour during two world wars resulted in women working in jobs previously the preserve of men. Also significant were the labour demands of capitalism that encouraged the exploitation of women as cheap labour, but at the same time led to new opportunities for semi-skilled machine operators in the forming stages of production. These machines de-skilled work that had previously been done by craftsmen and brought women operators into conflict with men who were keen to protect their traditional position. Nevertheless, these new jobs provided women with better pay and served to break down the sexual division of labour.

The women designers in the pottery industry between 1870 and 1955 designed domestic tableware and ornamental ware for both export and home markets and in this they were confined mainly to the design of decoration. Like other designers at the time, they used a variety of historical and modern styles, and like their male counterparts, they worked for both large and small pottery manufacturers. Their designs varied a great deal as popular taste and fashionable styles became bewilderingly diverse, covering the full spectrum from Regency to Modernist. Developments in technology and the introduction of new bodies and decorating techniques created immense possibilities for design, although traditional processes remained central to much pottery manufacture. At the same time, the vagaries of economic growth and the threat of foreign competition affected the design and marketing of pottery.

In the 1870s women designers such as Hannah Barlow, Helen Miles and Eliza Simmance came to prominence in the art pottery studios of Minton, Doulton and Wedgwood. These women designed decoration for salt-glazed stoneware and the new bodies invented by entrepreneurial Victorian potters. The employment of middle-class women in respectable, segregated studios provided a solution to one of the problems facing widowed or unmarried women without an income: that of making a living without threatening their status as ladies through contact with the commercial world. At an amateur level, women china painters decorated and exhibited pottery which exemplified the Victorian 'feminine' ideal of tireless industry, patience and dexterity, but which at the same time did not pose a serious challenge to the masculine world of 'high' art.

Other opportunities for women designers emerged within the context of the Arts and Crafts Movement in the late nineteenth century. In response to the theory and practice of the movement, the pottery industry established hand-painting sections. These offered openings for paintresses and women designers such as Louise Powell and Grace Barnsley who were keen to use craft decorating methods within an industrial context. As a result, traditional patterns and ornamental techniques were revived and put back into production. Another consequence of the Arts and Crafts Movement was the establishment of small independent art potteries such as the Royal Lancastrian pottery which employed the designer Gwladys M. Rogers. Like other art potters, she was interested in craft production methods and the design of both form and decoration. This unity of pottery shape and surface pattern, of design and production, was reinforced a few years later by the work of studio potters such as Katherine Pleydell-Bouverie. She provided a positive example to those women who were determined to challenge the stereotype of women designers as 'natural' decorators.

The interest in hand painting encouraged many women to train first as paintresses and then as designers in the reorganised art schools of Stoke-on-Trent. Some companies established hand-painting studios of their own and several of the studio-trained women went on to work in a variety of roles in the pottery industry: Grete Marks worked as a freelance designer; Millie Taplin and Freda

Beardmore were company designers; Susie Cooper was an independent designer and manufacturer; Clarice Cliff was an art director; and later in the 1930s, Agnete Hoy was employed by Bullers and at Doulton's Lambeth factory as a designer in a Scandinavian-style craft studio. Their designs were developed in response to the challenges of the time; they were keen to combine art and industry to produce moderately priced wares for the changing market.

This largely middle-class group of women enjoyed and utilised the political and social freedoms won by their sex in 1918 and 1928. To a large extent they established the right of other women to work as designers in the post-war pottery industry. Several women who had trained before the war, among them Jessie Tait and Peggy Davies, were engaged as designers by Midwinter and Royal Doulton, while others, such as Susie Cooper, re-established businesses which had been closed by war-time exigencies.

All these women have made a contribution to design. If history is to take proper account of the relationship of both sexes to design production, these women and others like them must be properly acknowledged. Design historians have played a large part in reinforcing assumptions about the roles and abilities of women designers. Isabelle Anscombe's *A Woman's Touch*, written in 1984, is typical of this. The book's title and its theme, which 'concentrates on those women designers whose work contributed to the modern home and its furnishings', reinforces patriarchal ideas about women as the discerners and arrangers of beauty in their 'natural' space – the home. Women designers, so Anscombe would have us believe, have a sex-specific 'touch' that transforms a house into a home.[16] Like other design historians Anscombe fails to recognise the historical formulations of patriarchy and the biased methodologies of historians' discourse. As a result, women's design is ignored and unrepresented. This book is an attempt to redress the balance.

To reach a fuller understanding of women designers' activities, historians must delineate the relationship between design and patriarchy. We need to challenge the terms which assign inferior status to certain design activities. The ideological assumptions behind labels such as 'feminine', 'delicate' and 'decorative' should be highlighted and analysed. We must examine the patriarchal basis of labour divisions that attribute certain design skills to women on the basis of biology. We should disclose the true reasons for the inclusion of only a handful of women in design history. These women have acted as the negative to the male positive; they have occupied the historical space left by men. If men's designs have been described as bold, assertive, calculated, then women's designs have been described as the opposite: subtle, intuitive or emotional. We should bear in mind that 'because of the economic, social and ideological effects of sexual difference in a western patriarchal culture, women have spoken and acted from a different place within that society and culture'.[17]

The failure to recognise the value systems of design history which have privileged an object's exchange-value over its use-value, and the professional site of production over the domestic site of production, has led to an emphasis on the role of design within capitalism. This has been compounded by the theory of Modernism and has resulted in the separation of craft from design history. Modernism has led to an emphasis on formally and technically progressive products made within a modern industrial context. As a result, Modernist design historians, in constructing their linear, progressive history, have ignored products that are traditional in style, material or production techniques.

Feminist design historians need to cut through these exclusive definitions of design and craft. In the pottery industry, we shall see that a rigid distinction cannot be drawn between industrial and craft methods of production, and that both coexisted within this particular area of design between 1870 and 1955.

In 1973, Sheila Rowbotham wrote: 'unbiased history simply makes no declaration of its bias, which is deeply rooted in existing society reflecting the views of the people of influence.'[18] More than a decade and a half later this book is an unambiguous feminist account of the women designers who made a career in the British pottery industry between 1870 and 1955. It is intended as a starting point, not a definitive statement, and it provides just one piece in the jigsaw puzzle that is the history of women in design.

Notes

1. Paintress is the word used in the pottery industry to describe the women who paint ware either on-glaze or under-glaze.
2. There is little specific published source material on women potters, although women are mentioned in some of the main texts on the pottery industry. In addition, there are several articles and unpublished theses on women workers in the pottery

industry, which I have listed in the bibliography. There are a few specialist books and articles on women pottery designers although these have often been written primarily with the needs of the collector in mind. See, for example, B. Bumpus, *Charlotte Rhead*, Kevin Francis Publishing, 1987; A. Eatwell, *Susie Cooper Productions*, Victoria and Albert Museum, 1987; and P. Rose, *Hannah Barlow: A Pioneer Doulton Artist*, Richard Dennis, 1985. Some of the best sources are nineteenth- and twentieth-century trade journals, art magazines and women's magazines.

3. Since 1983 there has been considerable debate within design history which has been informed by feminism. The first conference on 'Women and Design' was held at the Institute of Contemporary Arts, London in 1983; this has been followed by many conferences and study days including those at Leicester University in 1985, the Central School of Art and Design, London in 1986, and the ICA in 1988. Articles and reviews have been published in journals such as *Feminist Arts News, The Woman's Art Journal, Feminist Review, Design Issues, Block, Journal of Design History*, and *Art History*, dealing with the relationship of women to design by writers such as Judy Attfield, Pat Kirkham, Lynne Walker, Angela Partington, Phil Goodall, Jos Boys, June Freeman, Moira Vincentelli, Anthea Callen, Janice Winship, Suzette Worden and Tag Gronberg. Many of these are writing their own books on different aspects of design such as fashion, advertising, magazines, architecture, textiles, housing, interiors and craft. Useful introductions to some of their work can be found in G. Elinor, S. Richardson, S. Scott, A. Thomas, and K. Walker (eds), *Women and Craft*, Virago, 1987 and Judy Attfield and Pat Kirkham (eds), *A View from the Interior, Feminism, Women and Design*, The Women's Press, 1989. See also Tag Gronberg and Judy Attfield (eds), *A Resource Book on Women Working in Design*, The London Institute; Central School of Art and Design, 1986.

4. See for example, Nikolaus Pevsner, *Pioneers of Modern Design: From William Morris to Walter Gropius*, Penguin, 1975; Reyner Banham, *Theory and Design in the First Machine Age*, Architectural Press, 1975; Fiona MacCarthy, *A History of British Design, 1830–1970*, George Allen & Unwin, 1979; *History of Architecture and Design 1890–1939*, Open University, 1975; John Heskett, *Industrial Design*, Thames & Hudson, 1980. In these basic textbooks of design history, two

or three women are consistently mentioned. Some books, like those which form the Open University series, acknowledge more women designers, although in all cases the work of the women who make it into the history books could be described as Modernist. More recently, a few more women have been acknowledged by Adrian Forty in his book *Objects of Desire: Design and Society 1750–1980*, Thames & Hudson, 1986. Some historians have been careful to declare their biases when undertaking an analysis of a particular period, for example Penny Sparke in her book *An Introduction to Design and Culture in the Twentieth Century*, Allen & Unwin, 1986.
5. Consider as an example the silences about women's involvement in the Bauhaus. Although women were trained and taught at the Bauhaus, the vast literature on the subject makes scant reference to their presence (I include here Gillian Naylor's recent updated version of her early book on the Bauhaus). We know a great deal about Marcel Breuer, Walter Gropius, Lazslo Moholy-Nagy, Johannes Itten and Wassily Kandinsky, but how much do we know about their female counterparts – Marianne Brandt, Anni Albers and Gunta Stölzl?
6. The Irish-born designer Eileen Gray's gender has determined her designation as a 'feminine' designer. Unlike her contemporary Le Corbusier, her work has been consigned to the so-called 'decorative' arts. It is only more recently that historians have noted her role in the European avant-garde as a Modernist designer and architect. Margaret Macdonald and Louise Powell are examples of women designers whose work has been subsumed under their husbands' names. Louise Powell was a pottery designer at Josiah Wedgwood and Sons in the early twentieth century. She worked with her husband Alfred Powell and, until recently, it was he alone who was credited with their joint contribution to new design development at Wedgwood. Margaret Macdonald is another woman designer whose work has been left out of the history books. When it *is* acknowledged, it is done in order to account for a decorative element in work produced by her husband Charles Rennie Mackintosh which is inconvenient to a historical analysis of Mackintosh as a full-blown Modernist. See, for example, Thomas Howarth, *Charles Rennie Mackintosh and the Modern Movement*, Routledge & Kegan Paul, 1977.
7. Patriarchy as a concept has been defined by various feminist

theorists. An early definition is to be found in Kate Millet, *Sexual Politics*, Abacus, 1972, p. 25: 'Our society . . . is a patriarchy. The fact is evident at once if one recalls that the military, industry, technology, universities, science, political offices, finances – in short, every avenue of power within society, including the coercive force of the police is in entirely male hands.' The central problem with this definition of patriarchy is that it is a universal and trans-historical form of oppression that is being described. It presents specific problems for a Marxist–Feminist approach, which is located in historical analysis. In Britain, Sheila Rowbotham has argued in her essay, 'The Trouble with Patriarchy', *New Statesman*, 98, 1979, p. 970, that this 'implies a universal form of oppression which returns us to biology'. A useful definition of patriarchy which attempts to overcome this problem of universal oppression is outlined by Griselda Pollock 'Vision, Voice and Power: Feminist Art History and Marxism', *Block*, 6, 1982, p. 10: 'patriarchy does not refer to the static, oppressive domination of one sex over another, but a web of psycho-social relationships which institute a socially significant difference on the axis of sex which is so deeply located in our very sense of lived, sexual identity that it appears to us as natural and unalterable'.

8. An example of this is John Ruskin's essay 'Of Queen's Gardens', *Sesame and Lilies*, Collins, 1913. More recently, successive British governments have reiterated the importance of the woman's role in the preservation of the family. For example, the Conservative Party social services spokesman, Patrick Jenkin, told the Conservative annual conference in 1977, 'the pressure on young wives to go out to work devalues motherhood itself. . . Parenthood is a very skilled task indeed and it must be our aim to restore it to the place of honour it deserves': quoted in Anna Coote and Beatrix Campbell, *Sweet Freedom: The Struggle for Women's Liberation*, Picador, 1982, p. 85.

9. A division according to sex still exists today in different design activities. For example, in higher education more women students do courses in jewellery, fashion and textiles, and conversely more men students take architecture, industrial design and engineering.

10. For a discussion of the implications of the hierarchy of the arts in relation to the issue of gender, see R. Parker and G.

Pollock, *Old Mistresses: Women, Art and Ideology*, Routledge & Kegan Paul, 1981; and Elinor et al., op. cit., part two, pp. 55–104.

11. See D. De Marly, *Charles Worth*, Batsford, 1980.

12. An example of this is the work of Susie Cooper. According to the trade journals of the day her success in the 1930s was a consequence of her 'feminine' style, which was thought to appeal to women.

13. Of the many women designers that I shall discuss, only a handful designed both pottery shape and decoration.

14. Heidi Hartmann, 'The Unhappy Marriage of Marxism and Feminism: Towards a More Progressive Union', in Lydia Sargent (ed), *Women and Revolution. The Unhappy Marriage of Marxism and Feminism*, Pluto Press, 1981, p. 16.

15. As we shall see later, the importance of art school training in gaining access to the more prestigious jobs in the decorating stages of production cannot be overestimated.

16. Isabelle Anscombe, *A Woman's Touch: Women in Design from 1860 to the Present Day*, Virago, 1984, p. 11. See my review of this book in *Art History*, vol. 9, no. 3, September 1986, pp. 400–3 for a detailed critique.

17. Parker and Pollock, op. cit., p. 49.

18. S. Rowbotham, *Hidden From History*, Pluto Press, 1980, p. xvii.

CHAPTER 1

·

A Woman Potter's Lot

The Potteries, design and women workers

In her report for the Royal Commission of Labour on *The Employment of Women* in 1893, Clara E. Collet drew attention to the unusual nature of women's work in the Potteries.[1] 'The conditions of work and the system of payment of wages prevailing in the Staffordshire Potteries (Stoke-on-Trent, Hanley, Burslem, Tunstall, Fenton, Longton) are strikingly different from those under which women work in other industries.'[2] The Potteries, made up of these six north Staffordshire towns, was established as the centre of the British pottery industry by the early nineteenth century. Pottery manufacture dominated the area, although other local industries included coal-mining and iron and steel production (Figure 1). Women workers and young girls made up a substantial sector of the Potteries workforce: in 1861 they comprised 31 per cent, a figure which had grown to 61 per cent by 1959.[3] Apart from a temporary drop in women's numbers in 1931 due to the economic depression, this increase was gradual. Their jobs in the industry were various, although they tended to be concentrated in the lowest paid, least skilled work. This was particularly the case in the nineteenth century when pottery manufacture was dominated by hierarchical labour divisions based on craft skills and gender, which advantaged skilled men. Some erosion of these divisions of labour took place during the period, but even so in 1946 women were paid two-thirds the wages of men for undertaking the same work.[4]

Women's employment prospects were checked and controlled by the combined, though frequently conflicting, ideologies of patriarchy and capitalism. Patriarchy required women to occupy a different sphere from men, ideally a domestic one to correspond with their 'proper' roles as wives and mothers; while capitalism required a cheap, unskilled and dependent labour force that could be hired and fired at will. The relationship of women pottery workers to these dominant ideologies between 1870 and 1955 was in a state of flux: for example, due to the demands of capitalism for cheap labour, new job opportunities were offered to women in sectors of work previously designated as belonging to men. Although women were ultimately exploited in these jobs, they did challenge and transform some of the gender-based labour divisions that had been shaped by patriarchal ideology.

Unskilled women worked at all stages of the pottery production process between 1870 and 1955, although as the twentieth century progressed, some women took on new skilled and semi-skilled jobs in the forming sections of manufacturing. In the decorating stages, women were traditionally dominant and it was in these that pockets of skilled work for women had always been available. In these sections they worked in a range of occupations for which it was thought they had an inherent aptitude. This assumption of women's abilities allowed them access to skilled work such as designing surface patterns for pottery. However, the highly paid jobs such as art director and senior designer were more likely to be filled by men.

The Pottery Industry

The harshness of employment in the potteries in the nineteenth century was offset to some extent by the paternalism of large manufacturers such as Doulton and Wedgwood, who offered a more reliable and fair annual hiring contract. In this they were unusual, as most employers exploited the vulnerability of workers whose jobs were largely unprotected by regulatory legislation. Until such legislation was introduced later in the nineteenth century, pottery workers were disadvantaged by working practices established in the interests of the employers; on starting a new job 'the worker . . . virtually entered into servitude for one year'.[5]

Although there had been some worker combinations in the pottery industry in the eighteenth century, it was the years 1831 to 1850, following the repeal of the Combination Acts in 1824, which saw the rapid expansion of trade unionism for skilled pottery workers. Membership increased in response to the unemployment which had been caused by various trade disruptions. This period also saw the pottery workforce at its most radical.

Whereas the unions had been on the offensive in attempting to change working conditions and pay up to 1860, between 1870 and 1955 they had to defend their position against the erosion of pay levels, the introduction of new machinery and unemployment. The failure to amalgamate plagued the unions in their dealings with the employers. Sectional craft interests could be exploited by employers to break strikes and undermine wage demands. In 1890 the throwers, turners and handlers attempted to form a federation or association, but finished up in disagreement.[6] Craft unions such as the Hollow-ware Pressers' Society, the Flat-ware Pressers' Society and the Ovenmen's Society were dedicated to the protection and maintenance of their own privileges covering pay, status and entry to apprenticeships.

Conflict arose in the latter part of the nineteenth century as manufacturers attempted to substitute new machines with semi-skilled women operators, for skilled men workers: 'in this particular industry, women were unimportant until the introduction of machinery after 1845. By that date men feared the competition of female labour.'[7] The Hollow-ware Pressers' Society, 'did not oppose the new machinery itself but the implicit transformation of their work which jigger and jolly suggested'.[8]

The dual effects of new machinery and the labour shortages caused by the First World War added urgency to the proposals for a new combined union. Moves towards this had begun in 1906 when the Printers' and Transferrers' and the China Potters' Federation had joined the Hollow-ware Pressers' Society to form the National Amalgamated Society of Male and Female Pottery Workers (NASMFPW). By 1912, trade union membership in the potteries stood at 7650 out of a total labour force of 60,000.[9] This number had risen to 40,000 by the end of the First World War, due no doubt in part to the formation of the combined National Society of Pottery Workers (NSPW) in 1917. This superseded the NASMFPW and represented male and female, skilled and unskilled workers until 1970.

New technology provided pottery manufacturers with the means to increase profitability and production between 1870 and 1955. This was achieved across the production process and affected the forming, glazing, firing, decorating and packaging of ware. The switch from coal to electric and gas had the most visible impact on the area as the distinctive bottle oven kilns which once dominated the Potteries' skyline were replaced by tunnel kilns by the late 1950s (Figure 2).[10]

Design in the Potteries

As the system of manufacture shifted from craft to industrial production the form and decoration of pottery were transformed. The distinct craft basis of the industry had its origins in the eighteenth century when industrial pottery manufacture was first established in north Staffordshire. Improvements in the system of production and distribution, combined with the introduction of new bodies, better methods of glazing and higher quality transfer decoration meant that the potters' products were reaching a wider market. Increased levels of demand generated a greater degree of specialisation in the trade.[11]

Prior to the mechanisation of the pottery process, wares had varied from region to region according to local clays, distinctive glazes and the craft skills of the potter. Labour divisions in the newly organised factories of the late eighteenth century fragmented this unified design process and set the precedent for the next 150 years as designs were produced for distinct stages of the production process. Within this system the shape of the ware could be created without any consideration of the design of the surface decoration and vice versa. In fact, most manufacturers produced a limited range of pottery shapes to which they added different patterns. A small number of shapes suited mass-production techniques by allowing the standardisation of products to a high quality of finish. This became crucial if the status of pottery tableware was to be enhanced to attract the wealthier sectors of the market.

The design of both shape and decoration was stimulated by fashion as the market for pottery expanded beyond the confines of the local vicinity and national boundaries. This was true of both the large manufacturers such as Wedgwood, Copeland, Coalport and also of the smaller manufacturers who poached popular designs. Wedgwood's early commercial successes were a result of the careful exploitation of the fashions for Rococo and neo-classicism. By the middle of the nineteenth century, the stylistic eclecticism which characterised so much of Victorian design could be clearly discerned in the pottery industry. This was encouraged by technological developments such as improved casting methods, and superior transfer and lithographic printing which facilitated the copying of various

16

historical motifs and forms – Gothic, Baroque, Rococo and Italian Renaissance.

Traditional and modern decorating techniques were used in the nineteenth century by firms such as Minton and Doulton. These included slip-trailing, pâte sur pâte, sprigging, incising, tube-lining and relief decoration in or on the clay body. Decorating was done by a variety of means and took place at three different points in the manufacturing process. First, in its raw state prior to the biscuit firing, ware could be incised or sgraffito patterns could be scratched through additional coatings of natural or coloured slip. Alternatively, the clay body could be decorated with slip-trailing, sprigging and tube-lining. Secondly, ware could be decorated with hand painting and/or printed transfers after the biscuit firing (Figure 3). Thirdly, it could be decorated after its removal from the glost firing. This was the cheapest and most common form of decoration, although it was the least satisfactory because it tended to wear off with constant use.

Hand decorating, whether under-glaze or on-glaze, required great skill in using loaded brushes of colour directly on blank ware.[12] A variety of hand-decorating techniques was used, including banding, gilding and groundlaying. Hand decorating declined between 1900 and 1955 due to the increase in lithographic printing.

Lithographs radically altered the work of the decorating shops. As with the potting shops, this change was accompanied by de-skilling. Lithographic printing was done with success from about the 1880s using stones and later aluminium plates. The advantage to the manufacturer was that all colours for a design could be placed on one lithographic transfer which could then be applied to the ware in a single operation. It offered a great range of colour at relatively low cost. In the late nineteenth century, it was used as a means of reproducing painted decorations, but by the 1930s it was being exploited as a distinct medium to create subtle decorative effects.

Further diversity in design was created by the introduction of new glazes and wares. Majolica was a pastiche of Italian Renaissance maiolica and was produced by Wedgwood, Minton and several other firms in the mid nineteenth century. Brightly coloured glazes were introduced; notably *bleu de Deck*, a brilliant peacock blue glaze developed in France in 1861 and popularised in Britain within the context of the Aesthetic Movement. In the twentieth century other glazes were introduced such as *flambé*, a bright-red flame-like glaze, uranium orange and uranium vermilion. There was a great deal of interest in iridescent lustres between 1890 and 1929 due to the development of new commercial lustres and experiments undertaken by designers. Traditional lustres, which were time-consuming and costly, were produced by firing metallic salts in a reducing atmosphere. The new commercial lustres which were painted onto already glazed and decorated wares were adopted as a cheaper alternative by companies such as the Royal Lancastrian Pottery, G. L. Ashworth & Bros and Wedgwood.

The main aim of nineteenth-century pottery manufacturers in relation to the development of new bodies had been the production of a cheap durable white earthenware. The first version of this was ironstone, followed in the 1870s by granite ware which was the favoured body of the volume producers such as Johnson Bros and J. & G. Meakin.[13] Bone china was never out of fashion, but it was particularly favoured by some companies in the late nineteenth century. Another new body was Parian porcelain introduced by Copeland in the 1850s. This was a fine porcelain which could be tinted or coloured, and which was an ideal material for small-scale statuary. Wedgwood developed its own version, Carrara porcelain. Salt-glazed stoneware and jasperware continued to be produced throughout the period by the manufacturers Wedgwood and Doulton. Fewer new bodies were produced after the First World War, although Wedgwood introduced a pink, self-coloured, semi-translucent bone china in the mid 1930s.

The pottery industry has responded with varying degrees of enthusiasm and in different ways to the issue of design and to the employment of the designer. In many small potteries the master-potter fulfilled the role of designer which was often combined with that of manager.[14] In these companies design meant keeping abreast of new patterns, glazes and bodies, and being able to respond to market demands in a competitive business. It did not necessarily mean creating new patterns and shapes, or even adapting existing ones. Indeed, with the commercialisation of transfer printing and lithographs by companies such as Johnson, Matthey & Co. and Rataud in the 1890s, it was possible for these smaller manufacturers to buy already prepared surface designs for pottery. At the same time, the development of the new shapes was a massive investment which involved the production of new moulds and new tools. As a consequence, many small companies did not manufacture their own shapes, but bought in suitable blank ware from other producers.

Within the context of the larger companies, the owners became detached from the details of manufacture and more absorbed by the financial and management side of their companies as the nineteenth century progressed. This had not been the case with the original potters: 'The eighteenth century potter was the supreme arbiter of taste in his own establishment, Josiah Wedgwood not only supervised the shape and style of his productions but was directly responsible for some of the designs.'[15]

The translation of these designs into prototypes for mass-production was undertaken by skilled modellers and draughtspeople employed by the company. From the outset, Josiah Wedgwood employed the services of artists such as John Flaxman, George Stubbs, Lady Templetown and Lady Beauclerk to provide designs for manufacture.

The need to improve the aesthetic quality of manufactured products in British industry was regularly debated by government inquiries, independent agencies and interested individuals between 1870 and 1955. Economic considerations were a primary reason for this: it was believed that improvements in the design of goods would stimulate demand. As early as 1836 the report by Mr Ewart's Select Committee of the House of Commons on Art and Manufacture drew attention to the need for art instruction among the working classes and for the appropriate training of designers. In response to this the Normal School of Design was established in Somerset House, London, followed by branch schools in provincial cities in 1842 at Manchester, Birmingham and York. Then in 1843 came schools in Sheffield and Nottingham, and four years later at Hanley and Stoke. In 1853, art schools were opened at Burslem and Newcastle-under-Lyme, and from the outset the Potteries art schools had close links with the local industry. Early advocates of Hanley art school were three local potters – Herbert Minton, John Ridgway and William Ridgway. During the next hundred years, the Potteries art schools were to provide both the aesthetic and technical education for the skilled workers of the pottery industry, including designers of shape and decoration, mould-makers, casters, and decorators of ware.

The Potteries art schools raised the profile of design within the industry and provided a forum for debate about the relationship between art and industry. To many manufacturers design was a means of improving sales and exports, and the application of art to industrial pottery manufacture enhanced the status of products and signified greater commercial value. The label 'art' was often applied to wares to indicate this. In the 1860s and 1870s both Minton and Doulton established art studios which went a step further along this path by employing artists and designers to model and decorate one-off wares. Other manufacturers such as Wedgwood introduced 'art' wares which proved immensely popular. To some extent, these provided the impetus for the development of art pottery in the late nineteenth century and studio pottery in the twentieth century.

Prestigious companies such as Wedgwood and Minton employed an art director to take responsibility for aesthetic decisions within the company.[16] Further down the hierarchy of artistic professions were the skilled craftsmen and women whose artistic skills were required for modelling, throwing, engraving, free-hand painting, enamelling, tube-lining, banding, gilding and aerographing. These skills were either learned as apprentices, or at the Potteries art schools.

The application of art to industry was thought to be advantageous to manufacturers in the inter-war years. For many the initial interest in design was economic, although this was not the sole reason. Some were genuinely concerned to improve what they considered to be low standards of mass taste. The pottery industry was brought into these discussions through different means. Groups such as the Design and Industries Association, the British Institute of Industrial Art, and the Society of Industrial Artists which had a local branch in the Potteries, encouraged debate on these issues. Exhibitions such as the annual Ideal Home and British Industries Fairs, as well as one-off events such as the British Empire exhibition at Wembley in 1924, the Dorland Hall exhibitions in 1933 and 1934, and the British Art in Industry exhibition at the Royal Academy in 1935 brought manufacturers into direct contact with their critics. The economic dimension to design was demonstrated by the role of the government Board of Trade which produced several reports on the relationship of design to industry.[17] *Design in the Pottery Industry*, produced by the Pottery Committee of the Council for Art and Industry in 1937, directly addressed the problems of pottery manufacturers. It argued that,

> The position so long held by English pottery was . . . not unassailable. . . Foreign production has greatly improved and increased, and we are now faced with keen competition not only in markets abroad but even in our own home market. To meet

the challenge, English manufacturers are modernising their factories . . . lowering the price . . . but . . . it is necessary to link with it an appeal to the taste of the public through the still greater attractiveness of both ware and design.[18]

For designers after the Second World War, dominant themes were the need for modern designs to beat off the challenge from foreign competitors, the relationship of new technology and new markets to design, and the increasing modernisation and streamlining of production and business. Most manufacturers continued to produce a plethora of styles and shapes; designs that were considered modern and progressive were sold alongside traditional designs such as the willow pattern.

Women Pottery Workers

Pottery manufacture involved seven distinct stages which began with the mixing of clay and ended with the packing of ware. Women were employed at all these stages which spanned the two major sectors of production; the forming of clay, and the decorating of the ware. They worked as assistants to men throwers, turners, pressers and casters, and to the ovenmen who controlled the kiln firing. They were attendants to dippers, placers, packers and printers. At most points along the production line, they occupied unskilled jobs, except in transferring, decorating and some aspects of forming. Between ·1870 and 1955 their employment opportunities were governed by intricate labour divisions which privileged skilled men workers. These men were protected by craft unions representing the different sectors of the pottery trade, for example the Hollow-ware Pressers' Society, the Flat-ware Pressers' Society, the Packers' Society and the Ovenmens' Society. Until the First World War and the formation of one union to represent all the needs of the industry, women were virtually absent from the ranks of these craft trade unions.[19] Consequently they had little power to resist the control over their work that these exerted.

Underpinning work organisation in the pottery industry was an elaborate sexual division of labour which was constructed by patriarchal ideology. Patriarchy located women in a separate sphere; one which was defined by their biological differences from men. They were considered to have particular aptitudes for specific tasks; for example, they were thought to be more dextrous and better able than men to undertake repetitive, detailed work. Combined with this was the notion that women had a 'natural' facility for decorative work which affected pottery manufacturers' perceptions of their potential as designers. They were considered to be suited to the design of surface decoration rather than the design of pottery shapes. This was the case throughout the period 1870 to 1955, although as women secured greater economic and social independence in the twentieth century, some were able to overcome this division. Class played a crucial role in women's access to the skilled jobs of designer and paintress, but low earnings throughout Stoke-on-Trent ensured that working-class women worked wherever they could.

In contrast to the suitability of decorative work for women, work in the slip house or potting shops was thought to be dirty, unladylike and to expose women to the corrupting influence of men. Commentators and reporters on the pottery industry were shocked by the inappropriate roles occupied by women and the unconventional behaviour attributed to them. In 1841, Scriven recorded with horror the accounts of loose morals which were apparently in evidence in the potting shops,

> from the oral testimony of the magistrates and clergy, and from some of the manufacturers themselves, I find that sexual intercourse is of very common occurrence, and that bastardy, the natural result, is thought very lightly of.[20]

Fifty years later Clara Collet reported contradictory evidence from a woman who stated that, 'she came across a considerable number of cases of immoral conduct, but had never heard of one case in a factory nor of immoral relations between men and women working together in the factory'.[21]

To a certain extent, these women were an affront to patriarchal sensibilities. Jobs were available to them because manufacturers needed cheap labour, or because they worked as assistants to their potter husbands. Divisions in the industry were clearly centred on sex and craft skills, but the labour needs of capitalism brought transformations to the rigid sexual divisions, and the introduction of new machinery undermined the craft skill hierarchy. These issues were highlighted in the late nineteenth century with the debate about women machine operators.

Women were doubly disadvantaged by this hierarchy because access to the training for specific craft skills was itself determined by gender. At all stages of production there were clear contradictions between the idealised role for women prescribed by the social thinkers of the time, the sex-specific skills with which women were supposed to be equipped, and the realities of their labour. In the slip-house all skilled work, such as the mixing of clay, was done by men who had served apprenticeships for jobs which were then protected by their trade unions. Along with unskilled men, women worked in the slip-house as labourers doing jobs such as wedging and carrying clay. The double standards of patriarchy were demonstrated in the denial of apprenticeships to women on the grounds of inappropriate sphere, while at the same time their employment as wedgers and carriers of upwards of 75 pounds of clay was tolerated.[22]

In the potting shops where clay was formed into ware, women worked in a variety of roles. From the beginning of industrial pottery manufacture in the eighteenth century, they had worked as unskilled assistants to skilled men. They carried clay, ran the moulds and worked the treadles for the potters' and turners' wheels before the widespread introduction of steam-power.[23] They fettled, towed and sponged to clean off and smooth ware that had been thrown, cast or pressed. In these roles women were sub-employed by the men they assisted, rather than being directly employed by the manufacturer. During her visit to the Potteries in 1907, Sylvia Pankhurst observed that 'women workers were subordinated to men. Women turned the wheels for men throwers and trod the lathe for men turners. In each case a woman was employed by the man for whom she toiled – she was the slave of a slave' (Figure 4).[24]

This sub-employment system which was widespread in the nineteenth century had its origins in the seventeenth century when the potter would have been paid to produce a given amount of ware for a fixed price. To complete the order on time, the potter would supply assistants usually in the form of his own family or relations, and 'despite the development of factory industry, and of formalised relationships within the potbanks, craftsmen continued to sub-employ their own families'.[25]

Due to economic necessity, women often had to work outside of a family work group, particularly if, as was likely in the 1870s, their fathers worked in industries other than pottery.[26] This put women in a subordinate situation on two counts; first, if they were sub-employed within a family workgroup it was difficult to renegotiate work tasks and pay because this represented a challenge to the family and ultimately, the father. Secondly, if they were employed as assistants in a non-family situation, the women were in positions of greater weakness. Without kin loyalty, they were regarded as cheap labour only working to make up the family income and not working for themselves. The craftsman hired, fired, paid and laid down conditions of service for his assistants, who sometimes numbered as many as four. As one assistant said in evidence to Clara Collet in 1893, 'the girls have nothing to do with their employers and if anyone complained to the employers of the man under whom she worked the man would pay her out for doing so'.[27]

Manufacturers used women as cheap labour and as a means of breaking down craft opposition to new machinery. Undermining the power of craftsmen as sub-employers was a way of furthering their cause, and as a result, the first two decades of the twentieth century saw the replacement of the sub-employment system with direct managerial control over all employees.

The introduction of the jigger and jolley into the potting shops in the 1880s and 1890s highlighted the difficulties facing women who worked outside the socially sanctioned decorating stage. Because of increasing sophistication, machines such as the jigger and jolley de-skilled certain branches of the pottery trade such as throwing and turning. This led to the replacement of skilled men flat-ware pressers and hollow-ware pressers by semi-skilled women machine operators. By 1890 an estimated 1000 journeywomen flat-pressers were working in the industry using the new machines. But without trade union support, these women were unable to fight unscrupulous employers for comparability in pay.

Women threatened the job security and status of these craftsmen. To begin with they were paid at a half or two-thirds the craft rates which led to a lowering of the wages for the job. Manufacturers also used women as a means of redefining jobs and demanding increased output for the same wage. The apprenticeship system was almost destroyed in certain sectors of trade, as manufacturers realised that they had an almost limitless supply of cheap labour which did not require upgrading upon the completion of apprenticeships.[28]

With little tradition of co-operative action, the various craft unions were unable to argue collectively against the introduction of new machinery. Instead, they fiercely guarded their individual privileges, but were in agreement in their dislike of women workers taking over what they considered to be men's rightful work. Most of their arguments against women workers had their basis in patriarchy. The Hollow-ware Pressers' Society thought it inappropriate for women to work independently of men, and argued; 'we believe that for women to be employed at the jollies is wrong; when a woman works at a jolley she occupies an arduous and responsible position wholly unfit for women.'[29] The flat-pressers argued that a woman working on the jolley was neglecting her true occupation as a housewife: 'It is degrading to her position, lowers her in the social and moral scale, and deprives her of paying those attentions she owes to herself and her domestic surroundings, and will ultimately inflict upon herself and society an irretrievable injury.'[30]

The reality of women's employment in the pottery industry was conveniently ignored by the flat-pressers who were also angered that the financial gains of sub-employing women as cheap labour were being removed from their hands into the hands of the manufacturers. Casting was another site of conflict between men and women workers in the industry, and this continued into the twentieth century, as women were increasingly involved in the casting of small items of ware normally produced by the hollow-ware presser. By 1924 women were working as casters, but were being paid half as much as men.[31]

Trade union support for women came from the Women's Trade Union League (WTUL), founded by Emma Paterson in 1874. In the 1890s it attempted to organise women workers throughout the pottery industry. Its main object was to promote trade unionism among working women by establishing branches of the League in different industries across the country. These were to 'remain fully independent in the management of their own business and strictly self-supporting'.[32] Between 1893 and 1903, the WTUL was active in the Potteries, initially establishing three branches: two in Hanley for paintresses and clayworkers, and one in Burslem for paintresses. By 1893 these had a combined membership of 400 members which was consolidated in 1898 by the appointment of a General Secretary.

The north Staffordshire branch of the WTUL continually suffered from lack of funds and from the trade conditions which took a heavy toll on women's wages and therefore on their union subscriptions. Furthermore, although it had more ambitious aims, it was competing for the same membership as the Printers', Transferrers' and Decorators' Society which had been founded in 1899 out of the Amalgamated Printers' and Transferrers' Society. This was the main base of women's union membership until the formation of the combined union in the early twentieth century, and its women members, who numbered 1035 in 1900, were skilled workers with negotiating power.[33]

In the face of organisational and financial difficulties, the WTUL changed its tactics in the Potteries in the 1890s and 1900s. It ceased giving priority to recruitment and turned its attention to the mounting of effective campaigns for the introduction of protective legislation into the industry. In its 24th Annual Report protective legislation was urged 'in order to put a stop to the evils of this dangerous trade'.[34] Lead poisoning became one of its main campaigning issues. Jobs in the dipping section brought with them extra problems because of the health risk attendant on using the lead glazes. In her 1893 report Clara Collet noted that 'the girls in the glazing department looked very white and ill'.[35] Lead poisoning was made more likely by the poor cleaning facilities and lack of ventilation in many of the potteries, where essential items of factory hygiene such as sinks for washing were not always provided.

The use of lead was not completely prohibited until 1947. Prior to this the unions had campaigned against its use with little success. Their most effective action had been in 1891 when the Factory and Workshop Bill had come before the House of Commons. This Bill, which became known as 'the potters' charter for health', included the pottery industry within its remit because of successful lobbying by the trade unions. The effects of lead poisoning were wide-ranging; in a mild form it caused gastric disorders, but fully developed it caused blindness and paralysis. In the pottery industry this paralysis affected the dipping hand, and led to the condition known locally as 'wrist-drop'. Women were particularly vulnerable to the effects of lead poisoning with a rate of attack that was 2 to 3 times that of men.[36] Their reproductive system was especially prone to the effect of lead, causing miscarriage and still-birth, and giving rise to an infant mortality rate in Stoke-on-Trent that was one of the highest in the country. It also acted as an abortifacient; 'It was apparently a local "truism" that to marry a girl lead worker would ensure a marriage where family size could be easily limited.'[37]

The 1891 Factory Act covered the other major industrial disease of the pottery industry – pneumoconiosis. This was a dust disease commonly referred to as potters' rot or potters' asthma, first recognised in the eighteenth century. It was caused by the particles of clay dust which damaged the lungs and made breathing extremely difficult particularly among workers who processed and handled clay. It was not until after the Second World War that this disease was brought under control.

The WTUL was indefatigable in its efforts to force more effective controls on pottery manufacturers who were keen to avoid the extra costs and slowing of production which accompanied the new health recommendations. The 1891 Factory Act had made recommendations, not precise rules, and even though union pressure forced the manufacturers to introduce Special Rules in 1894 and a second set in 1898 governing health issues, the WTUL continued to lobby Parliament, through sympathetic MPs, for government legislation. As a result of an article by Gertrude Tuckwell entitled 'Commercial Manslaughter' which reported on the potters' lot, an official government inquiry was established in 1898.[38] In 1913 a detailed set of rules was established to protect the health of pottery workers under section 79 of the Factory and Workshop Act 1901. After this date severe restrictions were placed on the use of lead, and lead glazes were gradually withdrawn from the industry.

The organisation of women into trade unions became imperative as the twentieth century progressed. With the exception of those in the transferring and decorating shops, they were non-unionised and unskilled. It was the major upheaval of the First World War which precipitated trade union action on behalf of women pottery workers. In both the firing and dipping stages of production, women workers began to take on skilled work as a result of the labour shortages brought about by male conscription. The issue of women glost placers, who put the glazed ware into the kilns, focused attention on the replacement of skilled men by women who undertook the same job, but were paid only half or two-thirds their rates of pay.

It was the first combined union, the National Amalgamated Society of Male and Female Pottery Workers, which effectively defended the interests of unskilled women workers.[39] At the onset of war, the NASMFPW had 2000 women members, most of whom were skilled transferrers and decorators. The war acted as a stimulant to women's membership following the union's successful negotiations on their behalf. Initially it acted for women glost placers and then for other groups who were paid low wages for work that had been better paid when done by men. An agreement was reached with the Manufacturers' Association whereby women 'substituted' for men 'should be employed at the same prices and under the same conditions as those of the men whose places they have filled, providing that such work has generally been regarded by the trade as men's work and on the understanding that the men on their return should have first claims on old places'.[40] Some manufacturers were able to circumvent this agreement by claiming that jobs were different, and citing custom and practice. In most industries women did not achieve wage-equality with men; in fact, 'women pottery workers were amongst those who secured the least increase, or about 60 per cent'.[41]

By 1918 women pottery workers were substantially unionised with 20,000 members of the National Society of Pottery Workers (NSPW). This represented 60.9 per cent of its total membership, and accounted for 59 per cent of women employed in the industry.[42] This membership was a measure of women's support for a trade union which had acted on their behalf. To consolidate its female membership, the NSPW appointed a full-time woman organiser in 1917.

Wartime conditions brought to the forefront government debate regarding the employment of women. A report by the War Cabinet Committee was published in 1919 on *Women in Industry*. This followed other reports, the most important of which was the Royal Commission of Labour report on *The Employment of Women* of 1893. This covered the work conditions in various areas of manufacturing including the pottery industry. Its aims were to investigate first, the difference in wages of men and women; second, to examine alleged grievances; and third, to assess the effects of women's industrial employment on their health, morality and the home.

In this Clara Collet, the assistant woman commissioner responsible for reporting on the pottery industry, described the structure of the industry and outlined the type of roles undertaken by women. She addressed the three aims of the report; first, she commented on the method of calculating wages which was mainly piece rate for the dozen.[43] Some unskilled jobs were paid on a fixed weekly rate, although all pottery workers had to pay stoppages for a large number of facilities such as lighting, and sweeping up. Paintresses had to provide their own brushes until the Second World War.

Clara Collet described the sub-employment system and pointed out that 'in many cases husband and wife or child worked together'.[44] She highlighted the disadvantages of this system by including the evidence of one worker who complained that after the annual holiday, 'if the head man was a drunkard, the boys and girls assisting him could do nothing until he had recovered from his drinking bout, and were without work for days'.[45] Collet's report offered a detailed account of women's roles in the industry and their wages. Some discussion did take place around the issues of grievances, morality, health and the effect of work on women's home lives. Yet the report was mainly descriptive and unconcerned with broader issues governing women's social roles.

The experience of wartime highlighted areas of conflict between men and women workers. The 1919 *Report of the War Cabinet Committee on Women in Industry* attempted to address specific inequalities in pay and opportunity which had become evident during the war. Its brief was wider than its predecessors in that it examined notions of 'appropriate' work for women.

The report's arguments provide an excellent insight into the delineation of patriarchy at the end of the First World War, when 'normal' social relations between the sexes and indeed classes had been severely disrupted. It rehearsed key patriarchal propositions regarding women's roles; that they were naturally weaker and as a consequence less able to do certain types of heavy work; that they were less appreciated than men because it was thought that they 'ought not to be working'; and that their employment patterns were less stable because women expected to marry. Finally it was observed that women were less organised because 'they have for so long worked in the main as isolated units in the home result[ing] in their not attaining that power of organisation which, in the case of men, has enabled them, when settling wage questions, to meet the concentrated power of the employer on terms of increasing equality'.[46]

Once the main conclusion was drawn that women were poorly paid both in absolute terms and in relation to men, the Committee attempted to account for this through a variety of arguments. It observed that,

> the principal evidence before the Committee as to the causes of the low rates of payment to women, both absolute and in comparison with men, was from the societies of women. These causes were represented as mainly the artificial restrictions on training and employment, and as easily remediable. But a state of affairs that has come down through the ages and is nearly universal must have some origin in nature, however much the effect may have been accentuated by the action of man.[47]

The economists who contributed to the report argued that low wages were the only way to create demand for women's labour, if they were 'less appreciated, less stable, less well-trained and less organised [and are therefore] for productive purposes as a whole, inferior editions of men'.[48] Equal wages, it was proposed, worked against greater opportunities for women, which were 'hindered, too, by the cry for equal wages for men and women, as the powerful lever for increasing the opportunities of women is taken away if they are not to do the work cheaper'.[49]

Members of the Engineering and National Employers' Federation rated women's productive value at about two-thirds that of men, and argued that 'where a woman is paid more than 66 per cent of a man she ceases to be profitable as a producer'.[50] Mr Marjoribanks, who represented the engineering trades was in no doubt about what constituted 'women's work'. Women

> were admirably adapted for light repetition work. . . on piece-work a woman will always beat a man. . . On mass-production she will come first every time. . . We were never able on this particular class of work to get the men to cope with it, they would not stand it. Men will not stand the monotony of a fast repetition job like women, they will not stand by a machine pressing all their lives, but a woman will.[51]

The report concluded that it was inappropriate to pay women the same rate as men employed in the same class of work. Instead it encouraged greater trade union action on behalf of women to improve their lot, although it acknowledged with some realism that

> the fixing of a rate for men and women which shall be in equitable proportion to any less degree of physical endurance, skill or responsibility exacted from the woman or to any additional strain thrown on the men, and which shall neither exclude women on the one side nor blackleg men on the other, is one of the most delicate problems with which the trade unions are faced.[52]

Within the report there were significant shifts in attitudes regarding women working in industry. It was accepted that women had a right to work, and that their employment was economically useful. There were few assertions of the home as women's rightful sphere, although the report emphasised the great importance of motherhood as an occupation. The writers of the report were little concerned to ascribe to women their 'natural' roles, although their biological difference from men was used on several occasions to legitimise inequalities. Nevertheless the social basis of ideas about the appropriateness of the sexes for specific jobs was acknowledged. The point was made in the report that, although new opportunities for women had been created by the invention of new machinery such as the telephone and typewriter, 'if such things had been invented long ago, and owing to the conditions of that time the occupations connected with them had been made men's employments, women would probably have still been shut out of them.'[53] In its deliberations on the importance of physical strength, it was noted that 'Girls as a rule do not have as much spent on them as boys. If they were better fed and trained, their output would be bigger than it is now in occupations in which they compete with men.'[54]

To a certain extent, the report demonstrated a renegotiation of patriarchy. It was unlike nineteenth-century government reports which highlighted the dichotomy between the middle-class ideal of a separate domestic sphere, and the working-class experience of low wages which necessitated women's work. In these, women's employment was seen as an unfortunate reality that did not prevent the writers from voicing the conventional wisdoms of the day about the woman's place being in the home. In contrast, the *Report of the War Cabinet Committee on Women in Industry* made some progress in acknowledging the social and cultural reasons for the inequalities in women's employment and pay. It drew attention to the impossibilities of 'a conventional view of women's work, which still recognises for women ideals which are more or less incompatible with the facts of everyday life'.[55] Furthermore, the sexual division between work and home, and men and women, was not served forth in the report as some sort of 'truth'; rather it was renegotiated into a theory of appropriate work for women. This idea of appropriate work was in itself based on assumptions about women's intellectual and physical abilities which had their origins in patriarchy, but the report was more critical in its considerations. It contributed to a reassessment of the reasons why women sought employment, in its recognition of women as independent bread-winners providing crucial income to the family unit, and in its assertion 'that an adult woman ought to receive an independent living wage in respect of her work, whether she is domestically independent or not'.[56] It also raised the issue of the discriminatory nature of the family wage and pointed out that 'the fact that at present men receive larger wages is not a natural result of their being held responsible for the maintenance of their children, but a custom resulting from their stronger economic position'.[57]

Recommendations were made in the report against the introduction of 'the rate for the job' and 'equal time rates' because it was
argued that both these policies would drive women out of jobs. In
fact it was implicitly recognised in the report that these proposals
had been formulated by several skilled men's unions, notably the
engineers, to achieve just this. The rate for the job meant that a
certain rate of production would be set for a job which a given
worker would have to meet. The rates would be set according to
men's work capacity, not women's, and these could, therefore, be
used as a basis for excluding women from such work.

The report made specific points in relation to the pottery industry,
although it is interesting that some of these were based on a misrep-
resentation of the information. The report commented that women
were not qualified for skilled work in the making departments
because they had not served apprenticeships, although it omitted to
mention that women had been denied access to these. It also noted
that ·they did not have 'the physical strength for the heavy work in
other departments', which contradicted the reality of women's physical labour in the pottery industry.[58] It also argued that women's
output was markedly inferior to men's in both quality and quantity,
and that women were bad time-keepers. In conclusion, 'it was considered that the employment of women could only increase from
what it was before the war if the output of the factories was
increased'.[59]

This debate about women's place in the pottery industry continued through the inter-war years. Women workers remained
acceptable as a reserve labour force, but in times of economic
recession and high unemployment their place was back in the home.
This argument failed to solve the problem as manufacturers continued to employ women because they were cheaper than men. In
1945 the National Society of Pottery Workers grappled with the
issue in its policy document *Reconstruction in the Pottery Industry*.
It acknowledged that although women 'in the 1930s made up
approximately 55 per cent of total workers employed, their status
has always been inferior to that of men'.[60] To counteract this the
union proposed that women should receive the rate for the job,
though it failed to agree the criteria for establishing this rate. It also
recommended that apprenticeships should be open to girls as well
as boys.

The union's attitude to women workers was typical of the welfar-
ist policies of post-war Britain in which women's problems were

solved not by equal pay, but by a family wage for their husbands. 'If married women are to be set free from the economic compulsion to go out to work, and given the opportunity to choose for themselves, then there must be a reasonable wage and a "guaranteed week" for their husbands.'[61] In true patriarchal fashion, women's goal was to marry, not to work. In fact, lack of understanding characterised the union's deliberations on women pottery workers. This was graphically demonstrated when the union bemoaned the lack of women on its National Executive and their poor attendance at the annual conference, without taking stock of women's combined burden of work and domestic responsibilities. It is doubly ironic that women's lack of involvement in decision-making was ignored by historians of the NSPW who attributed the union's lack of radicalism to them.[62]

Women pottery workers' wages between 1870 and 1955 are extremely difficult to quantify given the numerous piece-rate prices which were negotiated for different sectors of the trade: 'Wages within the same occupation varied widely due to the complex variety of product, plant, ware, size, counts and design. Two hollow-ware pressers working in adjacent workshops on one potbank could be receiving weekly wages differing by 10 and sometimes 15 shillings.'[63]

Comparability between men's and women's wages is also difficult to demonstrate. Generally, unskilled pottery workers of both sexes were badly paid, but women especially so. Skilled women earned only a half or two-thirds of men's rates and unskilled women earned only a third. For example, in 1836 average weekly wages for men were 21s–28s, and for women they were 9s–12s.[64] Half a century later, women introduced to the new machinery as flat-pressers earned 18s per week, whereas their male counterparts earned 27s per week.[65] Skilled women paintresses and transferrers earning between 11s and 14s in 1893 were only getting about half of the rate of an equivalent male printer, who earned about 28s.[66] In 1911 women pottery workers were ranked eleventh in terms of pay out of the.fourteen principal women's industries.[67] Sam Clowes, General Secretary of the National Society of Pottery Workers from 1918 to 1924, described women's wages in one factory as being 'so low that it was generally known that they turned to prostitution in the evening'.[68]

The First World War did stimulate women's wages in the industry, but mainly as a result of 'substitution', and even then their wages were only 60 per cent of those for men. Between 1924 and 1963 women's wages averaged only half of men's; in 1924 warehousemen were paid on average 45s, whereas warehousewomen were paid 24s; men casters were paid 61s, and women casters 30s; men flat-pressers 55s, and women flat-pressers 37s.[69] In 1938 women's average weekly wage was £2 8s 4d, men's was £5 16s 8d.[70] Women again did men's jobs during the Second World War, but it did not greatly improve their wages, which in 1947 averaged £3 5s 9d as against £6 7s 9d for men.[71] It was not until the Equal Pay Act was enforced in 1975 that two price lists for men and women workers' piece-rates ceased to be produced. The effectiveness of this legislation to stamp out wage inequalities in the pottery industry is seriously questioned by recent statistical analysis of comparative wages.[72]

Most workers in the pottery industry began at 7 a.m. and worked until 6 p.m., with half an hour for breakfast and an hour for lunch which were unpaid. Until June 1919 when the union negotiated a 47-hour week, they worked long and irregular hours which were primarily determined by the vagaries of manufacturing output and demand. As Christopher Shaw explained in his book of 1903, *When I was a Child. By an Old Potter*: 'manufacturers did not disdain to accept the profit got out of seventy to eighty hours' labour per week from a child of nine years of age, while the child got one and six or two shillings'.[73]

Women's lives were made long and arduous from the double load of industrial and domestic work. Low wages in the major north Staffordshire industries of mining and steel meant that women had to work for family subsistence. In 1904, the Principal Lady Factory Inspectress found that 'since well-paid men's employment was scarce in this area, it was claimed that "a woman is looked upon as lazy unless she takes her share in contributing to the family income" '.[74] Skilled women in the pottery industry could earn as much as husbands employed in other industries.

Some women worked for other than purely financial reasons. Hilda Salt who worked in various jobs in the industry as a ground-layer, caster, flat-presser and for most of her working life as a gilder at Samson Bridges, Anchor China Works, liked to work because 'it got me away from the house'.[75] Gaining employment in the potteries, except during times of high unemployment, was relatively easy for trained workers. However as most women were unskilled they represented the most dispensable sector of the labour force. Many jobs were gained through word of mouth – workers at particular companies would pass on the information about new opportunities.

People who needed jobs were often 'spoken for' by family or friends at the factory; this led to the situation of one family dominating an area of production and reserving well-paid work for other family members. Ethel Hood was a caster in the 1930s along with her eleven sisters and her mother who cast anything from teapots to ewers.[76] In other instances, whole families would work in a variety of jobs in one company. Kenneth Gleaves' family worked for Harry Woods in Burslem in the 1930s. He was the assistant clay manager, his father built the bottleovens, his uncle was the decorating manager, his brother was a printer, and his cousins numbered an engraver, a colour mixer and secretary – all at the same factory.[77]

Ethel Hood worked wherever the money was good, and she was prepared to move around for this. This was unusual for the potteries' workforce where company loyalty was strong. Many women stayed in the company where they were trained for most of their working lives – a situation which suited manufacturers who obviously preferred trained workers. Ada Haynes worked as a paintress at A. E. Grays for most of her working life, while Florence Hancock and Doris Gleaves worked as banders for Susie Cooper from the ages of 15 and 17 respectively until her company ceased all production in the 1980s.[78]

Longevity of service had its advantages in that it could open up internal job ladders especially to skilled workers. Within the decorating side of the production process women who trained as paintresses could occasionally move into jobs as designers. This occurred in both the nineteenth and twentieth centuries, although in Stoke-on-Trent it was more likely after the reorganisation of the art schools in the 1910s which led to the systematic training of decorators.

Decorating offered women some of the best employment in the industry. It was not only reasonably well-paid and skilled, it also provided a relatively clean working environment. Paintresses were known for going to work in decent clothes, rather than dirty, old workclothes. Engravings in *The Queen: The Lady's Newspaper* from 1887 show women paintresses at Doulton's Lambeth factory wearing elaborate bustled gowns (Figure 5).[79] As Arnold Bennett wrote in 1902,

the paintresses form the noblesse of the banks. Their task is a light one, demanding deftness first of all; they have delicate fingers, and enjoy a general reputation for beauty; the wages

35

they earn may be estimated from their finery on Sundays. They
come to business in cloth jackets, carry dinner in little aprons,
and look startlingly neat and tidy.[80]   (Figure 6)

Conditions were not the same in all potteries. Clara Collet described
the work conditions of one group of paintresses in 1893, where 'the
ventilating holes in their room were all stuffed up', although she
acknowledged that generally, 'the burnishers and "paintresses"
seemed drawn from a rather different class; they were working
entirely separate from the men'.[81]

As skilled workers, who had served a seven-year apprenticeship,
their negotiating power was substantial and they were able to win
for themselves better pay and work conditions. Many of the paintresses came from slightly better-off families who could afford for
their daughters to attend art school. For many working-class
women, the necessity of art school training and the poor earnings
entailed by the apprenticeship period were barriers to the skilled
decorating jobs. Ada Haynes was born in 1906, the daughter of a
shoe shop owner. She won a scholarship when she was thirteen to
attend Burslem School of Art for three nights and two days every
week. After completing her scholarship she gained employment at
A. E. Gray as a paintress.[82] Other paintresses were trained directly
by the companies. Millicent Eaton was recruited in the 1930s by
Sam Talbot, A. E. Gray's designer, after he had seen her school art
work. She was offered a six-year apprenticeship by Gray's which
began in the early 1930s with a starting wage of 6s a week which
rose to 16s 8d. From this 'various deductions were made . . . to pay
for "infirmary" benefit (2d/week) and "teaching time" (4d per shilling reducing to 1d per shilling per week at age twenty-one)'.[83]

The decorating shops were often training grounds for working-
class women who became designers through hard work and design
ability, but who were without the educational advantages of their
middle-class sisters. Typical were Millie Taplin and Clarice Cliff,
although training restricted their role to designers of decoration.
This was reinforced by the sexual division between forming pottery
shapes and decorating ware, and by the view that women had an
innate facility for decoration. Other paintresses with a talent for
design were used unofficially by manufacturers, but did not receive
the rewards of pay and enhanced status. For middle-class women
with financial security and family support, there were increased
educational opportunities between 1870 and 1955. The national art

schools offered courses in design, while those in the Potteries provided more specific design education for the pottery industry. Theoretically, all these were accessible to women, although the Potteries
art schools provided a more practical training which served a direct
purpose for workers in the industry as a way of improving earnings.
Most of the women designers in the north Staffordshire pottery
industry were trained in Stoke-on-Trent art schools. The few who
trained outside the Potteries tended to be those who worked freelance and did not live in the area. Design was one of the most
prestigious jobs for women in the pottery industry, but there is little
doubt that it was made possible by women's dominance in the
decorating shops and their widespread involvement in industrial
pottery manufacture. As one commentator wrote: 'the trade in the
potteries is really in the women's hands'.[84]

Notes

1. Potteries with a capital 'P' refers to the Potteries region of
north Staffordshire.
2. Royal Commission on Labour, *The Employment of Women.
Conditions of Work in Various Industries in England, Wales,
Scotland and Ireland*, HMSO, 1893, p. 61.
3. J. Sarsby, 'Occupational Segregation and Women's Wages in
the Pottery Industry', *Feminist Review*, no. 2, Winter 1985, pp.
67–94; *Census of England and Wales. 1911.* vol X, part 1,
HMSO, 1914; *Census of England and Wales, 1921, County
of Stafford*, HMSO, 1923; *Census of England and Wales, 1931
Occupation Tables*, HMSO, 1934; and F. Burchill and R. Ross,
A History of the Potters' Union, Stoke-on-Trent: Ceramic and
Allied Trades Union, 1977, p. 173.
4. ibid., p. 224
5. ibid., p. 12.
6. R. Whipp, 'The Stamp of Futility: The Staffordshire Potters
1880–1905', in R. Harrison and J. Zeitlin, *Divisions of
Labour: Skilled Workers and Technological Change in
Nineteenth Century England*, Harvester Press, Sussex, 1985,
p. 136.
7. M. Hewitt, *Wives and Mothers in Victorian Industry: A study
of the effects of employment of married women in Victorian
industry*, Rockliff, 1958, p. 18.

8. Whipp, 'The Stamp of Futility', in Harrison and Zeitlin, *Divisions of Labour*, p. 138.

9. Burchill and Ross, op. cit., p. 163.

10. For additional information see R. G. Haggar, A. R. Mountford and J. Thomas, 'The Staffordshire Pottery Industry', in M. W. Greenslade and J. G. Jenkins (eds), *The Victoria History of the County of Stafford*, vol. 2, University of London Institute of Historical Research, 1967, p. 56; D. J. Machin and R. L. Smyth, *The Changing Structure of the British Pottery Industry, 1935–1968*, Dept of Economics, University of Keele, 1969; J. H. Thomas, *The Rise of the Staffordshire Potteries*, Adams & Dart, 1971; R. Whipp, 'The Art of Good Management, Managerial Control of Work in the British Pottery Industry, 1900–25', *International Review of Social History*, vol. XXIX, 1984, part 3, pp. 359–85.

11. L. Weatherill, *The Pottery Trade and North Staffordshire 1660–1760*, Manchester University Press, 1971.

12. This was particularly true of under-glaze decorating on biscuit-ware where mistakes could not be easily rectified. In contrast, mistakes made on-glaze could be wiped clean.

13. Creative Tableware company histories, *J. & G. Meakin* and *The Story of the Johnson Brothers*, 1983.

14. Master-potter is a term used in the pottery industry to refer to a skilled craftsperson; someone who has served a long apprenticeship and has great experience and knowledge in the industry. It is significant that there is no female equivalent for this term, and it is indicative of the industry's sexual divisions of labour which confined women to distinct areas of usually unskilled work. Other gendered terms include draughtsman, ovenman, fireman and paintress. Paintress is the only gendered term to describe skilled work as women's.

15. K. Niblett (ed.), *Wedgwood of Etruria & Barlaston*, exhibition catalogue, City Museum and Art Gallery, Stoke-on-Trent, 1980, p. 12.

16. Wedgwood employed Emile Lessore, Thomas Allen, John Goodwin and Victor Skellern; Doulton employed George Tinworth and Charles Noke whilst Minton employed Léon Arnoux and Louis Solon in this capacity. Additionally, most of the major companies employed designers and/or freelance designers who were accountable to the art director.

17. *See, for example, Report of the Committee Appointed by the*

Board of Trade under the Chairmanship of Lord Gorell on the
Production and Exhibition of Articles of Good Design and
Everyday Use, HMSO 1932; Report by the Council for Art
and Industry. Design and the Designer in Industry, HMSO,
1937.

18. Report of the Pottery Committee of the Council for Art and
Industry. Design in the Pottery Industry, HMSO, 1937, p. 3.

19. Skilled women transferrers were to be found in the
Amalgamated Printers' and Transferrers' Society founded in
1871; in 1898 this formally dissolved, but the majority of
members joined the Printers', Transferrers' and Female
Decorators' Society. The combined union, the National
Amalgamated Society of Male and Female Pottery Workers
had 2000 women members in 1914; four years later the National
Society of Pottery Workers which superseded it had 20,000
women members. Burchill and Ross, op. cit., p. 148.

20. Quoted from Children's Employment Commission, Report by
Samuel Scriven, Esq., on the Employment of Children and
Young Persons in the District of the Staffordshire Potteries: and
on the Actual State, Condition, and Treatment of Such Children
and Young Persons, 1841, by Sarsby, op. cit., p. 84.

21. Royal Commission on Labour, Employment of Women, p. 63.

22. Wedging was done by women until the introduction of the
pug-mill.

23. For a description of the work of a mould runner, see C. Shaw,
When I was a Child. By an Old Potter, David & Charles
Reprint, 1969, first published 1903, pp. 12–3.

24. R. Pankhurst, Sylvia Pankhurst. Artist and Crusader,
Paddington Press, 1979, p. 80.

25. Whipp, 'Stamp of Futility', in Harrison and Zeitlin, Divisions
of Labour, p. 126.

26. Sarsby, op. cit., p. 85.

27. Royal Commission on Labour, Employment of Women,
p. 63.

28. Whipp, 'Stamp of Futility', in Harrison and Zeitlin, Divisions
of Labour, pp. 138–9.

29. ibid.

30. ibid., p. 140.

31. Burchill and Ross, op. cit., p. 176.

32. R. Whipp, 'The Women Pottery Workers of Staffordshire and

Trade Unionism, 1890–1905', MA thesis, University of Warwick, 1979, p. 110.

33. According to Burchill and Ross, op. cit., pp. 146–7, there were approx 30,000 women workers in the pottery industry with under 5 per cent of these trade union members in 1893.
34. *24th Annual Report of the Women's Trade Union League*, 1898, pp. 10–11.
35. Royal Commission on Labour, *Employment of Women*, p. 62.
36. For additional information on this see: Whipp, 'Stamp of Futility', in Harrison and Zeitlin, *Divisions of Labour*, pp. 131–3 and C. Mallet, *Dangerous Trades For Women*, produced by the Womens' Liberal Federation, 1893.
37. R. Whipp, 'The Subjected or Subject of History? Women and the Social Organisation of Work in the Early Twentieth Century Pottery Industry', unpublished paper, 1985, p. 22.
38. Gertrude Tuckwell was the niece of Emilia, Lady Dilke, chair of the Women's Trade Union League from 1901.
39. In 1906 the Printers' and Transferrers' and the China Potters' Federation joined the Hollow-ware Pressers' Society.
40. B. Drake, *Women in Trade Unions*, Virago, 1984, p. 160.
41. ibid., p. 95.
42. ibid. Figures from Table I. According to Burchill and Ross, op. cit., p. 177, in 1921 the membership of the NSPW was 38,700; 14,500 men and 24,200 women.
43. In the pottery industry, workers were paid a fixed price per dozen produced. The dozen was not a fixed number; for certain items of ware such as plates, a dozen might indeed mean twelve, for other items such as bowls, a dozen could mean fifteen, and for large tureens it could mean eight. The basis of this was a calculation of how much labour was involved in the making or decorating of the piece.
44. Royal Commission on Labour, *Employment of Women*, p. 63.
45. ibid.
46. *War Cabinet Committee on Women in Industry*, HMSO, 1919, p. 71.
47. ibid., p. 69.
48. ibid., pp. 72–3.
49. ibid., p. 73.
50. ibid., p. 84.

51. ibid., p. 83.
52. ibid., p. 79.
53. ibid., p. 73.
54. ibid., p. 71.
55. ibid.
56. ibid., p. 174.
57. ibid., p. 176.
58. ibid., p. 95.
59. ibid.
60. National Society of Pottery Workers, *Reconstruction in the Pottery Industry*, Co-operative Printing Society Ltd, 1945, p. 27.
61. ibid., p. 28.
62. See, for example, W. H. Warburton, *The History of Trade Union Organisation in the North Staffordshire Potteries*, Allen & Unwin, 1939.
63. Whipp, 'Stamp of Futility', in Harrison and Zeitlin, *Divisions of Labour*, p. 129.
64. Haggar, Mountford and Thomas, op. cit., p. 48.
65. Whipp, 'Stamp of Futility', in Harrison and Zeitlin, *Divisions of Labour*, p. 128.
66. Royal Commission on Labour, *Employment of Women*.
67. Drake, op. cit.
68. Burchill and Ross, op. cit., p. 161.
69. ibid., p. 176.
70. Haggar, Mountford and Thomas, op. cit., p. 51.
71. ibid.
72. Sarsby, op. cit.
73. Shaw, op. cit.
74. Hewitt, op. cit, p. 193.
75. Interview by author with Hilda Salt, 29 May 1985.
76. Interview by author with Ethel Hood, 28 May 1985.
77. Interview by author with Kenneth Gleaves, September 1986.
78. This was even after Susie Cooper had been taken over by Wedgwood. At this point she was producing ware on a small scale.
79. 'The Work-Table: Women's Industries, Pottery Work and China Painting', *The Queen: The Lady's Newspaper*, 1 October 1887, pp. 403–5.
80. A. Bennett, *Anna of the Five Towns*, 1902.
81. Royal Commission on Labour, *Employment of Women*, p. 62.

82. Interview by author with Ada Eardley, *née* Haynes, September 1986.
83. K. Niblett (ed.), *Hand-painted Gray's Pottery*, Stoke-on-Trent City Museum and Art Gallery, 1982, p. 13.
84. Whipp, 'Stamp of Futility', in Harrison and Zeitlin, *Divisions of Labour*, p. 135.

CHAPTER 2

■

A Private Space in a Public Sphere

China painters and decorators

Not the least important amongst the many hitherto closed doors to which the more liberal feeling of men, and the determination and enterprise of women during the latter half of this century, has proved an Open Sesame, is the wide field of industry which may be included under the one general term of 'The Art of the Potter'.[1]

■

During the second half of the nineteenth century women rose to prominence as designers and decorators in the Minton and Doulton art studios. Both Colin Minton and Henry Doulton were keen to improve the aesthetic quality of ornamental pottery by employing students from the recently established schools of design. These schools offered training for middle-class women who were unmarried or widowed and in need of respectable employment. In 1872 *The Art Journal* declared: 'Marriage is undoubtedly woman's happiest vocation. But as all women are manifestly *not* "called" to the happiest lot, it is a little hard that they should not be fitted for some other business.'[2]

Opportunities for women pottery designers and decorators were enhanced by the example of Minton and Doulton as well as of Josiah Wedgwood in England and earlier precedents in the continental factories of Sèvres and Meissen. Women had worked on the European continent as pottery designers and decorators as early as the eighteenth century. Among their number were the designers Sabina and Anna Elisabeth Auffenwerth, Seraphina Susanna Magdalena Schick and Pierrette Caudelot Perrin. Sabina and Anna

Elisabeth worked with their father the goldsmith Johann Auffenwerth in Augsburg. They produced chinoiserie silhouette designs
in gold and silver for the Meissen porcelain factory between 1720
and 1760. These designs for tea and coffee pots, cups, saucers and
plates were described as 'imaginatively conceived family scenes in
indoor settings, comedies and musicians after Watteau, cavaliers
and their ladies, hunting and battle scenes, portrait busts and finally,
mythological and allegorical themes'.[3] Sabina continued to design
for Meissen following her marriage in 1731 to the engraver and
publisher Isaak Heinrich Hosennestel.

Seraphina Schick worked with her husband, Adam Friedrich von
Löwenfinck, at Meissen, and from 1749 she designed for the German
faience manufacturer, Haguenau. After his death in 1754, she succeeded her husband to the post of art director at the Haguenau
pottery, where she remained until her employment as co-director of
the faience factory of Ludwigsburg in 1763. From 1773 until her
death in 1805, she was in sole charge of the factory. In France,
Pierrette Caudelot Perrin ran the Marseilles faience company Vauve
Perrin from 1748 to 1793, after the death of her husband, Claude
Perrin. She was responsible for the establishment of the factory as
a centre of excellence in faience production, and her designs, which
exploited the era's fascination with Rococo and Orientalism, 'are
the legacy of one eighteenth-century woman's imagination, resource-
fulness and business acumen'.[4]

In Britain, Sarah Wilcox, daughter of the painter and potter
Thomas Frye, worked as decorator and designer at Bow; while at
Josiah Wedgwood women were active as designers. The women who
worked at Wedgwood formed two distinct groups; first were those
of the nobility and aristocracy who included Lady Diana Beauclerk,
Lady Elizabeth Templetown and Emma Crewe; and then there were
professional artists such as Elisabeth Vigée-Le Brun and Angelica
Kauffmann. These well-established women artists played less
important roles because they did not produce designs specifically for
Wedgwood. Instead, aspects of their art were copied by skilled
modellers for bas-reliefs and cameos. This interest in the work of
contemporary artists demonstrates Wedgwood's policy of employing
artists to improve the standard of manufactured products. Other
artists employed by Wedgwood included John Flaxman and George
Stubbs, whose work for the company contributed to the establishment of neo-classical taste in Britain in the late eighteenth century.

Aristocrats such as Lady Diana Beauclerk (1734–1808) and Lady

Templetown (d. 1829) attended on the ladies of the royal household, and occupied themselves with feminine leisure pursuits: embroidery and certain types of painting. They were keen amateur artists and Lady Beauclerk, like many of her female contemporaries, was particularly skilled in her use of pastels for portraiture. She was also known for her designs for interiors and decorated two of her own houses. Lady Templetown became a noted landscapist, an interest stimulated by the Picturesque Movement: 'As ... the English drawing-room began to open out into the countryside, ladies of leisure began taking views in water-colour.'[5]

She retired from art on the death of her husband in order to run his estates. Samuel Smiles said of her, 'had Lady Templetown been a poorer women [sic] she might have made a fortune by her wonderful work'.[6] Both women produced designs for Wedgwood based mainly on domestic themes of children and women sewing or teaching their children (Figure 7).

Many women pottery designers prior to the nineteenth century worked anonymously, and from this, nineteenth-century commentators 'inferred, from the absence of proof to the contrary, that women took no active participation either in the production or decoration of any of the beautiful works of art, or of those of utility which owed their origin to the potter's wheel, until the early part of this century'.[7] Major women designers such as Pierrette Perrin and Sabina Auffenwerth have consequently been unacknowledged in the histories of pottery manufacture. Seraphina Schick did sign her designs, but in the manner befitting an eighteenth-century society lady, her career at Haguenau and the Ludwigsburg faience works was unaccounted at the time. Of the Wedgwood artists, Josiah Wedgwood's usual custom of never mentioning artists in his catalogue was broken in the case of Lady Templetown whose name was cited in his 1787 catalogue.

Opportunities for the employment of women as pottery designers came about for a variety of reasons in the mid nineteenth century. There was a great deal of debate about the quality of design in British manufacturing industry from the 1830s onwards. The 1836 report by Ewart's Select Committee of the House of Commons on Art and Manufactures drew attention to the problems facing British industry by highlighting the difficulties of manufacturers unable to find artists or designers willing to work for them, and at the same time, pointing out the dangers of copying foreign work, particularly French. France was the acknowledged producer of high-quality decorative arts and, as a consequence, its products were widely copied. The committee warned of the dangers of this tactic on the grounds that it was better to develop an indigenous style than to copy a foreign style badly, as most British manufacturers seemed to do. It concluded 'from the highest branches of poetical design down to the lowest connexion between design and manufactures, the Arts have received little encouragement in this country'.[8]

The report recommended the establishment of schools of design, the aim of which would be to train designers who would work in industry to improve the aesthetic quality of manufactured goods. It was agreed that designers who could make practical interventions into specific industries were required, rather than artists. The schools' curriculum should be to emphasise 'the direct application of the arts to manufactures'.[9]

Educating Women Designers

Shortly after the founding of these schools for male artisans, the Female School of Design was opened, in 1842. The Council of the School of Design proposed that:

> The fitness of such an occupation for females; the various branches of ornamental manufacture for which their taste and judgment are adapted; the desirableness of enlarging the field of employment for well-educated women; and the successful precedent of a similar institution on the continent, appeared to the Council to furnish strong grounds for adopting this measure.[10]

From the outset the Female School of Design had no difficulties in attracting students; indeed, there was a reserve list for those who could not be accommodated due to lack of space. This problem plagued the School from the date of its initial location in ground-floor rooms at Somerset House.[11]

The Female School was similar in most respects to the Normal School except that it was only open during the day. As a result it was mainly non-working middle-class women who were able to attend. In contrast the Normal School offered evening classes for male industrial workers as well as day classes. The rules of eligibility for the Female School were prepared with the intention of discouraging women who were seeking training principally for an accomplishment. The first rule stated that:

The School of Design for Females having been established strictly with a view to the benefit of those who desire to study Ornamental Art with reference to its use in some industrial occupation, no one who wishes to study drawing merely as an accomplishment can be admitted.[12]

Fanny McIan, head of the Female School, was scrupulous in her interviewing procedure and only admitted women who had demonstrated their financial need to work. The success of the School and Fanny McIan's determination to run it in her own way without the interference of the new management committee provoked 'jealousy of the Female School on the part of those in charge of the [Normal] School of Design, and the ensuing series of hostile actions perpetrated against the Female School can only be attributable to that jealousy, and to the threat of competition it presented'.[13]

After Henry Cole's appointment as head of the Normal School of Design in 1852, the Female School was forced to cut its operating costs and to increase its fees. This meant that middle-class women without means or training, who had been the school's original target, could no longer afford course fees. Instead middle-class women with means wishing to gain further qualifications or who wanted to enhance their accomplishments took most of the places. The School was already experiencing practical problems caused by its abrupt removal from Somerset House in 1848 to the three floors above a soap manufacturer's shop in the Strand. This had been done by a hostile management committee that had also attempted to confine the women students to the production of small-scale works with no pretensions to art. This view reinforced 'contemporary preconceptions associating females with the careful, detailed execution of small-scale work, and also the assumption that there were certain (unspecified) types of work "suited" to the feminine nature'.[14]

Following the establishment of Henry Cole's new Central Training School in 1852 which accepted both male and female students, government support was withdrawn from the Female School in 1859 on the grounds that its services were no longer needed, a move that showed 'an obvious misunderstanding of the special nature of the Female School of Art, and of the special category of needy gentlewoman for whom it provided the means to an independent living'.[15] The Female School was unique in that it offered a large number of middle-class women a socially acceptable means of acquiring specific career skills. To prevent its closure a successful appeal was made for financial support and this enabled it to move to new buildings in Bloomsbury in 1861.

Underlying the management committee's hostility was a desire to limit women to their appropriate sphere. The women trained at the Female School had successfully competed for prizes which had previously been won by men, thereby breaching the established sexual order; they had moved out of the separate sphere which had defined and limited their artistic roles.

Economic necessity was the main reason why middle-class women worked. The plight of untrained women who had little hope of marriage or who were widowed and had no means to earn a living was of growing concern to nineteenth-century social commentators. A dilemma faced Victorian society as it struggled to come to terms with the shortcomings of one of its central tenets – the division between the professional and domestic spheres. In 1872 women outnumbered men by nearly a million, and three million out of the six million adult women in Britain had to support themselves and their dependent relatives.[16] Not only were some women unable to secure husbands, many were ill-equipped to support a family after the death of a husband. It was pointed out that of the women in employment, 'a great part of the applicants for work are either widows or mothers of families – that is to say, women who have "fulfilled their natural destiny" '.[17]

The debate about education highlighted two questions in relation to women. First, should women be educated for the likely event of earning their own living; and secondly, what sort of living should they be trained for? Increased education and training provision was proposed as a solution to women's employment needs, although it was noted that there were other factors which affected their professional opportunities. Teaching, which was considered to be 'women's special work', was a case in point. In 1872 only three of the 117 schools of design were run by women, and only five of 338 art night-classes were taught by women.[18] Commentators debated this at length: 'it may be that women cannot at once rise to the level on which men stand after ages of culture and of conscious freedom.'[19] But it was thought more likely that women's domestic duties left them with little of the uninterrupted time required to achieve excellence. Also, without the discipline of apprenticeships, they could not be fully committed to long-term training.

Nineteenth-century writers on art were convinced of women's suitability for specific types of art work, and it was during this century that the stereotype of women's art as delicate, sensitive and decorative was most effectively delineated.[20] Journals were filled with discussions regarding the abilities of women and their appropriateness to particular aspects of art practice. The *Magazine of Art* declared that 'the instinctive perceptions of woman are often more subtle and finer than those of man; and her heart will guide her to the interpretation of delicacies of sentiment which pass unrecognised by his stronger genius'.[21] Evident in most of these writings is a hierarchical ordering of different branches of art. It was suggested that a woman of great ability (considered a rarity) could work in fine art. But if she combined only intellect and manual skill and lacked the spiritual quality thought to be the distinguishing feature of genius, then 'she may be said to have talent, and may be a worker in a lower sphere. To her the branches of decorative art are open.'[22]

The status of design, the so-called decorative arts, was affected by the notion that women had inherent design skills which originated in their role as home-makers. Woman's 'true mission' was to order and arrange the home: 'Designing seems to offer peculiarly suitable work for women. To whom should we so confidently apply for all that concerns the beautifying of home-life as to the presiding spirit of the home?'[23]

Women's artistic ambitions were to be fulfilled as 'angels in the house'. In this they exercised their intrinsic facility for good taste which could not be confined by the mere use of the brush, but was to be found:

> in the training of her little one's taste . . . in touching their dress
> with the beauty of bright embroideries and graceful
> shapes . . . in aiding their amusement by drawing little pictures
> for them to paint . . . such a woman will give artistic beauty to
> a spray of ivy or feathery tamarisk by wreathing it round a
> mirror. . . It depends on her artistic taste whether her table
> looks like a mere feeding-board or a hymn to nature, the mother
> of food.[24]

In the nineteenth century design was tainted not only by its connection with manual skills, but by this perceived link with women's 'nature' and its growing identification with their art. Fine art and genius were intimately identified with men by romantic theory, which equated masculinity with the qualities of driving ambition, commitment and self-immolation apparently required of this branch of art. In contrast, it was observed that 'with a very large class of feminine artists the great object is not to become famous, but to earn a livelihood'.[25] Any disruptions to the natural order were to be minimised: as *The Magazine of Art* was pleased to report, 'there is happily a large class of women who have no need to earn their bread, and to whom art and the practice of art may yet be a solace and a delight'.[26] There was, however, an equally large group of women who had to earn their living, especially if working-class women were included in the numbers. Many of these women were married, but because of the low wages paid to workers in manufacturing industries, they were required to work from necessity.

China painting and the formation of the Minton and Doulton Studios

China painting was considered to be an appropriate occupation for middle-class women by the 1860s and 1870s. *The Art Journal* commented in 1872,

> there is perhaps no branch of Art-work more perfectly womanly
> and in every way desirable than painting on china. The
> character of the designs brings them within the reach of even
> moderate powers, and it must be admitted that painting flowers
> and birds and pretty landscapes, or children's heads, is work in
> itself more suitable for women than men.[27]

In this role middle-class women paralleled the skilled and semi-skilled working-class women who worked as paintresses and decorators in the north Staffordshire pottery industry.

The pottery manufacturer Colin Campbell Minton was one of the first to provide regular employment for the women trained in the schools of design. This followed the successful completion of the decoration of the grill-room at the South Kensington Museum which had been designed by Sir Edward Poynter, and executed in ceramics by Minton and a group of women students from the National Art Training School. The authorities at South Kensington approached Minton with a view to founding an Art Pottery studio for the purpose of employing women artists. Although the Minton factory was based in Stoke-on-Trent, it was proposed to establish the studio in London. The Commissioners of the 1851 Exhibition granted a five-year lease for a plot of land in South Kensington near the Albert Hall. The studio, which occupied two floors, was opened in 1871 with William S. Coleman as art director. Coleman, a well-known illustrator, had become interested in pottery decoration and had approached Minton's in the late 1860s with the intention of learning the potter's skills. He was given a studio in the factory and was assisted by the fifteen-year-old George Woolliscroft Rhead.[28]

The aim of Minton's Art Pottery studio, which attracted a great deal of public attention, was to raise the standard of design in pottery decoration and to provide employment for the students of the National Art Training School. A press announcement stated: 'there are from twenty to twenty-five educated women, of good social position, employed without loss of dignity, and in an agreeable and profitable manner'.[29] The physical surroundings were crucial to the success of the enterprise as strict codes and conventions governed the environment considered suitable for women of the 'better classes'. The products of the studio included plaques, bowls, vases, tiles and other small pieces of decorated ware. The blank ware was brought from Stoke-on-Trent for decoration, although the firing of the ware took place in the studio's own enamel kiln. The painting techniques taught by Coleman were 'decorative in character, and depend for their expression on good outline, with well-distributed masses of detail and harmonious colouring'.[30] He rejected any attempt to create the effects of pictorial art on pottery such as depth and three-dimensional modelling. Instead, he advised that decorators should work with the flatness of the surface and the qualities of the material used.

Hannah Bolton Barlow was one of Minton's workers, though she later made her reputation as senior designer at Doulton's Art Pottery studio. According to Rhead, she had a particular interest in drawing animals which caused 'consternation among her feminine fellow-workers, from her habit of bringing mice, frogs, and other live stock to the Studio in her pockets'.[31] Most of the other designers from the Minton studio remain anonymous, although it is thought that Coleman's sisters, Rebecca and Helen, worked there. Rebecca Coleman's work was praised in *The Magazine of Art* in 1884 for showing skill in handling and purity of colour.

Various categories of work were produced in the Minton Art Pottery studio, including wares that had been decorated on the biscuit-ware in under-glaze colour and wares that combined under-glaze decoration with on-glaze decoration to increase the colour range. Also there were the highly worked pieces with,

free, artistic treatment . . . in which the whole range and force
of the vitreous pigments at the command of the artist are
brought to bear in producing objects which, so far, have taken
their position as works of Art, and created a demand which
cannot fail to have a marked influence upon the industrial arts
of this country generally.[32]

With the success of his privately produced plaques which sold at
between £30 and £50 each, Coleman lost interest in the studio and
left in 1873. The studio lacked direction after his resignation and
Coleman's successor, Matthew Elden, the designer of the decorative
relief panels on the new Wedgwood Institute at Burslem, proved to
be unsatisfactory. When the studio burned down in the summer of
1875, Minton was provided with a reasonable excuse for closing
down an enterprise that had turned into something of a disaster.
Describing the whole episode of the studio's existence Rhead stated
that,

> The failure can scarcely be said to be Messrs. Minton's fault.
> The head of the firm was not a potter, as was Josiah Wedgwood
> and his own predecessor Herbert Minton; he was simply an
> employer of labour – all the difference in the world between
> the two things. He was largely in the hands of his
> representatives. . . He had shown himself enterprising and
> broad-minded in the encouragement which he gave to Coleman
> in the first instance.[33]

Colin Campbell Minton also had the foresight and lack of prejudice
to create a studio that offered attractive employment to middle-class
women. In this, he had established an important precedent and
offered encouragement to other manufacturers. Unfortunately the
studio's reliance on Coleman left it ill-prepared to survive his
departure.

Undoubtedly the efforts of Minton provided an incentive to Henry
Doulton who was interested in forming an art studio to produce
salt-glazed ornamental stoneware at his Lambeth pottery. This enterprise was unusual due to the nature of the products made by the
Doulton company. These were acid-resisting stonewares for the
chemical and allied industries, insulators for the telephone, telegraph
and electricity supply companies, and salt-glazed vitrified stoneware pipes and conduits needed for the new drainage and sanitary
systems. The only ornamental wares to be produced by the company

before the setting up of the Doulton Art Pottery studio were relief-figured hunting jugs, mugs, tobacco jars, tea and coffee pots which were made continuously until the closure of the Lambeth factory in 1956. Henry Doulton's decision to 'make Lambeth the centre of a real art product' was closely connected with the activities of the Lambeth Art School and its head, John Sparkes.[34]

The Lambeth School of Art had been founded in 1854 as a branch of the Normal School of Design. Sparkes, who became head of the School two years later, believed that 'a school situated in the heart of a settlement of potters ought to do something to advance the beauty as well as the utility of pottery'.[35] Sparkes approached Henry Doulton with his ideas, only to have them quickly dismissed as impractical. Contemporary with this initiative was the discovery of *grès de Flandres* by Doulton's friend and business colleague, Edward Cresy. This was the name given to Rhenish stoneware which had been imported into Britain and many other European countries from the sixteenth century onwards. Cresy showed this to Doulton and suggested that he might be interested in producing a similar type of ware at his Lambeth pottery. Doulton rejected this proposal, but did allow one of his potters to try to copy a piece of Cresy's *grès de Flandres*. The results were unsatisfactory since the cobalt blue colour fled during firing to produce a dull surface of brownish grey. Nevertheless it was this piece, shown at the International Exhibition of 1862 along with Doulton's utilitarian wares, that encouraged John Sparkes to continue his nurturing of Doulton. After Henry Doulton joined the management committee at Lambeth Art School in 1863, Sparkes successfully promoted his plans for a collaboration between the pottery and the Art School.

The unofficial collaboration between Doulton and the Lambeth Art School continued when George Tinworth, one of Sparkes' most promising students, was given a job as modeller at Doulton's pottery in 1867. It was Tinworth who designed the first set of stoneware jugs, tankards and vases under the direction of Sparkes and Cresy in the manner of Rhenish stoneware with raised bosses, beaded runners and incised concentric lines, which were then filled in with blue or brown or the tops were dipped in blue glaze. The limited colour range resulted from the difficulty of finding colours that could withstand the high temperature of salt-glaze firing (Figure 8).

The firm's success with its wares at the 1867 Paris International Exhibition, when French critics had praised 'these attempts to ornament the green clay in graceful lines of extreme simplicity', persuaded Henry Doulton to establish an art studio,[36] once he had gained an assurance from Sparkes that he would direct some of his students to the Doulton pottery. George Tinworth designed the second set of vases and jugs which were then decorated by Hannah Barlow and her brother Arthur, two of the art school's most promising students who started as freelance designers in 1870, before being taken on as permanent employees in 1871. Doulton's aim at this point was to produce ware for the 1871 International Exhibition at South Kensington. After 'seven months of intense activity and many disappointments two or three hundred pots were made and of these 70 were eventually selected by Sparkes as being good enough to exhibit'.[37] The ware was a great success. *The Art Journal* commented:

> The objects produced by Messrs. Doulton include many beautiful forms that have descended to us from antiquity... We never weary of contemplating them and return to them with increasing admiration after considering the abuses of proportion and vulgarity of ornament induced by desire for novelty.[38]

Among the purchasers were Queen Victoria, the South Kensington Museum and the ceramic expert Professor Arthur H. Church.

Church, a ceramic chemist, was consulted by Doulton on the technical problems experienced with the firing and colour. Firing presented particular difficulties due to the ferocity of the salt-glazed kiln and the fact that the stoneware was fired with the industrial ceramics which required several days in the kiln. Added to this the wares could not be protected by the fireproof saggars normally used in the pottery industry. The problem was that the colours were either scorched by the intense heat or the salt failed to react with them. As a result 'the blues often turned black in the firing and the browns and yellows muddy; sometimes the whole of a week's artistic endeavours by Tinworth and Arthur and Hannah Barlow came from the kilns stunted, cracked or discoloured, or marred beyond recognition by grit which had dropped from the roof or the walls of the kiln.'[39] The solutions to these difficulties were developed through experience; the position of the ware in the kiln was changed, the kilns were modified, and, with the assistance of Church, new bodies and glazes were developed to resist the fierce heat of the firing. By examining German and Flemish stonewares, Chinese flambé porcelains, and through the use of oxides of tin and chromium, Doulton and Church began to extend the range of colours from blue and brown.[40]

The new Doulton wares marked a revival in the production of salt-glazed stoneware in Britain and Henry Doulton delighted in its success by showing visitors round the factory and pointing out the production process. John Ruskin was a great supporter of the studios and frequently visited them. He accepted a piece of ware as a gift after one of his visits, selecting a jug by Hannah Barlow which had 'little piggies scurrying round under the handle'.[41]

In two papers read to the Society of Arts in 1874 and 1880, John Sparkes described the wares produced at Doulton's and the role of the Lambeth Art School. The fundamental design principles were first, that there should be no copying of old work, and second, that there would be no duplicates made of each item of Doulton ware.[42] In this, the Doulton ware was 'the precursor of a movement to foster the production of hand-made and hand-decorated pottery'.[43]

Sparkes outlined the different decorative techniques used in what by this time had become known as Doulton sgraffito.[44]

This was supplemented in the 1870s and 1880s by the introduction of new techniques such as pâte sur pâte and a decorated earthenware which Sparkes described as faience.[45] This became one of the company's wares from the 1870s and Sparkes began to train his students in faience decoration.

By the 1880s some 1600 different shapes had been produced, most of which had been thrown on the wheel by hand. Doulton was unusual in this respect since the craft of hand throwing was being superseded in Stoke-on-Trent by semi-automated methods of forming. Doulton's hand-thrown wares were individually decorated, and even in the 1880s, when ware had to be produced in series to meet popular demand, each piece was still hand-thrown and finished.

When the Doulton Art Pottery first opened, the artists' accommodation was temporary, just a section of the showroom separated from the public by screens. With the expansion of his enterprise, Henry Doulton realised that more suitable accommodation was required that would allow all the artists to work together. Urgency was given to this by the employment of several new women designers in 1873 who, for the sake of propriety, needed proper work spaces. Doulton's experiences in Staffordshire had initially set him against the employment of women in his pottery, but he later changed his views:

In Staffordshire I have seen women and young girls employed in the most coarse and degrading labour, such as turning the wheels, wedging the clay, etc. I always declined to employ female labour in the ordinary work of the factory, and it was not until Mr Rix had placed before me a well-organised scheme that I agreed to employ girls and women in our art department.[46]

A block of workmen's dwellings built within the Doulton factory which had not been used for their intended purpose were found to be suitable for the new art studios. The row of houses had numerous small rooms which, following repair, provided excellent work spaces. The women, whose numbers had risen to 74 by 1876, were housed either individually or in small groups. By 1881, when the number of women artists, decorators and trainees had risen to 231, Doulton extended this building to provide fifty separate studios (Figure 9).

The studios brought about changes in design practice for the designers. For the first eighteen months Hannah Barlow had been the only woman designer and had finished each piece herself. After the opening of the studios and following the usual system in Stoke-on-Trent, the production process was organised on hierarchical lines. The head was the senior designer who was in charge of a senior and perhaps several junior assistants. This 'ensured that much of the routine detail, beading, painting and such like, was delegated by the head of the studio'.[47]

Entry to employment at Doulton's came after art school training and a trial month in the factory. If the students showed aptitude for the work they were offered permanent employment which began with a seven-year apprenticeship, first as junior and then as senior assistant to one of the designers. Between 1878 and 1899 some 1000 students were trained by Rix, the art director.[48] Wages for the women working in the studios were much better than those earned by women decorators in the north Staffordshire potteries. In 1896 a Miss Earl, who was a senior assistant, earned £1 7s 7d for a 57½-hour week, whereas in Stoke-on-Trent in 1893 skilled paintresses and transferrers were earning between 11s and 14s for a 57-hour week.[49] To many of the middle-class women in the studio the indignity of having to earn a living was keenly felt. Hannah Barlow recalled that 'in all the years I have worked at Lambeth, I never once had the sensation that money was the ultimate object of my art'.[50]

With more women involved at different stages of training, the responsibility for particular designs was shared among several designers and decorators. By the 1880s senior designers like Hannah Barlow would add their contribution to an already partly decorated piece.[51] Hannah Barlow was one of the few women to throw some of her own pots, although this was not normal practice and most ware was thrown by men. New designs were worked out by the designer, but then executed by several others in addition. To speak therefore of *a* Hannah Barlow – or indeed *a* George Tinworth piece of ware poses problems of attribution for the historian.

Doulton's Women Designers and Decorators

The women designers who worked at Doulton's included Hannah Bolton Barlow and her sisters Florence and Lucy, Louisa J. Davies, Emily J. Edwards, Louisa E. Edwards, Edith D. Lupton, Eliza Simmance and Eliza S. Banks. In the faience department were Edith Rogers, Esther Lewis, Alice Marshall, Ada Dennis, Linnie Watt and Florence E. Lewis. Little is known of the lives of several of these women designers, but more is known of their work thanks to John Sparkes' articles on the Doulton Art Pottery studio.

Best known and indeed typical of the women who found employment at Doulton's was Hannah Barlow (1851–1916) (Figure 10). The death of her father in 1866 forced Hannah, one of nine children, to consider ways of making an independent living. Little in the preceding fifteen years had prepared her for the possibility of earning a living. She had had virtually no formal education, but had developed a facility for drawing from nature in the Essex countryside surrounding the family house.

Ceramics had interested her since childhood when she had watched an itinerant thrower produce a pot on a wheel. After being introduced to John Sparkes by Edith Rogers, a family friend who was attending the Lambeth School of Art, she decided to enrol. At Lambeth, Hannah Barlow developed a distinctive style of drawing directly from nature and later from memory. Her sketchbooks were filled with hundreds of sketches of animals which captured 'the spirit of the beasts and birds represented' (Figure 11). Specific areas of art and design which she learned at Lambeth were general design, painting and modelling. General design included different aspects of pottery decoration. Sparkes described her 'Japanese facility of representing the largest amount of fact in the fewest lines'.[53] Hannah Barlow's work was clearly inspired by the Japanese products which were widely seen in Britain following the 1862 International Exhibition at South Kensington. The calligraphic and formal techniques of Japanese prints were arousing keen interest in art and design circles by the 1870s. Designers admired the economy of line, the use of pattern and simplicity of form evident in Japanese objects. Retailers such as Liberty of Lower Regent Street capitalised on this craze by importing a variety of oriental products: fans, prints, silks and blue and white ceramics.

Hannah Barlow's first meeting with Henry Doulton at the Lambeth pottery was recorded by his biographer Edmund Gosse:

> She was going downstairs early in 1871 and was met by a
> gentleman tearing up the staircase, two steps at a time, who,
> nevertheless, paused to take off his hat to her, and to give her
> a very charming smile. 'I wonder who that is' said Miss Barlow
> to herself, 'whoever it is, I feel sure he must be a delightful man
> to work for.'[54]

He proved to be a supportive employer who actively encouraged her work and that of her brother, Arthur.

By the mid 1870s, Hannah Barlow had developed a characteristic style which was much simpler and more spontaneous than her later work. A writer in *The Lady* in 1887 wrote: 'She knows the anatomy and ways of animals by *cumulative experience* and scratches the forms on to the clay . . . a method demanding a precision of touch rare even among artists of distinction.'[55] Usually these incised or sgraffito designs comprised groups of animals set in natural surroundings with simple, decorative borders of scrolls, beads or dots (Figures 12 and 13). At the same time she experimented with different decorative techniques such as carving, which can be seen in a vase of 1872 modelled in high relief with a continuous, circular design of deer being attacked by wolves. The base of this in blue and grey to contrast with the browns of the main body was decorated with incised lines (Figure 14). Hannah Barlow was a great animal lover and kept a small menagerie at home which included a deer, Shetland pony, goose and donkey. However, her depictions of animals were rarely sentimental and there are no examples in her work of animals taking on human characteristics.

Florence Barlow joined her sister and brother at Doulton's in 1873 (Figure 15). She shared many of her sister's interests as a designer, and specialised in painting birds (Figure 16). By some private arrangement made around 1877, Hannah Barlow agreed to confine herself to animal motifs and Florence Barlow to bird motifs. The two sisters shared a studio and were briefly joined by a third sister, Lucy, who worked at Doulton's for three years between 1882 and 1885 before becoming her sisters' housekeeper.

Initially, Florence Barlow used the sgraffito technique. In *The Doulton Lambeth Wares*, Desmond Eyles suggested that 'in their early incised work, both Florence and Hannah were influenced by Jean-Charles Cazin, a French landscape artist and stoneware potter who succeeded Alphonse Legros as a teacher at the Lambeth School of Art in the early 1870s'.[56] After 1878 she began to experiment with pâte sur pâte, described by John Sparkes:

> [she] has recently executed some very charming paintings in coloured clays – of birds especially, which give a conventional light and shape and colour treatment to her desires, very helpful on the score of variety.[57]

Her particular skill was to produce an effective sense of light and shade in the pâte sur pâte medium (Figure 17). Like the other women designers at Doulton, she worked on the whole range of the studio's products: these included faience, marqueterie, impasto, silicon, and Carrara ware. By the late 1880s Hannah Barlow's work had become more elaborate and complex, combining different decorative techniques such as pâte sur pâte with sgraffito and faience. An example of this is a faience moon flask with painted decoration of cows in a field, and with borders by Katie Blake Smallfield (Figure 18). About the same time, Doulton ware began to attract some adverse criticism mainly as a result of the complicated designs introduced to stimulate new sales. Mark V. Marshall, a designer at Doulton's from 1879, wrote a poem, 'Lambeth Laments', which attacked what he described as the 'Roman Splendours' of the current ware:

> Away! bad dreams, oh: cease to care
> For Italy's voluptuous craze.
> Look back at Barlow's modest ways
> The love and zeal of early days,
> of Doulton Ware.[58]

By the 1880s Hannah Barlow was a celebrated artist. Her work was praised in magazines such as *The Lady* and *The Queen: The Lady's Newspaper*. She exhibited a terracotta relief entitled 'Our

Pet' at the Royal Academy in 1881 and at numerous other venues both at home and abroad. Hannah Barlow left in 1913.

One of Hannah Barlow's earliest colleagues was Eliza Simmance. She was trained at Lambeth School of Art and began work at Doulton's in 1873 where she remained until 1928. She worked collaboratively with the Barlow sisters and also independently. Her range of skills was enormous; she worked in various techniques on stoneware and on the new silicon ware. This was a hard smooth stoneware with a fine texture that could be decorated by a variety of techniques including sprigging, sgraffito and pâte sur pâte, as well as being stained with colour which permeated the body of the ware. Eliza Simmance specialised in sgraffito and pâte sur pâte, and during her fifty-odd years at Doulton her designs responded to new artistic ideas. Her early designs were typically of finely incised flowers and blossom, and demonstrate her knowledge of fashionable Japanese products. John Sparkes wrote of her:

> she excels in painting the 'pâte sur pâte' patterns. There are examples of her work . . . which are so eminently graceful and well-drawn as to emulate the qualities in the work of the Italian Ornamentalists. She, too, has so many ideas to spare – more than she can work out by herself – that she keeps a staff of rising artists occupied carrying out her instructions.[59]

At the end of the century she began experimenting with the Art Nouveau style, becoming one of the Doulton Art Pottery's major exponents. To create the free-flowing lines of Art Nouveau, she developed a form of tube-lined decoration which allowed her to make thin, relief patterns on the surface of ware (Figures 19 and 20).

Louisa E. Edwards and Louisa J. Davies worked at the Doulton studios from about 1873 until 1890–5. They were both interested in Persian and Indian designs and were influenced by the work of William De Morgan, who designed and decorated pottery between 1872 and 1911. De Morgan had researched Persian and Moorish decorative motifs, and these inspired his highly formalised animal and bird designs decorated in red, blue and green enamels and lustres. Sparkes described Louisa Edwards' work as being 'drawn with clear lines of perfect construction, and distributed with judicious thought, taste, and skill' (Figure 21).[60] Of Louisa Davies he said she 'has treated certain natural plants – notably, reeds, sedges, and grasses – with a masculine vigour and power' (Figure 22).[61]

This method of analysing design according to so-called 'masculine' and 'feminine' characteristics was common as we have seen in Victorian art and design criticism. Louisa Davies's salt-glazed stoneware vase of 1882 is deeply incised with blue flowers and brown leaves on a pale olive-green ground. It is much less detailed and graphic than most of the studio's output (Figure 23). But although there was a distinctive Doulton style, arguably it had more to do with use of different techniques and various bodies than with the sex of the maker.

Emily J. Edwards was one of the first women designers to be taken on at the Doulton studios, working there from 1871 to 1876. Her work demonstrated an intimate knowledge of classical forms which she used in an abstract way. According to Sparkes it was 'ornament, made up of an ingenious mixture of classical or conventional forms with natural growths' (Figure 24).[62]

In addition to the many other women artists who designed for salt-glazed stoneware, including Edith D. Lupton, Eliza S. Banks and Edith Rogers, who worked in the studios from 1876–*c*.90, 1874–84 and 1881–88 respectively, a large number of women worked in the faience department. Like Edith Rogers, whose father was Alfred Rogers, woodcarver to Queen Victoria, many of these women designers were the daughters or wives of men associated with the studios (Figure 25). Ada Dennis, who worked at Doulton's between 1881 and 1894, was the wife of Walter Gandy, a longstanding associate of the studios who had a wide knowledge of historical art and ornament which Henry Doulton frequently drew upon. Ada Dennis designed for faience, Carrara and marqueterie wares; an example of her work is a faience jug from 1894 depicting children painted in the style of Kate Greenaway's illustrations (Figure 26). John Sparkes' wife Catherine was a talented artist who did freelance work for Doulton's throughout the 1870s. Alice Marshall worked at the studios between 1897 and 1914, and specialised in floral decoration on faience. She was the daughter of Mark V. Marshall, who worked as a designer at Doulton's from 1879 to 1912.

Male artists and designers often helped their female relations to opportunities in art and design, thereby creating a family framework for such activities by providing encouragement, tuition and practical support. Conversely, they could also handicap their wives' and daughters' progress by overshadowing or making invisible their work. Certainly, subsequent historians have been more interested in fathers, sons and husbands than mothers, daughters and wives. This can be seen in the case of Arthur Barlow, brother of Hannah and Florence. Arthur, like other male designers working alongside the women designers at Doulton, was given disproportionate recognition by writers on the Doulton Art Pottery.[63]

The faience department provided three women in particular with an outlet for their creative talents. Linnie Watt, Esther Lewis and Florence E. Lewis were employed at Doulton's from the 1870s to the 1890s. Faience was especially suited to painterly decoration, and designers such as Esther Lewis specialised in landscapes and seascapes. An example of her work which was described as 'equally good decoration and good art' is 'Old Bridge, North Wales', a faience wall-plaque designed in 1877.[64] In 1884, her work was described in the *Magazine of Art* as 'amongst the most notable efforts in the decorative representation of scenery contributed by an English lady'.[65]

Linnie Watt was a talented artist who exhibited at the Royal Academy. Her work at Doulton, which was characterised by rustic scenes and figure painting, was praised by Sparkes: 'Miss Linnie Watt has a most distinguished gift for conveying the impression of a picturesque scene with rustic figures in excellent colour and with artistic breadth of effect, quite admirable in its truth.'[66] To the writer in the *Magazine of Art*, her designs were the epitome of grace and beauty, and perfectly suited to their decorative role in the home, and, 'taken together, the decorative pictures of Miss Linnie Watts are perhaps the most novel and satisfactory product of the taste for paintings on china in England'.[67]

Florence Lewis studied at Lambeth School of Art and worked at Doulton from 1874 to 1897.[68] According to Eyles, she was a much more substantial artist than Sparkes gave her credit for and regularly exhibited at the Royal Academy, the Royal Institute and major London galleries. Sparkes described her 'remarkable power of design and skill in painting . . . whether she is working out a large design or a small tile, her energy and power are equally shown'.[69] At the Doulton studios she designed for the whole range of wares including faience, Crown Lambeth and marqueterie, and 'played an important part in the development of these wares by directing for several years a group of some seventy young women as trainee painters'.[70]

In addition to her role as a designer, Florence Lewis was a noted writer on pottery design. Her book *China Painting*, published in 1884, outlined the basic rules and techniques of decorating china. By the mid 1870s china painting was an acceptable form of art practice for middle-class women. George and Frederick Rhead, writing in *Staffordshire Pots and Potters*, 1906, attributed its popularity to the success of the Minton and Doulton studios which 'directly created that interest or "craze" for pottery decoration which became almost universal throughout the country during the 'seventies, and, amongst a good deal of downright bad work, a certain proportion of good was done'.[71]

The interest in china painting stimulated the firm of Howell and James to organise annual competitions of paintings on china from 1876. These competitions were patronised by members of the royal family who provided prizes, and judged by distinguished Royal Academicians such as E. J. Poynter, and architects such as Richard Norman Shaw. The competitions were open to both amateurs and professionals, and women designers from the Doulton and Minton studios exhibited there. In some circles it was noted with satisfaction that 'the art within certain limits has steadily improved, and the distinction between amateur and professional work has steadily diminished'.[72] In others, its amateur and therefore non-threatening status was emphasised. It was described as ornamental, graceful, harmless and charming – all terms which linked china painting with women and their separate sphere.

At the height of its popularity there were 350 artists working in the Doulton studios, although at the time of Henry Doulton's death in 1897, there were under a hundred. After this date the market for the expensive Lambeth wares gradually diminished, and as women designers left they were not replaced.[73] Like most middle-class Victorians, Henry Doulton believed in the essential goodness of women and that the 'true sphere of woman is the family and household, and I believe that the contact of women with the strifes and rivalries in which public men are involved would weaken that beneficent influence which they exert over our sex'.[74] He recognised the inevitability of women working, but thought that if women had to work, then it 'should be as far as possible restricted to occupations not involving severe labour, and as much as practicable to the Arts that beautify and adorn life'.[75] This is his own justification for employing women designers and decorators, a decision he did not regret once the issue of satisfactory accommodation had been resolved. Commenting on the employment of women in the art studios, he wrote:

'The effort, like most good ones, had a small beginning. It was tentative. But the admirable organisation triumphed, and it has given me from that time to this, the most absolute and perfect satisfaction.'[76] The sentiment was reciprocated by the women artists when they presented Henry Doulton with two commemorative volumes in 1882. In these beautifully illustrated volumes signed by 229 women artists and assistants, they wrote:

> Ten years having now elapsed since the introduction of female employment into the Lambeth Art Pottery we the undersigned being the whole of the Lady Artists and Assistants now engaged in the studios upon work, desire to take the opportunity of expressing our obligation to you for the origination of an occupation at once interesting and elevating to so large a number of our sex. We also desire to record our very high appreciation of the arrangements made for our comfort and convenience.[77]

Henry Doulton's undoubted commitment to art pottery is interesting in that it was apparently an unprofitable enterprise which he subsidised.

Decorating the signed pages of the commemorative volumes were numerous illustrations of women working in the pottery. These idealised images of wholesome, healthy women in elegant, aesthetic gowns captured perfectly Henry Doulton's intention in establishing the Doulton Art Pottery (Figure 27). It provided pleasant and remunerative employment for middle-class women with artistic ability but without means. His initiative, combined with the radical theories of the Arts and Crafts Movement, provided a framework within which women pottery designers could work between 1880 and 1914.

Attitudes to women pottery designers and decorators in the nineteenth century, and the opportunities open to them, were shaped by a matrix of complex and sometimes contradictory factors. Their status, either amateur or professional was important, as was the status of their designs, which depended on whether they were signed. An art and design education in anticipation of a career, as opposed to training for additional ladies' accomplishments, was enormously significant in the second half of the nineteenth century. This was made easier by class position for eighteenth-century aristocratic women designers.

For those women like Lady Templetown who were employed by

Wedgwood, the issue of status was contentious both in contemporary accounts and subsequent histories. Aristocratic women produced paintings, architecture, embroidery and ceramics as an extension of ladies' amateur 'accomplishments'. However, their employment by Wedgwood alongside male counterparts, John Flaxman and George Stubbs, placed them in a professional context. From the comments of contemporaries, it is clear that these aristocratic women were paid fees for their designs, although most business arrangements were conducted with due respect for etiquette by Josiah Wedgwood I.[78] It is significant that although design historians have placed emphasis on Wedgwood's enlightened attitude to design through his employment of artists in the latter part of the eighteenth and early part of the nineteenth centuries, little has been said about the women designers whom he employed.

At Doulton's Lambeth studio, the women designers and decorators were trained and employed as professional artists, although within the context of the separate sphere. The new art schools had trained them in those aspects of artistic production considered particularly appropriate for their sex and those which did not bring them into competition with men – in the lesser, decorative or applied arts. Women's 'nature', it was thought, equipped them for small-scale design, and like the aristocratic women at Wedgwood seventy years earlier, appropriate subject matter included pretty scenes of children, home, gardens, birds and flowers which was thought to be intrinsically 'feminine'. This separation of women's artistic domain from men's, which was maintained in pottery by identifying women with the design of surface pattern and decoration, and men with the design and modelling of shapes, enabled women to operate as professionals without undermining the gender divisions of Victorian middle-class society. Although earning their own living in a professional and industrial arena, the Doulton women worked in good clothes in comfortable, private studios away from the taint of commercialism and the glare of male eyes, designing – with the important exception of Hannah Barlow – surface patterns. At Lambeth, then, Henry Doulton offered women a private space in the public sphere.

All the women designers so far discussed signed their wares. This has meant that their existence is indisputable, although the quality of their designs and the importance of their roles is open to interpretation. To date most of the interest shown in the work of these women pottery designers has come from collectors who are not so hidebound by designers' gender. Although informed by their own value-systems, collectors seem less concerned to construct a progressive and essentially Modernist account of pottery design and designers than historians. This latter group appear all too willing to accept that women's designs look the way that they do because of 'nature' and biologically-determined ability, rather than as a consequence of ideology. They seem largely unconcerned to analyse the reasons why 'decorative' and 'sensitive' should signify 'female', and why these qualities are valued less in a hierarchy which prizes their opposites.

From this discussion of women designers in the nineteenth century, we can see that these women worked the way that they did as designers for specific social and ideological reasons, not because they were biologically predisposed that way. Owing to the construction of gender in the nineteenth century, women existed within the confines of the separate sphere which limited their access to certain types of jobs, training and art; ultimately their roles were defined in a relation of difference from men's. However, these positions were not accepted without conflict nor did they remain fixed and unchallenged. That women such as Lady Templetown, Hannah Barlow and Florence Lewis were able to work as designers is indicative of the struggle, albeit modest, in which they engaged.

Notes

1. 'The Work-table: Women's Industries, Pottery Work and China Painting', *The Queen: The Lady's Newspaper*, 1 October 1887, p. 403.
2. 'Art-Work For Women I. The Work To Be Done', *Art Journal*, 1872, vol. XI, p. 65.
3. R. Berges, 'Woman Power in Eighteenth-Century Ceramics', *Antique Dealer and Collector's Guide*, June 1980, p. 80.
4. ibid., p. 82.
5. G. Greer, *The Obstacle Race*, Secker & Warburg, 1979, p. 286.
6. L. S. Rakow (Mrs), 'The Feminine Touch in Wedgwood', *The Wedgwoodian*, proceedings of the 12th Wedgwood International Seminar, Smithsonian Institute, Washington, 1967, p. 156.
7. 'The Work-table', *The Queen*, 1887, p. 403.
8. F. McCarthy, *A History of British Design, 1830–1970*, Allen & Unwin, 1979, p. 9.

9. R. Haggar, *A Century of Art Education in the Potteries*, Stoke-on-Trent (no publisher), 1953, p. 3.

10. *Report of Council of School of Design*, 1842–3, p. 6.

11. ibid., 1843–4, p. 23.

12. ibid.

13. A. Callen, *Angel in the Studio. Women in the Arts and Crafts Movement 1870–1914*, Astragal, 1979, p. 29. See Chapter 1, 'Design Education for Women', pp. 19–49 for a full discussion of these issues.

14. ibid., p. 30.

15. ibid., p. 35.

16. 'Art-Work For Women II. Why the Work is Not Done', *Art Journal*, 1872, vol. XI, p. 103.

17. ibid.

18. 'Art-Work For Women I', *Art Journal*, 1872, p. 65.

19. 'Art-Work For Women II', *Art Journal*, 1872, p. 102.

20. See R. Parker and G. Pollock, *Old Mistresses: Women, Art and Ideology*, Routledge & Kegan Paul, 1981, for a fuller discussion of this.

21. L. Scott, 'Women at Work: Their Functions in Art', *Magazine of Art*, vol. VII, p. 98.

22. ibid.

23. 'Art-Work For Women I', *Art Journal*, 1872, p. 65.

24. Scott, op. cit., p. 99.

25. ibid.

26. ibid.

27. 'Art-Work For Women I', *Art Journal*, 1872, p. 66.

28. G. W. Rhead and F. R. Rhead, *Staffordshire Pots and Potters*, E. R. Publishing Ltd, 1977 (first published by Hutchinson & Co., 1906), p. 348.

29. 'Minton's Art-Pottery Studio', *Art Journal*, 1872, vol. XI, p. 100.

30. ibid.

31. Rhead and Rhead, op. cit., p. 355.

32. 'Minton's Art-Pottery Studio', *Art Journal*, 1872, p. 101.

33. Rhead and Rhead, op. cit., p. 81.

34. E. Gosse, *Sir Henry Doulton. The Man of Business as a Man of Imagination*, Hutchinson, 1970, p. 360.

35. ibid., p. 60.

36. ibid., p. 73.

37. D. Eyles, *The Doulton Lambeth Wares*, Hutchinson, 1975, p. 20.
38. ibid, p. 21.
39. ibid, p. 23.
40. Gosse, op. cit., p. 183.
41. ibid., p. 85.
42. J. Sparkes, 'On some recent inventions and applications of Lambeth stone ware, terra-cotta, and other pottery for internal and external decorations', *Journal of the Society of Arts*, 1 May 1874, vol. XXII, p. 561.
43. Eyles, op. cit., p. 23.
44. These techniques included scratching or cutting a pattern in the clay soon after it had left the potter's wheel; cutting into the clay at the 'green hard' stage, that is, some hours after it had been thrown; and whitening the body or dipping the ordinary brown body into coloured slips which could then be cut through to reveal the body underneath. Other techniques comprised carving on the surface of ware; applying moulded clay dots, discs, rosettes or figures to the surface; and stamping patterns into the clay.
45. Doulton faience was different from the tin-glazed maiolicas which were its inspiration because it was decorated on biscuit-ware prior to glazing. The original maiolicas were painted on an opaque unfired lead glaze containing tin oxide; it was this that gave the ware its whiteness.
46. Gosse, op. cit., p. 209.
47. P. Rose, *Hannah Barlow. A Pioneer Doulton Artist*, Richard Dennis, 1985, p. 23.
48. Callen, op. cit., p. 68.
49. Callen, op. cit., p. 64, and Royal Commission on Labour, *The Employment of Women. Conditions of Work in Various Industries in England, Wales, Scotland and Ireland*, HMSO, 1893.
50. Gosse, op. cit., p. 181.
51. Rose, op. cit., p. 23.
52. ibid., p. 11.
53. Sparkes, 1874, op. cit., p. 562.
54. Gosse, op. cit., p. 81.
55. 'Lady Artists: Miss Hannah Bolton Barlow', *The Lady*, 1887, p. 215.
56. Eyles, op. cit., p. 92.

57. J. Sparkes, 'On the further development of the fine-art section of the Lambeth Pottery', *Journal of the Society of Arts*, 12 March 1880, vol. XXVIII, p. 349.

58. Rose, op. cit., p. 29.

59. Sparkes, 1880, op. cit., p. 350.

60. ibid., p. 350.

61. ibid.

62. Sparkes, 1874, op. cit., p. 562.

63. See Eyles, op. cit.

64. Sparkes, 1880, op. cit., p. 354.

65. C. Monkhouse, 'The "Royal Academy" of China-Painting', *Magazine of Art*, 1884, vol. VII, p. 248.

66. Sparkes, 1880, op. cit., p. 354.

67. Monkhouse, op. cit., p. 249.

68. Eyles, op. cit., p. 130.

69. Sparkes, 1880, op. cit., p. 353.

70. Eyles, op. cit., p. 130.

71. Rhead and Rhead, op. cit., p. 361.

72. Monkhouse, op. cit., p. 246.

73. According to Rose, op. cit., p. 38, a pair of faience vases cost 52s 6d in 1882.

74. Gosse, op. cit., p. 209.

75. ibid.

76. ibid.

77. Commemorative Volumes (2) presented to Henry Doulton, dated from 1871–1881, p. 1. Held at Minet Library, Lambeth, London.

78. Rakow, op. cit.

CHAPTER 3

∎

Alternative Roles for Women
The hand painting revival and art potters

In many of the Continental countries the woman potter in the past has played no small part, for irrespective of the war-time shortages of labour, it has been recognised that a woman can be not only a successful potter but also an artistic one.[1]

∎

The revival of interest in craft processes and products that took place in Britain between 1880 and 1919 opened up new opportunities for women pottery decorators and designers. The fear of foreign competition and the effect of the First World War galvanised pottery manufacturers into debate and action on design. Manufacturers such as Josiah Wedgwood and Sons responded to the success of competitors like Doulton and to the theories of the Arts and Crafts Movement by reviving hand painting within a mass-production system. Women designers and paintresses played a crucial role because of the assumption that they had a special facility for hand decoration. At the same time, the Art Pottery Movement created a suitable environment for women who wished to work as artist–potters and as hand decorators. Improved training and employment possibilities opened up for women artists and designers towards the end of the nineteenth century, and centres of progressive art and design education emerged in Glasgow and the Potteries. These provided the starting point for many women wishing to embark on careers in design for industrial pottery manufacture.

In the small potteries of Della Robbia, Bretby, Pilkington, Bernard Moore and Burmantofts, women who worked as designers, makers and decorators included Dora Billington, Gwladys M. Rogers,

Esther Ferry, Florence Tooth and Liza Wilkins. These potteries were inspired by the example of Arts and Crafts theorists and practitioners who had outlined an alternative, radical design practice. In this, the hierarchical and elaborate divisions of labour common in the large potteries of north Staffordshire were rejected in favour of small-scale series production by a limited number of craftworkers. A different response to the same craft theories was exemplified in the work of women designers Louise Powell and Daisy Makeig-Jones, who occupied important positions in the development of the hand-painting studio at Wedgwood in the early twentieth century.

Arts and Crafts Theories into Practice at Wedgwood

From the 1860s, Josiah Wedgwood and Sons underwent a process of modernisation and expansion. This had been made necessary by the precarious financial position resulting from decades of neglect and reliance on a reputation established in the eighteenth century. New wares were introduced such as Parian, a translucent porcelain-like body which was left unglazed and used for statuary, and Majolica, introduced in the 1860s following the success of the Minton prototypes. Under the Majolica heading was a range of products which illustrated Wedgwood's desire to establish its reputation as an art ware producer in order to capitalise on the expanding market for artistic products in the late nineteenth century. During the 1870s Wedgwood employed many apprentice paintresses who, like their London counterparts, were art school trained, middle-class women, and not the artisan or working-class women who normally made up the ranks of paintresses in the potteries of Stoke-on-Trent.

The range of wares produced under the Majolica label included Tremblay, Argenta and artistic faience.[2] The latter had been developed by the French artist Emile Lessore, who worked for Wedgwood from 1860 after a brief spell at Minton. Lessore established a school of decorative art pottery at Wedgwood's Etruria factory which attracted critical approval after the 1862 Paris Exhibition. Lessore's appointment marked a recommitment to the employment of artists, something which had been a cornerstone of the first Josiah Wedgwood's approach to pottery design.

Other artist–designers such as Christopher Dresser, Walter Crane, William De Morgan, Helen J. Miles and Thérèse Lessore were associated with Wedgwood at this time. Thérèse Lessore, the daughter of Emile, was employed by Wedgwood from the mid

1870s. Helen J. Miles was trained at South Kensington before working extensively as an illustrator and painter between 1860 and 1883. Her work was known through periodicals and regular exhibition. She designed tiles after their reintroduction by the company in 1875. Many of her designs demonstrate knowledge of the Aesthetic Movement and the fashion for Japanese products. 'Months', a printed and hand-painted design, was clearly inspired by Kate Greenaway's illustrations of children in idyllic, rural settings wearing the simplified, peasant or artistic dress so beloved of the design reformers of the Aesthetic Movement (Figure 28).

The Aesthetic Movement, or Queen Anne style as its architectural form was known, developed in Britain in the 1870s and 1880s. It 'introduced Japanese art to children's story books and red brick Queen Anne architecture to the streets of London; it led to changes in fashionable dress, to the first garden suburb and to the vogue for painted dark green or Venetian red front doors and railings'[3], and marked an attempt to improve the standards of mass-production by highlighting the importance of art and the role of the designer. The application of 'Art' to everyday objects such as 'Art Furniture', 'Artistic Dress' and 'Art Pottery' was one of its main characteristics.

The movement originated in the debates about design which took place in the mid nineteenth century and was inspired by the Gothic Revival, the writings of the art critic John Ruskin, the designs of William Morris and the newly imported art products from Japan. From the Gothic Revival came an emphasis on the appropriateness of form and decoration, and the concept of design as a whole, rather than a variety of styles lacking unity. From Ruskin and Morris came a reassessment of the artistic hierarchy which had separated the 'high arts' of painting and sculpture from the 'lesser arts' of design. Ruskin in his writings and Morris in his design practice rejected the division of labour in manufacturing industry for dehumanising the workers and debasing the aesthetic quality of products. They proposed instead a revival of craft methods and the use of natural forms as a source for the designer, rather than copying historical styles. It was Morris's desire to improve the aesthetic quality of everyday objects which was of the greatest importance to the designers of the Aesthetic Movement. Unlike Ruskin and Morris, its supporters were less concerned with the moral arguments against the industrial system, although they appreciated the simplicity and unadorned beauty of craft objects. Japanese art and design provided one of the primary visual sources for the Aesthetic Movement, and from the

1870s onwards it was common to find an array of products such as fireplaces, metalware, textiles, furniture and pottery decorated with bamboo, cherry blossom, kimono-clad women, cranes and fans.

Pottery manufacturers responded to the Aesthetic Movement in two main ways; first, they copied its motifs by incorporating Japanese patterns onto blue and white wares. These were usually transfer printed on mass-produced pottery, and within the context of the time, they were considered to be of better quality than other, more elaborate products. Secondly, manufacturers set up art potteries such as those at Minton and Doulton, or they established art sections like the one at Wedgwood. During the 1880s, the development of 'Art Pottery' was also linked to the activities of William Morris's followers who formed the Arts and Crafts Movement. These included some of the designers employed by Wedgwood such as William De Morgan, Walter Crane and Alfred and Louise Powell. Inevitably, these influenced the company's direction in art pottery and its use of hand-decorating techniques over the next thirty years.

The Arts and Crafts Movement represented a radical approach to design which had far-reaching effects on design theory and practice between 1880 and 1914. To some extent it overlapped with the Aesthetic Movement; they had common origins in the Gothic Revival and both were concerned to reform design. However, the essence of the Arts and Crafts Movement was its belief that 'society produces the art and architecture it deserves'.[4] This view originated in the writings of Ruskin and Morris and in their conviction that the improvement of standards of design would not be achieved solely by the employment of specially educated designers in manufacturing industry. Instead, they saw the impoverishment of Victorian design as a consequence of modern production methods which were based on the division of labour. As John Ruskin wrote:

> We have much studied and much perfected, of late, the great civilised invention of the division of labour; only we give it a false name. It is not, truly speaking, the labour that is divided, but the men: divided into mere segments of men – broken into small fragments and crumbs of life; so that all the little piece of intelligence that is left in a man is not enough to make a pin.[5]

To both writers, the degradation of industrial labour left its dull imprint on mass-produced designs. Their solution to the problem of good design was to reject mass-production methods. They proposed a return to craft processes in which the designer and maker were combined in one role and had a thorough understanding of materials and hand techniques. This, they believed, would lead to a better quality product. This reassertion of the validity of craft represented not only the restoration of pre-industrial production techniques, but also of social values. Initially, Morris's conviction that 'you cannot educate, you cannot civilise men, unless you give them a share in art', and his realisation that 'art cannot have a real life and growth under the present system of commercialism and profit-mongering' led him to a vision of the Middle Ages as a model society.[6] Later in his life, this view was reformulated within a socialist framework.

The practical effect of these theories on design objects was the use of natural materials and craft methods of production, often within the context of a guild. The medieval guild was the ideal for work and social organisation because of its stress on learning through direct experience and on collective action. In these guilds, craftworkers and designers produced a range of everyday products based on simple, vernacular forms. Within this framework, it was believed, art would be made 'by the people and for the people, a joy to the maker and the user'.[7] But paradoxically products made according to the strict principles of the Arts and Crafts Movement were expensive and hence mainly restricted to the wealthy consumer. At a popular level, the Arts and Crafts Movement was partly responsible for the vogue for hand-decorated or hand-finished products.

Women designers were active within the context of Arts and Crafts practice. But although it was a politically and socially progressive movement, 'with often radical social aims, which should have contained the potential for an equally radical reassessment of the personal and practical relations between men and women, [it] turned out to be reactionary in its reinforcement of the traditional patriarchal structure which dominated contemporary society'.[8] This was manifested in a sexual division of labour which was contrary to the true principles of the Movement, but which seems to have been widespread in areas of design with strong gender associations such as embroidery. Within this division, men were the designers, while their wives, daughters or sisters were the executants. In the case of the pottery industry, the prevailing sexual division of labour which cast women in the role of designers of decoration, and men as designers of shape was largely maintained in the newly created art studios and hand-craft sections. Women designers in the pottery industry had few opportunities to work as designers of both shape and decoration, as shown by the example of Hannah Barlow and George Tinworth at Doulton. Although Barlow did throw pots at the wheel, this was unusual, and it was Tinworth who was responsible for the production of the different ranges of Doulton shapes.

Louise Powell

Ada Louise Powell (1882–1956) and her husband Alfred Hoare Powell (1865–1960) introduced some of the ideas of the Arts and Crafts Movement to the Wedgwood company in the early years of the twentieth century. Wedgwood had to some extent lost its artistic direction in the closing years of the nineteenth century, a situation made more critical by the poor economic climate. The export market on which the company relied was uncertain, and changes in the home market had left it vulnerable. Added to this, both Cecil and Frank Wedgwood went off to fight in the Boer War, leaving Kennard Wedgwood to run the company. However, 'Mr Kennard proved extremely efficient and thoroughly justified his charge; in fact, his period of control signalised the commencement of a new era in connection with the Wedgwood business.'[9] This new era began with a programme of rationalisation and reductions in the product range. New markets were sought in Europe and John Goodwin was appointed as art director.

Goodwin had been trained in the Stoke-on-Trent art schools. He started an apprenticeship as a designer of pottery decoration at the age of fourteen and was taken on at Wedgwood's Etruria factory in 1893. His period as art director was marked by the overhaul of the product range which saw the withdrawal of elaborate Victorian wares. These were replaced by shapes and patterns that were relatively simple and echoed the company's neo-classical beginnings. At the same time Wedgwood began to target some of its products at the expanding middle-class domestic market. Freelance artists continued to be employed, including the French designers Marcel Goupy and Paul Follot. Goodwin's main priority was to improve the commercial, mass-produced ranges, whereas Louise and Alfred Powell's brief was to develop the art wares.

Their association with Wedgwood began when Alfred Powell submitted designs in 1903. The progressiveness of these was recognised by the company which was keen to develop a range of wares that catered for modern tastes. The principles of the Arts and Crafts Movement were already gaining a wider audience through shops such as Liberty, which commissioned designs for texiles, dress, metalware and jewellery in an Arts and Crafts idiom. From this first speculative contact and following his marriage in 1906 to Ada Louise Lessore, whose family had strong connections with the Wedgwood company, a working relationship began which was to last until 1940.

Alfred Powell had been articled to the architectural practice of J. D. Sedding. Sedding was an early exponent of the vernacular style which was to prove particularly influential towards the end of the nineteenth century. At Sedding's office Powell became friends with the other apprentices, Ernest Gimson and the brothers, Ernest and Sidney Barnsley. Like them he was keen to work according to Arts and Crafts principles using traditional building and design techniques. In 1901, he joined them in the Cotswolds, eventually designing his own house at Tunley near Cirencester from which he ran his architecture and design practice.

Powell's decision to become involved with a large manufacturer highlighted the problems facing the Arts and Crafts Movement in the early twentieth century. The ideals of the Movement and their practical realisation in the production of beautifully wrought objects made in idyllic, though isolated, rural guilds presented intractable difficulties, not least of which was the remoteness of the guilds from their sophisticated London market and the expensiveness of their designs. Gradually some members of the Movement began to acknowledge the potential of machines to produce goods of a reasonable quality at a lower price, if used appropriately. Indeed support for this view could be found in William Morris's own writings. Towards the end of the 1880s he had argued that 'those almost miraculous machines, which if orderly forethought had dealt with them, might even now be speedily extinguishing all irksome and unintelligent labour, leaving us free to raise the standard of skill of hand and energy of mind in our workmen'.[10] Powell's involvement with a manufacturer such as Wedgwood then, was not unprecedented, within this context of reassessment, although it was also evidence of his own pragmatism.

Louise Lessore was established as a craftworker and designer before her marriage to Alfred Powell. Her artistic interests were encouraged by her family; her grandfather was Emile Lessore, her father was Jules A. Lessore, a well-known marine painter and exhibitor at the Royal Academy and Paris Salon, and her aunt Thérèse worked at Wedgwood in the 1870s. Her sister, Elaine Thérèse

Lessore, was a painter and founder of the London Group of artists. Elaine designed for Wedgwood in the 1920s, and in 1926 the painter Walter Sickert became her second husband. Their brother Frederick was a portrait sculptor who opened the Beaux Arts Gallery in 1923. Louise Powell was trained at the Central School of Art and Design, which was run by the Arts and Crafts theorist William Richard Lethaby from its foundation in 1896 until 1911. The teaching staff included other Arts and Crafts practitioners such as Edward Johnston and Sidney Cotterell who taught calligraphy and illuminating. These were the areas of design in which she specialised, becoming a member of the Society of Scribes and Illuminators. She also worked with Johnston's successor Graily Hewitt on several major commissions, including two incomplete Morris manuscripts, one of which was *The Aeneid of Virgil*. Her designs for illumination provided an excellent grounding for her role as designer at Wedgwood. Contemporary with this, she produced decorative schemes for furniture designed by Ernest Gimson.

From 1906, Louise and Alfred Powell worked together as designers. Some of their work was jointly signed, while some was identified by their personal monograms. It is difficult to identify their individual contribution to jointly produced work, although Alfred Powell tended to use figurative and pictorial motifs, whereas Louise Powell was more interested in calligraphic and heraldic motifs.

The success of the early designs which Alfred Powell produced at Wedgwood led to a more formal agreement being made with the company. The result of this was the establishment of a studio, the employment of two assistants in London, and the provision of a small studio with facilities at Wedgwood's Etruria, factory. Both Louise and Alfred Powell were paid fixed sums as designers, and they produced designs for both shapes and decoration. A prototype shape was produced by the Wedgwood thrower to the Powells' specification and under their supervision. This was then mass-produced in earthenware and either decorated in their London studio or at Etruria, where it was also fired. Louise and Alfred divided their time between London, their house in Gloucestershire, and Stoke-on-Trent, visiting the latter four or five times a year for periods of up to a month. During this time, they oversaw the production of their new designs and trained the paintresses in hand-decorating techniques.

Some of their early pieces in the Arts and Crafts Exhibition at the Grafton Galleries in 1906 were favourably reviewed. In October of the same year, the *Staffordshire Sentinel* commented on their 'fresh style of decorated pottery' which was shown at a Wedgwood exhibition in Liverpool.[11] On display were some of the revived eighteenth-century designs that Wedgwood reintroduced at the suggestion of Louise Powell. She had come across some of the original pattern books during one of her visits to Etruria. These designs, modified to suit contemporary tastes, were painted in a traditional manner and included a large amount of free-hand painting. The revival of eighteenth-century patterns proved a commercial success owing to the growing appreciation of Georgian and Regency design in the first twenty years of the twentieth century. The patterns which included 'Vine', 'Oak Leaf' and 'Crimped Ribbon and Wreath' were sold through mainstream stockists such as James Powell of Whitefriars and Harrods, but they were also popular with progressive stores such as Dunbar Hay (Figure 29). They were described by the *Staffordshire Sentinel* as 'the most exquisite example of Josiah Wedgwood with all the original details and exactitude of finish'.[12]

The majority of the designs produced by Louise Powell were free-hand painted wares including jugs, vases, plaques, ginger pots, bowls and small containers. They were decorated in bold, stylised patterns derived from nature but with a strong calligraphic quality (Figure 30). The influence of Islamic and Renaissance pottery and her debt to the Arts and Crafts potter William De Morgan are evident in her use of striking colour combinations and lustre decoration. De Morgan's pottery was inspired by Persian and Italian pottery particularly in terms of pattern and colour. He was a pioneer in the use of the copper, silver and gold lustres which became popular in the early twentieth century.

The designs of Louise and Alfred Powell represented a compromise between the mass production of pottery and the theories of the Arts and Crafts Movement. Although the shapes were mass produced, they were vernacular and medieval in appearance (Figure 31). The craft aesthetic was achieved through the decoration which was based on free-hand painting techniques, deep earthy colours and stylised motifs from nature. This is evident in the Bicentenary vase specially designed in 1930 by Louise Powell to celebrate the founding of the Wedgwood company two hundred years earlier (Figure 32). With its double handles, heraldic lettering and stylised leaf motifs, it signified a commercial response to the Arts and Crafts Movement.

Their designs for bone china tableware were simpler and were based on small repeated leaf and flower patterns handled in a traditional way (Figure 33). Some of Louise Powell's designs were extremely complex in terms of pattern, and required modification by the art director, John Goodwin, for easier production. The Rhodian and Persian ornamental wares, introduced by Wedgwood in 1920 at the British Industries Fair, were examples of this (Figure 34). Although not designed by Louise and Alfred Powell, the shapes and patterns illustrate their powerful influence on Wedgwood's product range. By the mid 1920s some fifty of their designs had been put into production. Probably the major effect of their involvement with the company was the increased commitment to hand-painted wares which led to the establishment of a small handcraft studio at Etruria in 1928. They also played an important role in training two young women who were to be designers at Wedgwood in the 1930s, Millicent Taplin and Star Wedgwood.

Alfred Powell outlined their attitude to pottery design and decoration in a series of articles. In a manner typical of Arts and Crafts designers, they believed that 'it is really no easy matter at the present time to find a piece of modern industrial pottery that could be called by a properly constituted judge "beautifully painted" ',[13] and attributed this to the financial priorities of pottery manufacturers:

> the pottery industry as it is today represents such a good
> expenditure of money and effort that all the energy of the
> factory owners is absorbed by the attention which they have to
> give to their material interests.[14]

Arts and Crafts tenets were demonstrated by their commitment to a conducive working environment. They argued that 'beauty of workmanship (unconscious, plain, doing it well) would seem to be particular about surroundings and conditions'.[15] For the pottery industry, they advocated:

> uncovering the love of beauty-in-work. . . Instead, we put little
> girls – susceptible to all the usual delights of childhood, to sit
> in factories day after day placing little dabs of green and red on
> printed patterns until they turn into automatons, their little
> minds stiffen up to the dull work and do it professionally, but
> it is a real tragedy and a loss that pottery cannot afford.[16]

The distinction which they draw between the activities of the majority of paintresses who undertook the mundane decorating jobs, and the free-handers who worked in the Etruria factory is an interesting one. They believed that this latter group of paintresses had a more intelligent and practical involvement in the production of the wares which removed them from the realm of monotony:

> We have to learn to rely on ourselves – as used to be the rule. . . Quick minds – clever fingers – gentle hearts, and especially in Staffordshire, the native debonair gaiety that is so notable to strangers – these are some 'lines' to develop![17]

The legacy of Louise and Alfred Powell at Wedgwood was enormous. In 1936 Louise Powell's designs were exhibited with a new range of Wedgwood wares at the Grafton Galleries. However, because of technological developments in the 1930s, their approach became outmoded. Elaborate hand-decorating techniques began to be superseded by less complicated effects which brought much reduced time and labour costs.

Grace Barnsley and Thérèse Lessore

The Powells' example pointed the way for other designers, including several women, who were interested in working with large manufacturers such as Wedgwood. Wedgwood employed a number of designers on a freelance basis including Margery and Jessie Jack, Thérèse Lessore and Grace Barnsley. Grace Barnsley worked at Wedgwood in the 1910s and 1920s. Her contact with the company came through Louise and Alfred Powell from whom she learned hand painting. She was the daughter of Arts and Crafts designer Sidney Barnsley, a close friend and colleague of Alfred Powell. Initially she had no formal working relationship with Wedgwood and, like several other designers who were connected with the company at the time, she bought blankware to decorate. From the late 1910s she began to work closely with Wedgwood, designing patterns which were then hand painted either by herself or the company's own paintresses. These designs were clearly inspired by the example of Louise Powell with an emphasis on stylised, natural forms such as berries, vines, leaves and flowers handled in a loose painterly fashion (Figure 35).

Elaine Thérèse Lessore (1883–1944) trained at the Slade School of Art as a painter in the early twentieth century. In this she continued the family tradition in art and design, and in her work at Wedgwood she followed the example of her sister, Louise Powell. Her introduction to pottery design came through her sister, although

Walter Sickert, with whom she shared a studio, also decorated Wedgwood pottery. Between 1920 and 1924, Thérèse Lessore designed a series of plates and dishes with figurative designs of contemporary scenes. These were painted in under-glaze blue, polychrome enamels and copper and silver lustre. As co-founder of the London Group in 1913 with her first husband, Bernard Adeney, she was connected with the avant-garde in British painting and knew the Bloomsbury artists, Duncan Grant, Roger Fry and Vanessa Bell. This artistic context is apparent in her Wedgwood designs, as in the earthenware tea set in grey and pink lustre which has a figurative design of a bather disrobing. The formal depiction of the figure and the handling of paint relates to the work of the Bloomsbury group of painters, particularly Duncan Grant and Vanessa Bell (Figure 36). These artists had developed an interest in modern French painting, notably that of the Post-Impressionists and the work of artists like Henri Matisse. From the mid 1920s, Thérèse Lessore exhibited her pottery alongside her paintings, and it was through her that the Bloomsbury group established contacts with Wedgwood.

Daisy Makeig-Jones

One of Wedgwood's most prolific and important women designers in the early part of the twentieth century was Daisy Makeig-Jones. She was born in 1881 in Yorkshire and christened Susannah Margaretta, but was always known as Daisy. She was the daughter of a doctor who in 1899 moved his seven children, of whom Daisy was the eldest, to Torquay. Daisy Makeig-Jones was educated at home by governesses in typical middle-class manner before attending a boarding school for young ladies in Rugby. It was here that she developed an interest in art that was encouraged by her art teacher and which continued at Torquay School of Art from about 1899, and in a studio in the family home.

With family support, Daisy Makeig-Jones looked for a professional opportunity in art. It was to this end that, through a family friend, she was put in contact with the Wedgwood company in 1909. Wedgwood insisted that if she were to join the company then she had to learn the essentials of pottery manufacture by starting on the factory floor and learning the skills of the paintress. Typically she was pushed into the 'feminine' side of the production process. Cecil Wedgwood, who was managing director of the company, was convinced that given her family background she would not enjoy work in a pottery factory.

She trained for two years along with the other young paintresses under the art director John Goodwin and the senior designer James Hodgkiss. During the seven-year apprenticeship, the wages of the paintresses gradually increased from 2s a week for the first year, to 2s 6d for the next two to three years and finally to 3s 5d for the remainder of their training. They then moved on to piece rates. In August 1911, Daisy Makeig-Jones finished her training and was placed on the staff at an annual salary of £52.[18] She first worked in John Goodwin's studio before moving to her own studio in 1914 when she was given an increase in salary and promoted to designer.

Her first designs for Wedgwood were for nurseryware and consisted of patterns for children's earthenware porridge bowls, plates, mugs and jugs. The earliest of these, which were figurative and illustrated scenes of animals and people drawn in a naïve way, were Brownies from *c.* 1913, Noah's Ark from *c.* 1914, Cobble and Zoo from *c.* 1917 and Thumbelina from *c.* 1916 (Figure 37). Women's dominance as nurseryware designers was clearly linked to contemporary perceptions of intrinsic female skills. Underpinned by biological determinism, it was thought that women were specially suited to this in the same way that it was believed that their reproductive and maternal roles gave them special insight into the design of children's books.

Contemporary with these designs for nurseryware were experiments in lustre which preoccupied her for the next ten years and earned her an international reputation. Ornamental wares had taken second place to the production and marketing of tablewares at Wedgwood in the early years of the twentieth century. This had been done for economic reasons, but once the commercial standing of the company was secured, a desire to develop a new ornamental range of wares emerged. The first step in this direction came with the introduction of powder-blue, an imitation of the *bleu soufflé* developed in China at the end of the seventeenth century. This was produced in 1912 after collaborative experiments between James Hodgkiss, George Adams, the company chemist, and Bernard Moore, the artist–potter who was ceramic consultant to Wedgwood. Powder-blue inspired a revival in ornamental wares at Wedgwood, and provided the impetus for Daisy Makeig-Jones' own experiments with lustre.

Her experiments were not with the traditional reducing techniques of lustre production, but with the newer in-glaze commercial lustres which were painted onto already glazed and decorated wares. Under-glaze decorating techniques such as staining, stippling and mottling were combined with lustring and gold printing to create the extraordinary effects of the ordinary and Fairyland lustres. These processes were expensive and time-consuming but they produced exotic, iridescent patterns such as the Dragon, Bird, Fish and Butterfly ordinary lustres from 1914, and the magnificent Fairyland lustres introduced from 1915. The lustre production process was dependent on a high degree of craft skill from the paintresses, and could involve as many as five or six firings (Figure 38).

Daisy Makeig-Jones was fascinated by the notion of Fairyland, and Fairyland lustre allowed her imagination to run wild. She incorporated elves, fairies, pixies and gnomes into bizarre landscapes with toadstools, stars and spiders' webs. Initially, lustre colours purple, ruby, pink, blue, green, yellow, orange, mother-of-pearl and copper-bronze, were soft and harmonious. Later, following the introduction of Flame Fairyland lustre, strong primary colours were introduced (Figure 39). Lustre wares were extremely popular throughout 1915–29, although the elaborate hand painting and complex production process inevitably made them expensive luxury items. In the early 1920s, an ordinary lustre Imperial bowl nine inches high cost £2 7s 6d, while a Fairyland lustre version of the same bowl cost £5 4s 6d.[19]

'Celtic Ornaments' was another design of Daisy Makeig-Jones. It was based on decorative motifs from the sixth-century *Book of Kells*, a replica of which Wedgwood had obtained. The company was clearly aiming to capitalise on the vogue for Celtic art which emerged in the early twentieth century. It was manufactured on bone china teaware, and ornamental bowls and vases, but it apparently met with little commercial success.

The effects of the American Stock Market crash of 1929 were felt strongly by Wedgwood for it depended on the North American market for the sales of its expensive, ornamental designs. Almost immediately it instigated a reappraisal of all designs, including the lustres, which proved to be among the first casualties; price cuts could not restore dwindling sales. The new management team, which had been brought together in 1930, asked Daisy Makeig-Jones for her resignation, and after a tremendous row in April 1931 with the new managing director, Josiah Wedgwood V, during which she was told that there was no future for the lustres at Wedgwood, she agreed to leave.

By all accounts, Daisy Makeig-Jones was a formidable woman with a forceful personality who was prepared to stand her ground. She was unconventional in her appearance and working practices. After twenty-two years at Wedgwood her departure was largely unexpected. To the new all-male management team she represented a system of design and production that they were keen to leave behind. Tighter design controls were introduced at Wedgwood during the 1930s, and there was little room for the type of individualism which characterised Daisy Makeig-Jones' approach. Nevertheless, she was a major designer at Wedgwood, exerting a strong influence on the company's product range between 1915 and 1929. After her departure she moved southwards to live with her mother and sister, and in 1945 at the comparatively young age of sixty-three she died.

Women Designers at the Omega Workshops and Poole Potteries

The contacts which the Bloomsbury group had established with Wedgwood through Thérèse Lessore proved useful when the Omega Workshops opened in 1913 and the group required good quality blankware for decoration. The Omega Workshops were intended to be an extension of the art critic Roger Fry's commitment to developing Post-Impressionism in Britain. His premise was that Post-Impressionism should be tied to the public's everyday life by 'extending it to the applied arts, and thus introducing it more fully into our homes in the shape of mural decorations, upholstery and decorative furniture of all kinds'.[20] The workshops also offered profitable employment for artists who were unable to make a living solely from their painting.

Omega's founder members included Clive and Vanessa Bell, Roger Fry and Duncan Grant. Initially they were self-taught in pottery design, however they were eventually offered facilities for throwing and firing at the Poole Potteries in Dorset. After the Omega Workshops closed in 1919, some of its members continued to produce pottery with the assistance of Phyllis Keyes, a potter who had her own workshop and kiln. Roger Fry was the group's theorist and it was he who defined their approach to pottery. Although a convinced Modernist, Fry was a traditionalist when it came to pottery design. His writings reveal an Arts and Craft commitment to craft working methods and the social function of design products. He was against the machine which he believed led to 'dead mechanical exactitude and uniformity' and argued that 'wherever the machine enters, the nervous tremor of the creator disappears'.[21] Until a working relationship with the Poole Potteries was established all Omega pottery was hand-thrown. From 1914 moulds were made at Poole which enabled quantity production of Omega Pottery to begin.

Women were always involved in the production of this pottery. The artist Vanessa Bell hand-painted wares that were mainly thrown by Fry, and later she worked collaboratively with Phyllis Keyes. Vanessa Bell's decorative designs were comparable to those done by Thérèse Lessore for Wedgwood. They were figurative and portrayed fashionable women in contemporary scenes. In her handling of colour and form, Vanessa Bell demonstrated her knowledge and understanding of modern art; her later designs for pottery were abstract arrangements of colour and pattern.

The Poole Potteries employed a number of women designers, modellers and paintresses from around 1914–15. The company had started in the mid nineteenth century as an architectural pottery producing faience, glazed and terracotta wares and plain floor tiles.[22] It was not until the early twentieth century that the company showed serious interest in the production of ornamental and tablewares. Under the works designer, James Radley Young, a new unglazed ware was developed just before the First World War, and it was for the production of this ware that he trained a team of women throwers and decorators. The ware was left unpolished and had the irregular appearance of hand-finished products; in this it demonstrated the contemporary interest in craft. At about the same time, the Carter family who owned the Poole Potteries were involved in experiments which led to another new ware which came to characterise the Poole product range. The new style of ware was inspired by traditional Delft-wares, and was created on an off-white stoneware which had been dipped in a creamy-white slip and then a clear glaze. The hand painting was done before the firing, and as a result the colours tended to fuse into the slip and glaze to produce a soft, blotted effect.

The designers Truda Adams (1890–1958) and her husband John Adams (1882–1953) were responsible for a large number of patterns and shapes for these new ornamental wares. Truda Adams, who was divorced from Adams towards the end of the 1920s, and later married Cyril Carter, the Chairman of the Poole Potteries, was trained at the Royal College of Art. Truda and John Adams started at Poole in 1921 along with several art school trained paintresses, including Margaret Holder, Anne Hatchard, Sissy Collet and Ruth Pavely. Truda Adams immediately began to design floral patterns for wall plaques, vases, bowls and dishes, using a distinctive colour range of dull blues, reds, yellows and browns (Figure 40). These designs were adapted to different-shaped wares by the senior paintresses Margaret Holder and Ruth Pavely who 'stepped outside their role as decorators and were allowed not only to interpret established patterns, but also to offer original designs'.[23] During the 1930s, Truda Carter also produced several patterns for the 'Streamline' tableware which was designed by John Adams. Most of these were sparsely decorated with small floral motifs.

Throughout the 1920s and 1930s, Truda Carter was the resident designer at Poole, where she was joined periodically by several other women designers. These included Olive Bourne, Irene Fawkes, Dora M. Batty, and the textile designer Minnie McLeish. In 1950 John Adams described Truda Carter's 'considerable influence on design as she did many of the shapes and most of the characteristic painted patterns'.[24] Truda Carter's involvement in both the design of pottery shapes and decoration was sanctioned within the company by the example of other women who had thrown and modelled wares. Most important of these were Phoebe Stabler, Minnie McLeish's sister (d. 1955), and the Gilham sisters, Lily (1897–1968) and Gertie (1902–74). It was nevertheless unusual for women to design both pottery shape and decoration, although Arts and Crafts principles which encouraged this were brought to Poole by Harold and Phoebe Stabler.

Phoebe and Harold Stabler worked at Poole from about 1921 until the mid 1930s. Both were established designers before their contacts with Poole and had a kiln in their London home. Harold Stabler was well known in progressive design circles. He had been on the first committee of the Design and Industries Association, which had been established in 1915 to promote better standards of design in British industry, and he was a founder of the British Institute of Industrial Art. At Poole, Phoebe Stabler modelled a series of figures, including 'The Lavendar Woman' (1913), 'The Bull' (1914) designed with her husband, and 'The Piping Boy' (1914–22). She was an astute businesswoman and sold similar designs to Royal Doulton, the Ashtead Pottery and Royal Worcester.[25]

Lily and Gertie Gilham were taught throwing and modelling by

James Radley Young. He encouraged variety and individuality in pottery design, and in response to this Lily modelled insects and reptiles for garden pots and other ornamental wares. In addition she learned various decorating techniques such as tube-lining, and later went on to throw her own thin, fine wares. Her sister Gertie became the company's chief thrower in the 1920s and was better able to design for the demands of mass production than Lily. Gertie also taught throwing at Poole and Bournemouth Schools of Art.

During the 1930s, the range of ornamental and tablewares at Poole became standardised and commercially viable. They were exhibited with success at various exhibitions: 'the Pottery had gained an enviable reputation, in the eyes of contemporary observers, for distinctive and distinguished wares.'[26] The Poole Potteries initially responded to the themes of the Arts and Crafts Movement, but by the 1930s this had been superseded by an interest in mass production and good quality design in industry. The wares designed by women at Poole were produced in response to these considerations. Some displayed the qualities of hand painting and small-scale craft production, whereas others accorded with the desire to mass produce a modern product. In both these phases women played an important role that challenged the sexual divisions dominating pottery design in the north Staffordshire industry. The example of the Arts and Crafts Movement, with its emphasis on the unity of the design process, provided the framework for this challenge.

Women Art Potters

The interest in craft manifested at Wedgwood and Poole was also evident in the large number of art potteries established between 1880 and 1920. The work methods and organisation of these differed, although some were run like an independent Doulton Art Pottery studio. Others provided the prototype for the studio potteries set up in Britain from the 1910s onwards. Women designers often found opportunities within these art potteries, although there is little documentation of their lives and work. Best known at the time were Hilda Beardmore and Dora Billington, who worked as designers at the Bernard Moore Pottery in Stoke-on-Trent, Gwladys M. Rogers who worked at Pilkingtons, Esther Ferry and Rachel Smith who were based at the Burmantofts Pottery on the outskirts of Leeds, and Liza Wilkins, Ruth Bare, Violet Woodhouse, Hannah

Jones, E. M. Rope, A. Pierce and Lena Pierce at the Della Robbia Pottery, Birkenhead.

The Della Robbia Pottery was started in 1894 by Harold Rathbone and the sculptor Conrad Dressler to produce architectural relief panels. From 1898 the production of art pottery, which had been a small aspect of the company's manufacturing, was expanded following the arrival of an Italian sculptor, Carlo Manzoni, who had been running a pottery in Hanley, Stoke-on-Trent. Former art students were employed at the pottery as designers, in addition to artist/designers like R. Anning Bell, who went on to become head of Glasgow School of Art. An article in 1896 in the *Magazine of Art* reported that 'Employment is found at the Birkenhead Potteries for many young people of both sexes who show artistic taste.'[27]

Among the women designers was Hannah Jones who was described as a gifted colourist and Liza Wilkins who worked at Della Robbia until its closure in 1906, and who excelled in the use of Art Nouveau-style decoration. The pottery specialised in decorating techniques such as sgraffito and the use of coloured enamels to create the effects of Italian maiolica. An example of this is a cylindrical vase with flared rim from about 1900 which had decoration designed by Liza Wilkins. The vase was decorated with olive-green and yellow enamels and a green glaze; the stylised organic motifs clearly relate to the Arts and Crafts Movement and Art Nouveau.

Ruth Bare was another of the woman designers at Della Robbia; she specialised in both the design of ware and decoration (Figure 41). Art Nouveau was the dominant stylistic influence on her work, and a typical example of her design is a two-handled jar from 1903, which has modelled female heads with flowing hair in yellow, green and brown.

The aim of the pottery was to offer opportunities for students to work independently in order to bring out 'the full fancy and orig-inality of each individual worker'.[28] As well as ornamental wares, the pottery produced tableware – marmalade pots, porridge plates, egg stands and muffin dishes. In this it adhered to a fundamental Arts and Crafts principle, 'that the chief object of a manufacture of this kind. . . [is] the application of artistic qualities to objects of ordinary domestic use'.[29]

The Royal Lancastrian Pottery established by the Pilkington Tile and Pottery Company in 1900 provided employment for a group of talented young designers. These included Gordon M. Forsyth,

1. Line drawing of the old Etruria Works, after an original mid-nineteenth-century wood cut The view shows the Trent and Mersey canal.

2. Architect's drawing for the proposed Barlaston factory. Designed by Keith Murray, 1938.

3. A woman transferrer (left) and rubber-on (right) with printer (middle) workin on the American Commemorative View Ware at the Wedgwood factory c. 1936.

4. Painting by Sylvia Pankhurst 'Women in a Pottery Factory', 1907.

5. Hand paintresses at wo at Wedgwood's Etruria factory c. 1900.

6. Wedgwood women slip decorators with the compar designer, Harry Barnard, 1898.

Blue and white Jasper teapot with cupid finial and bas reliefs from the 'Domestic Employment' series by Lady Templetown, modelled by William Hackwood. c. 1802.

Early salt-glaze Doulton wares typical of those shown at the 1867 Paris Exhibition.

9. Hannah (left) and Florence (right) Barlow at work in their studio at Lambeth, 1887.

10. Hannah Bolton Barlow and her dog 'Rufus Darwin', 1913.

11. A page from Hannah Barlow's sketchbook, 1872.

Three salt-glaze Doulton wares
[in]cised decoration of animals and
[bird]s, relief beading and stippling by
[Hann]ah Barlow. Left: jug, 1895.
[Middl]e: tobacco jar and cover, 1895.
[Righ]t: jug, 1895.

[S]alt-glaze Doulton umbrella
[stand] with incised decoration of
[deer] by Hannah Barlow, 1874.

[S]alt-glaze Doulton vase
[mode]lled in high relief and
[depic]ting deer being attacked by
[wolv]es by Hannah Barlow,
.

[F]lorence Barlow at work on
[one o]f her pots. Undated.

16. Salt-glaze Doulton vase with slip outline decoration and pâte-sur-pâte painting of birds.

17. Three salt-glaze Doulton vases with pâte-sur-pâte paintings of birds by Florence Barlow. From right to left: vase, 1886; vase, 1883; vase, 1899.

18. Doulton faience moon flask painted by Hannah Barlow with border scrolls by Katie Blake Smallfield, *c.* 1885.

19. Three salt-glaze Doulton vases by Eliza Simmance with tube-lined decoration. Left: vase with leaves and flowers, 1906. Middle: tall vase with pomegranates, 1910. Right: vase with birds, 1916.

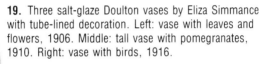

20. Salt-glaze Doulton vase by Eliza Simmance with tube-lined Art Nouveau style decoration, 1907.

21. Three salt-glaze Doulton wares by Louisa Edwards with incised decoration. Left: vase with leaves and flowers, 1881. Middle: vase with flowers and foliage, 1879. Right: jug with plants and flowers, 1878.

22. Salt-glaze Doulton vase by Louisa Davis with incised decoration of foliage, 1878.

23. Salt-glaze Doulton vase by Louisa Davis with deeply incised decoration of flowers and leaves, 1882.

24. Four salt-glaze Doulton wares by Emily Edwards with incised decoration of foliage and bands of beading. Left to right: jug, 1872; jug, 1873; dish, 1876; jug, 1872.

25. Two salt-glaze Doulton vases by Edith Rogers. Left: vase with incised foliage overpainted in pâte-sur-pâte, 1882. Right: vase with incised scroll decoration with plaques inscribed with names of Scott, Keats and Burns, 1882.

26. Doulton vase designed by Ada Dennis with motifs of children playing and beaded work, c. 1893.

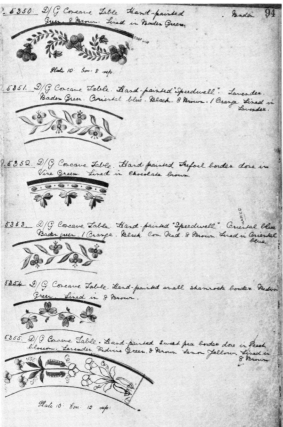

27. Page from the Commemorative volumes presented to Henry Doulton the women artists and assistants in 1

28. One of the original water-colour designs by Helen Miles for the 'Month series, *c.* 1877.

29. Page from Wedgwood pattern bo showing the 18th century patterns re by Wedgwood in the 1900s.

30. Earthenware mug painted in under-glaze blue and purple lustre and designed by Louise Powell for Wedgwood, 1910–1920.

31. Earthenware and bone china tablewares designed by Louise and Alfred Powell. Decorated with hand painting and stencilling by the Powell-trained paintresses, *c* 1910–1930.

Queen's Ware vase designed by ...ise Powell to commemorate the ...entenary of Josiah Wedgwood's ...h (1730–1930). Decorated in ...er lustre.

... Bone china and earthenware ...ewares designed and painted ...Louise and Alfred Powell ...Wedgwood, 1910–1930.

34. Freehand paintress
working on a Persian
ornamental vase at
Wedgwood's Etruria
factory, c.1926.

35. Two jugs and a bo
designed and hand
decorated by Grace
Barnsley for Wedgwoo
c. 1920.

36. Earthenware teaset
grey, pink and silver lus
painted by Thérèse
Lessore.

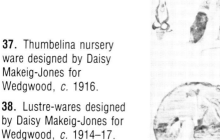

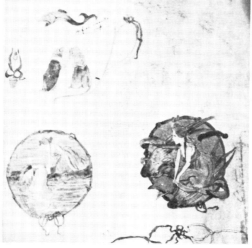

37. Thumbelina nursery ware designed by Daisy Makeig-Jones for Wedgwood, *c.* 1916.

38. Lustre-wares designed by Daisy Makeig-Jones for Wedgwood, *c.* 1914–17. From bottom right clockwise: Fish, Butterfly, Humming Birds, Dragon and Fairyland lustres.

39. Lustre-ware bone china plaque decorated with the design 'The Stuff that Dreams are made of' by Daisy Makeig-Jones, 1920.

40. Dish in red earthenware covered with a white slip adapted from an existing design by Truda Carter, 1921–5 for the Poole Potteries.

41. Plaque in red earthenware with incised design by Ruth Bare for the Della Robbia Pottery, 1899.

42. Earthenware bowl with reductio fired lustres in blue, gold, and red designed by Gladwys Rogers for Pilkington. 1907–8.

43. Earthenware tobacco jar and cover designed by Dora Billington, 1923.

44. Cream jug and sugar bowl by Jessie M.King with lead glaze and enamel colours, early twentieth century.

45. 'Sun-lit' pattern (in centre) on cane ware designed by Millie Taplin for Wedgwood, *c.* 1930.

46. 'Falling Leaves' pattern for bone china tableware designed by Millie Taplin for Wedgwood, *c.* 1934.

47. 'Winter Morn' pattern for bone china tableware designed by Millie Taplin for Wedgwood, *c.* 1934. From a pattern book at Josiah Wedgwood & Sons Ltd.

48. 'Moonlight' pattern on coffee cup and saucer designed by Millie Taplin for Wedgwood, *c.* 1934.

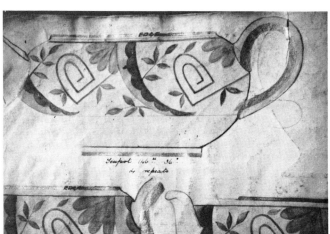

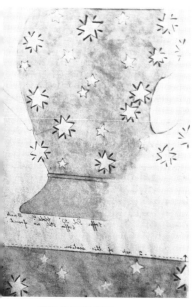

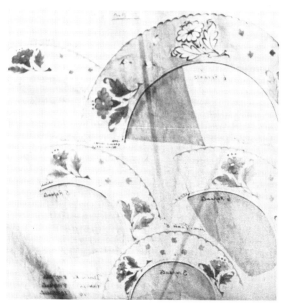

49. 'Stars' pattern for bone china tableware designed by Star Wedgwood for Wedgwood, *c.* 1935. From a pattern book at Wedgwood & Sons Ltd.

50. 'Lady Jane Grey' pattern for bone china tableware designed by Star Wedgwood for Wedgwood, *c.* 1935. From a pattern book at Josiah Wedgwood & Sons Ltd.

51. 'Coronation' pattern on bone china coffee pot, cup and saucer designed by Star Wedgwood for Wedgwood to celebrate the coronation of George VI in 1937.

52. Two designs by Charlotte Rhead for Wood & Sons' company, Bursley Ltd. Left: Trellis pattern (number 726) on white ground with orange fruits and green leaves on 'Cosy' teapot. Right: fruits and leaves pattern (number 735) on red lustre ground, *c.* 1926.

53. Two designs by Charlotte Rhead for Burgess and Leigh under the trade name Burleigh Ware. Left: 'Sylvan' pattern (number 4100) of trees, mountains and snow, 1927. Right: 'Garland' pattern (number 4101) of leaves and apples tube-lined in black on a white ground.

54. 'Florentine' pattern (number 4752) designed by Charlotte Rhead for Burgess and Leigh's Burleigh Ware, 1932.

55. 'Byzantine' pattern (number 2681) designed by Charlotte Rhead for A. G. Richardson under the trade name Crown Ducal. With stylised flowers and leaves within a border, 1932.

56. 'Persian Rose' pattern (number 4040) designed by Charlotte Rhead for A. G. Richardson's Crown Ducal range. With formalised rose heads and leaves on a beige ground.

57. 'Foxglove' pattern (number 4953) designed by Charlotte Rhead for A. G. Richardson's Crown Ducal range. With pink, mauve and blue flowers and green leaves and border on a white ground.

58. Fruit, flower and leaf design (number T.L.5) in orange, yellow, pink, blue and green designed by Charlotte Rhead for H. J. Wood.

59. Yellow and green leaf design (number T.L.2) designed by Charlotte Rhead for H. J. Wood.

60. 'Oakleaf' pattern for bone china tableware designed by
Freda Beardmore for E. Brain & Co.'s Foley China, *c.* 1931.

61. 'Carillon' pattern designed by Freda Beardmore for
E. Brain's Foley China and contributing to the Harrods
exhibition, 1933–4.

62. Pattern based on crocus flowers designed by Susie Cooper for A. E. Gray & Co. Ltd, c.1929. Yellow, green and purple with brown lining and gilt on earthenware 'Paris' shape jug.

63. 'Polka Dot' pattern in blue and 'Kestrel' shape earthenware hot water jug and cover, coffee cup and saucer designed by Susie Cooper for her own company, The Susie Cooper Pottery, c. 1934.

64. Wash-banded pattern in grey, blue and green on 'Kestrel' shape earthenware teapot designed by Susie Cooper for The Susie Cooper Pottery, c. 1932.

65. Leaf pattern in grey/blue on 'Kestrel' shape, earthenware hot water jug and cover designed by Susie Cooper for The Susie Cooper Pottery, *c.* 1933. Copyright: authors.

66. Wash and solid banded pattern in grey, brown and purple on 'Curlew' shape earthenware tureen and cover designed by Susie Cooper for The Susie Cooper Pottery, *c.* 1932.

67. 'Dresden Spray' lithograph pattern with blue/green shaded banding on 'Kestrel' shape earthenware tureen and cover designed by Susie Cooper for The Susie Cooper Pottery, *c.* 1935.

68. The Susie Cooper Pottery Ltd stand at the 1938 Britisn Industries Fair showing 'Falcon' shape with aerographed and sgraffito decoration on octagonal table and 'Spiral' shape with 'Endon Border' lithograph pattern on large rectangular table.

69. 'Iris' lithograph pattern with grey/blue shaded banding on 'Kestrel' shape earthenware soup bowl designed by Susie Cooper for The Susie Cooper Pottery, c. 1938.

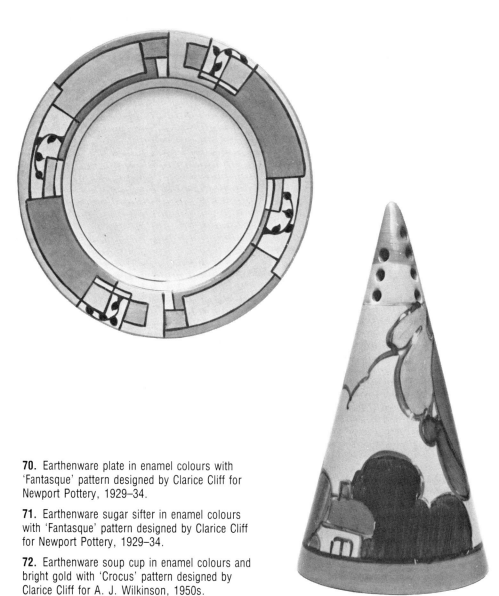

70. Earthenware plate in enamel colours with 'Fantasque' pattern designed by Clarice Cliff for Newport Pottery, 1929–34.

71. Earthenware sugar sifter in enamel colours with 'Fantasque' pattern designed by Clarice Cliff for Newport Pottery, 1929–34.

72. Earthenware soup cup in enamel colours and bright gold with 'Crocus' pattern designed by Clarice Cliff for A. J. Wilkinson, 1950s.

73. Earthenware teapot with moulded body and handle, enamel colours, and 'Celtic Harvest' pattern. Designed by Clarice Cliff for Newport Pottery, 1935–42.

74. Earthenware mug, moulded handle in the form of an elf, enamel colours, designed by Clarice Cliff for A. J. Wilkinson, 1930–42.

75. Milk jug in bone china designed by Grete Marks for E. Brain's Foley China, *c.* 1938.

76. Plate from the Grete Pottery designed by Grete Marks, *c.* 1938.

77. Vera Huggins decorating a stoneware vase at Doulton's Lambeth pottery.

78. Salt-glaze Doulton stoneware cylindrical pot with bird decoration. Designed and decorated by Vera Huggins, *c.* 1925–30.

79. Three salt-glaze Doulton stoneware pots designed by Vera Huggins. Left: vase with incised foliage on a mottled blue ground, *c.* 1925; Middle: bowl painted with pink and blue flowers against a brown ground, 1926; Right: vase glazed in green, blue and brown with incised and raised patterns, *c.* 1925.

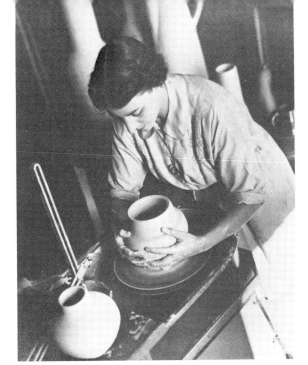

80. Joan Cowper throwing a pot at Doulton's Lambeth pottery, *c.* 1937.

81. Group of stoneware pots designed by Joan Cowper for Royal Doulton, *c.* 1938.

82. Agnete Hoy throwing a stoneware vase on the wheel in her studio at Doulton's Lambeth Pottery.

83. Salt-glaze Doulton stoneware bowls, dishes and vase designed by Agnete Hoy for Royal Doulton, 1952–56.

84. Stoneware Doulton punch-bowl designed by Agnete Hoy with carved and under-glaze painting in grey, pink, yellow and blue.

85. Stoneware cat modelled by Agnete Hoy for Royal Doulton with incised and painted decoration. 1955.

86. Peggy Davies painting one of her modelled pieces.

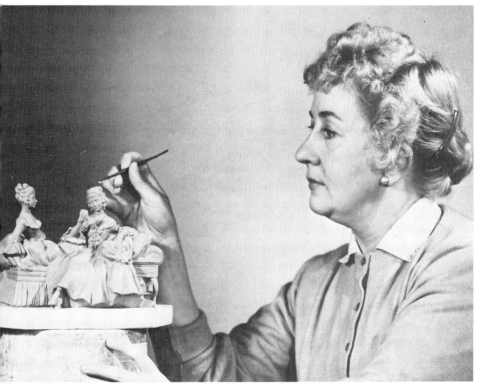

87. 'Blue Star' lithograph pattern on 'Quail' shape bone china coffee pot and cover, and hot water jug and cover designed by Susie Cooper for The Susie Cooper Pottery, *c.* 1951.

88. 'Wild Strawberry' lithograph pattern on bone china plate designed by Susie Cooper for The Susie Cooper Pottery, *c.* 1953.

89. Sgraffito and painted 'Dot' pattern on aerographed and white china teapot and jug designed by Susie Cooper for The Susie Cooper Pottery, *c.* 1954.

90. Sgraffito decoration applied onto an aerographed 'Quail' shape coffee pot by a freehand paintress at the Crown Works, *c.* 1952.

91. 'Stylecraft' shapes designed 1953 by Roy Midwinter with 'Homeweave' pattern by Jessie Tait.

92. 'Fashion' shapes designed 1955 by Roy Midwinter with 'Capri' pattern by Jessie Tait.

93. 'Festival' pattern designed by Jessie Tait for W. R. Midwinter's 'Fashion' shapes.

94. 'Primavera' designed by Jessie Tait for W. R. Midwinter's 'Stylecraft' shapes.

Richard Joyce, Charles E. Cundall and Gwladys M. Rogers. Forsyth, who was put in charge of art direction in 1906, was particularly keen to develop lustre decoration. Great emphasis was placed on artistic expression and designers were encouraged to produce new shapes and decoration. Gwladys Rogers designed lustre ware and lapis ware, which was introduced after 1928. Her designs, which span the first twenty-five years of the twentieth century, illustrate the changing artistic climate. Her early work revealed an interest in Arts and Crafts motifs such as natural forms and stylised repeat patterns (Figure 42), while her later work demonstrated knowledge of the 'moderne' style which became popular in Britain in the 1920s. The sources for this new style were found within modern art, the work of French designers such as Paul Follot and Paul Poiret, and African art which had attracted the interest of artists such as Picasso. The 'moderne' style was angular and geometric and exploited decorative effects such as lustre to create highly decorative surfaces. Gwladys Rogers' designs from the 1920s were a direct response to this new style.[30]

The Bernard Moore Pottery was established in 1905 in Stoke-on-Trent. Moore, a glaze chemist, was particularly interested in the glaze effects found on oriental ceramics. He produced several versions of Chinese glazes, including a *rouge flambé*, as well as lustres. Dora May Billington trained at Tunstall and Hanley Schools of Art until 1913, then attending the Royal College of Art where she eventually taught ceramics. She also taught at the Central School of Arts and Crafts and was President of the Arts and Crafts Exhibition Society. She worked at the Bernard Moore Pottery along with Hilda Beardmore and Hilda Lindop (Figure 43). Dora Billington exhibited widely and was well respected in both design and education circles. She played an important educative role both at the Royal College of Art and at the Central School of Art, teaching younger women such as Katherine Pleydell-Bouverie and Norah Braden, who became important contributors to the studio pottery movement in Britain in the 1920s and 1930s.

Design Education and Opportunities for Women

Opportunities for women in art and design education were very important if they were to gain wider access to jobs in design. This was especially true when close links were established between manufacturers and art schools. From the 1870s the proliferation of art schools and art classes meant that there were better facilities for women. Except for certain trades such as bookbinding, and gold and silversmithing, women were given almost equal access to training. Certain art schools were more progressive than others: included in this category were those in Glasgow and the Potteries.

Glasgow School of Art saw an increase in the numbers of women students from the early 1890s when they accounted for about a third of all students, to 1910 when they numbered a half. Twenty-seven women staff worked at the school during the same period, including Jessie Newberry, Annie French, Ann Macbeth and Jessie King.[31]

Jessie King (1875–1949) was trained at Glasgow in illustration, bookbinding, fabric and pottery design. In 1902 she won a gold medal at Turin where she exhibited in the Glasgow section along with Charles Rennie Mackintosh, Margaret Macdonald and her sister Frances, and Herbert McNair. In the same year she was made an instructor at the art school in Glasgow and her work was illustrated in *The Studio*.[32] Her designs for pottery were in the tradition of the Arts and Crafts Movement and emphasised stylised natural forms and simple decorative effects (Figure 44).

Schools of art and design were established in the Potteries, at Hanley and Stoke in 1847 and Burslem in 1853. From the outset, they were closely tied to the manufacture of pottery. Stoke art school was known as the Minton Memorial Institute after the pottery manufacturer Herbert Minton gave £500 to its construction, and the new art school building in Burslem, completed in 1873, was named the Wedgwood Institute after its sponsor. By the early twentieth century, Hanley and Burslem art schools were well established with good reputations; *The Studio* carried articles about Burslem in 1904 and 1906. By this time Burslem had developed a co-ordinated programme of art instruction which linked infant, elementary and further education. Its aim was to build on art skills acquired at each stage of education thereby encouraging a cumulative learning process. Thirty scholarships for three years of full-time study were provided at the art school to enable particularly talented students to continue their art training.[33] The Potteries art schools responded to the practical needs of the pottery industry by teaching modelling, design, chemistry and basic technical skills.

In 1920 the art schools were brought under the control of the Superintendent of Art whose job was to co-ordinate education and training facilities throughout Stoke-on-Trent. Gordon Mitchell

Forsyth (1879–1952), a pottery designer who had previously worked at Pilkingtons was appointed. Forsyth established Burslem as the principal school with both full and part-time courses during day and evening; the other schools at Hanley, Stoke and Longton offered evening classes only. By 1930 there were some 1100–1200 students attending the Potteries art schools. In 1925 a Junior Art Department was established at Burslem. This aimed to raise the standards of apprenticeships by producing artistically educated men and women suitable for employment in the pottery industry. Forsyth's plans involved 'reorganising the existing art schools on purely industrial lines. Up to that time people had been rather inclined to regard the art schools of the Potteries as being much more concerned with the fine arts than industrial requirements, and as something divorced from reality.'[34] Forsyth firmly believed that 'it was only by art that the pottery industry would gain fresh ground and find new fields to conquer'.[35]

The direction of the art schools during the inter-war period was essentially vocational; it was argued that 'there are no pin-money students here, no dilettantes'.[36] Art education was discussed by various groups associated with the pottery industry including the trade union whose 1920 report, *The Appropriate Education of Persons Occupied or Interested in the Pottery Industry*, recommended a variety of educational opportunities for the pottery worker, some purely recreational, others vocational. In this the union was supported by Forsyth who believed that 'it is not only necessary for the manufacturers to see virtue in art. The rank and file of the pottery workers must realise it also.'[37]

Forsyth played a critical role in opening opportunities for women, both as designers and as decorators. In an article of 1932, he acknowledged that there were not enough women designers in the industry.[38] His encouragement of women in the art schools enhanced their employment opportunities as designers in the pottery industry. The art schools also offered training to other women who, without the financial resources required for full-time studies, were able to attend evening classes to acquire specific skills for work in the industry. The educational changes implemented in the Potteries art schools, which had been begun in the early twentieth century and were fully developed under Forsyth, offered benefits both to women undertaking training and to the pottery manufacturers. Forsyth took an active role in bringing the two groups together to facilitate worthwhile employment for women and to improve design for the industry.

In the early years of the twentieth century, the sexual divisions in pottery design which led men to design shape and women to design decoration were undermined by the work practice of some women designers who were able to design both. At the same time other women such as those at Wedgwood were confined to more conventional roles as designers of decoration by the 'feminine' stereotype. The theoretical justification for women's changing role in pottery design originated in the radical proposals of the Arts and Crafts Movement in which the importance of craft process and the involvement of the designer in all stages of production were emphasised. Unity of shape and decoration was essential to Arts and Crafts theorists, and within this context alternative roles were available to women which did not merely reinforce the patriarchal divisions of Victorian society.[39] As we have seen, Ruth Bare, Truda Carter and Dora Billington provided successful role-models to subsequent women by working in non-stereotypical ways within the Art Pottery Movement as designers of shape and decoration.

Unlike the Poole Potteries where women had consistently thrown and modelled wares, rigid distinctions existed between the skills of men and women designers at the Wedgwood factory. For Grace Barnsley, Thérèse Lessore and Daisy Makeig-Jones, being a designer at Wedgwood entailed the production of patterns for the surface decoration of ware. In this they were like their nineteenth-century Doulton counterparts working within the parameters of the separate sphere, using their 'intrinsic' feminine skills. In contrast, and no doubt due to her status as a freelance designer and her involvement with Arts and Crafts practice, Louise Powell was one of the few women designers working at Wedgwood to design both shape and decoration.

As part of a husband and wife design partnership, Louise Powell's contribution to design at Wedgwood has been overshadowed by that of her husband, Alfred. As spokesperson, it is Alfred's record of their employment and role which is available for today's historians. Although Louise Powell signed many of her Wedgwood wares – thereby demonstrating her involvement with the company – numerous jointly attributed pieces add to the difficulties.

Attribution is a crucial issue for the historian in the case of husband and wife design teams, although in the case of the pottery industry it is often inappropriate to pin responsibility for the appearance of a particular piece of pottery to any one person. Many people were involved in the production of a particular design and several influenced its appearance; that is in addition to economic, marketing, technical, social and cultural determining factors. Many hand-painted wares from this period had several stamps or marks of attribution on the base, including the company's, the paintress's and the designer's, whereas some wares were completely unmarked. For these reasons it is problematic to attribute specific designs to individuals such as Louise and Alfred Powell.

For the feminist design historian, attribution presents particular theoretical problems given that, on the one hand, it is important to demonstrate the role of women designers in the pottery industry using evidence such as signed wares, but, on the other hand, it is too simplistic to construct a history of design which hinges merely on a list of names, women's or men's.

As I have tried to show in this chapter, women designers made a contribution to the history of pottery design between 1900 and 1920, but at the same time, the nature of their involvement and the type of pottery design with which they were concerned depended upon diverse factors. Most important here were the progressive theories of the Arts and Crafts Movement regarding the role of the designer, combined with traditional nineteenth-century notions of 'feminine' design skills.

Notes

1. 'Female Labour in the Pottery Industry', *Pottery Gazette and Glass Trade Review*, 1 May 1919, pp. 478–80.
2. See M. Batkin, *Wedgwood Ceramics 1846–1959*, Richard Dennis, 1982.
3. E. Aslin, *The Aesthetic Movement, Prelude to Art Nouveau*, Ferndale editions, 1981, p. 13.
4. G. Naylor, *The Arts and Crafts Movement*, Studio Vista, 1980, p. 7.
5. ibid., p. 28.
6. ibid., pp. 108–9.
7. ibid., p. 108.
8. A. Callen, *Angel in the Studio. Women in the Arts and Crafts Movement 1870–1914*, Astragal, 1979, p. 17. See Lynne Walker's response to Callen's argument in J. Attfield and P. Kirkham

(eds), *A View from the Interior. Feminism, Women and Design*, The Women's Press, 1989.

9. 'Retirement of Pottery Art Director', *Pottery Gazette and Glass Trade Review*, 1 November 1934, p. 1353.

10. Naylor, op. cit., p. 109.

11. S. Gater, 'Alfred and Louise Powell – An Introduction', unpublished paper, Wedgwood Museum, Barlaston.

12. ibid.

13. A. Powell, 'New Wedgwood Pottery', *The Studio*, vol. 98, 1929, p. 879.

14. A. Powell, 'Painting of Pottery', *Decorative Arts of Great Britain and Ireland*, catalogue for exhibition organised by the British Government at the Louvre, Paris, 1914.

15. Powell, *The Studio*, 1929, p. 880.

16. ibid.

17. ibid.

18. Una des Fontaines, *Wedgwood Fairyland Lustre*, Sotheby Parke, 1975, p. 26.

19. ibid.

20. J. Collins, *The Omega Workshops*, Secker & Warburg, 1983, p. 46.

21. Crafts Council, *Omega*, exhibition catalogue, 1984, p. 63.

22. See J. Hawkins, *The Poole Potteries*, Barrie & Jenkins, 1980.

23. ibid., pp. 78–9.

24. J. Adams, 'Potters' Parade', *Pottery and Glass*, October 1950, p. 57.

25. Hawkins, op. cit., p. 71.

26. ibid., p. 110.

27. M. Haslam, *English Art Pottery, 1865–1915*, Antique Collectors' Club, 1975, p. 79.

28. ibid., p. 77.

29. ibid., p. 79.

30. See A. Lomax, *Royal Lancastrian Pottery*, Abraham Lomax, 1957.

31. E. Bird, 'Women Designers and the Glasgow Style, 1890–1920', conference paper, 1983.

32. W. R. Wilson, 'Miss Jessie M. King and her Work', *The Studio*, vol. 26, 1902, pp. 177–88.

33. E. N. Scott, 'Co-ordinated Art Education at Burslem', *The Studio*, vol. 32, July 1904, pp. 132–6.

34. 'Art and Technical Progress in the Potteries', *Pottery Gazette and Glass Trade Review*, 2 June 1930, pp. 974–6.

35. G. M. Forsyth, 'Art: Its Effect Upon the Pottery Industry', *Pottery Gazette and Glass Trade Review*, 1 August 1921, p. 1220.

36. 'Art and Technical Progress', op. cit., p. 976.

37. 'Art: Its Effect', op. cit., p. 1220. See also National Council of the Pottery Industry, Second Report, *Appropriate Education of Persons Occupied or Interested in the Pottery Industry*, July 1920.

38. G. M. Forsyth, 'The Pottery Designer. What the Industry Needs', *Pottery Gazette and Glass Trade Review*, 1 April 1932, p. 513.

39. For further consideration of these debates see Anthea Callen, 'Sexual Division of Labour in the Arts and Crafts Movement'; and Lynne Walker, 'The Arts and Crafts Alternative', in Attfield and Kirkham, op. cit., pp. 151–64, 165–83.

CHAPTER 4

■

What the Ladies Think!
Designers for industry

An educated woman of first-class intelligence would be the one to cater for her own sex . . . she would understand the feminine mind and their desire for fresh ideas.[1]

■

Women designers played an important part in the inter-war pottery industry. They were involved in the debates on the relationship between art and industry, and they responded to the changing theories of design. They contributed to the formulation of specific design strategies in several different companies: Millie Taplin, Star Wedgwood, Jessie Van Hallen and Freda Beardmore occupied conventional roles as in-house designers, whereas Susie Cooper, Charlotte Rhead and Clarice Cliff worked in a less traditional manner as, respectively, an independent manufacturer, a designer at a succession of companies and an art director. Women's employment prospects as designers and paintresses did not present a progressive development towards greater opportunities during the 1920s and 1930s. Both middle- and working-class women designers were responsive to social and political changes which allowed some personal choice and flexibility. A few women were able to take new initiatives within a framework of innovative design education with the financial support of their families, while others succeeded in jobs which were normally beyond their class expectations.

The social and economic conditions within which these opportunities occurred were contradictory. The chief beneficiaries were middle-class women whose status was most effectively enhanced by legislative changes in the 1910s and 1920s such as in 1918 the right for those over 30 to vote and in 1923 the Matrimonial Causes Act which enabled women to divorce adulterous husbands. 'The new freedom belonged to the middle-class young. It never included older married women, and barely affected working-class girls.'[2] With the exception of Millie Taplin and Clarice Cliff, the women who established successful careers as pottery designers were from the middle classes.

Because of the severe economic difficulties facing the industry, working-class women pottery workers were a target for men who feared unemployment. Pressing issues for manufacturers to confront were the loss of pre-war export markets and the effects of the General Strike and miners' strikes in the 1920s. These problems stimulated debate about women's 'proper' sphere and forced some of the women who had been substituted for men during the First World War out of their jobs.[3] Whereas in 1919 *The Pottery Gazette and Glass Trade Review* could confidently assert that 'the part which women have played in keeping the works going has entitled them to be fully considered in every future development of the industry',[4] only five years later when the unemployment level in the potteries averaged 13 per cent, the same trade journal reported the male pottery workers' demands that 'a clear dividing line . . . be drawn between what is considered to be the work of a man and a woman. The operatives further claim that female labour shall be eliminated entirely as regards placing and dipping.'[5] Placing and dipping were sites of conflict between 'substituted' women and skilled men who considered the work to be rightfully theirs. However, some women retained these jobs in the face of male opposition because they were cheaper to employ than men:

> 'Rationalisation', wage cuts, the substitution of women for men, speed-up and the reduction in the power of trade unions through unemployment meant that there were objective reasons for antagonism between men and women workers. Women were obvious scapegoats. There was a widespread belief that the employment of women actually caused unemployment.[6]

Women's employment prospects in design and decorating were not threatened. In these jobs they followed the tradition established in the nineteenth century by women china decorators, and they reinforced the gender-based artistic stereotype by designing pottery decoration. At the same time, social and political changes in the inter-war years allowed women to reshape these roles into less conventional forms. Some women designers ran independent businesses, sold their design skills on a freelance basis, managed their own design studios or designed both pottery shape and decoration. They worked in ways quite alien to their nineteenth-century forerunners, and due to the extended provision of design education available in Stoke-on-Trent, women from the working class as well as from the middle class were theoretically (although not always practically) able to move into the field of design.

Instances of direct opposition to these new roles were uncommon, although scepticism accompanied patronising comment in the trade press. Most often they were legitimised on the grounds that women designers were intrinsically qualified to respond to the needs of the female domestic tableware consumer. It was said of Susie Cooper's success in the 1930s: 'what matters very definitely in regard to pottery sales is what the ladies think. And Miss Cooper designs for the ladies from a ladies' standpoint, for she designs first and foremost to please herself.'[7]

Design and Industry

During the inter-war period, design was high on the agenda in the debates about the economic prosperity of the industry. Design was seen as a useful tool in helping British companies to recapture their former overseas markets and to fight off the challenge of cheap foreign imports. Japan and Czechoslovakia were the two principal threats to the pottery industry's home and export markets from the 1920s onwards. Various articles appeared in the trade press on the unfairness and unscrupulousness of Japanese potteries, as well as articles in defence of the import tariffs introduced at the height of the depression. Tariffs imposed a duty of 50 per cent, then 20 per cent and finally $33^1/_3$ per cent on foreign pottery imports in this period.[8] Pottery manufacturers responded to design with differing degrees of enthusiasm. Prestigious companies such as Josiah Wedgwood & Sons led the way by employing in-house and freelance designers, while smaller manufacturers such as A. E. Gray, E. Brain, A. J. Wilkinson, Susie Cooper and Wood & Co. were committed to improving design standards. Other manufacturers considered design to be an expensive and dispensable extra in economically difficult times. They preferred to wait and let others test the market before risking their own capital.

The design reformers, who operated under the aegis of the British

Institute of Industrial Art, the Design and Industries Association and the Society of Industrial Arts, promoted design as a way out of the industry's problems. The British Institute of Industrial Art organised a conference on pottery in 1923 which aimed to 'secure . . . the maximum co-operation between the different interests and the different contributions – the contributions of designer, the manufacturer, the craftsman, the merchant and the consumer'.[9] Interested groups and individuals urged manufacturers to employ designers to help revitalise the pottery industry. Improved quality in design was considered a prerequisite to an increase in exports; and the designer, it was argued, could play an important role in identifying specific products for different markets. According to Gordon Forsyth, the industrial pottery designer 'had to be capable of creating stylish and sensible productions that would appeal to the general public at home or abroad'.[10]

The reformers and the educators used these organisations to promote a Modernist approach to design. They stressed that the designer should use modern materials, mass-production techniques and new technology to create a contemporary product. In 1932, at the second public meeting of the Potteries branch of the Society of Industrial Artists, Forsyth outlined the relationship between modern art and pottery manufacture. The 'rationality, orderliness and clear thinking of modern art' were recommended to the pottery manufacturer as being entirely appropriate to mass-production processes. This was challenged by a manufacturer who declared 'that if the manufacturers followed without question . . . Mr Forsyth's advice, they would all go bankrupt'.[11] Support for modern design was often won on the strength of its apparent logic and functionalism and its potential cheapness through mass production. Ironically, in an industry that still relied a great deal on craft skills, the 'rational' modern look was frequently achieved by these very skills. The matt glazed wares designed for Wedgwood by the designer Keith Murray, and widely promoted at the time as exemplary 'machine' products, were actually thrown and turned by hand.[12] The majority of manufacturers, including the volume producers Enoch Wedgwood, Carlton, Johnson Brothers and J. G. Meakin, were content to produce a variety of styles to appeal to all potential markets and were largely uninterested in pioneering the introduction of Modernist designs.

The activities of organisations such as the Society of Industrial Artists were supported by a number of eminent manufacturers committed to promoting a progressive, modern approach to design. It was within these companies that opportunities for women designers could be found. Within the larger of these, the roles of women designers were more rigidly and traditionally defined, whereas in the smaller companies women were able to design with greater flexibility.

Millicent Taplin

At Josiah Wedgwood & Sons, several women designers had been trained as free-hand paintresses by Alfred and Louise Powell. Two of the most notable were Millicent Jane Taplin (1902–80) and Cecily Stella (Star) Wedgwood (b. 1903). During the 1920s and 1930s Wedgwood pursued the policy of modernisation and rationalisation initiated in the early years of the twentieth century. Wedgwood responded to the world recession by streamlining its product ranges in order to be more competitive and to appeal to a wider market. From the early 1930s it began to concentrate on the production of moderately priced china tableware, rather than the expensive ornamental wares, which were phased out. The intention was to capture a significant sector of the domestic tableware market. Opportunities for both Millie Taplin and Star Wedgwood were closely linked to these design and manufacturing policy changes. Unlike Victor Skellern, who succeeded John Goodwin as art director in 1934, and the freelance designer Keith Murray, both women were largely uninvolved in the formulation of Wedgwood's new design strategy.

Millie Taplin was one of the few working-class women to become a professional designer in the pottery industry, although the path of her successful career was not easy. Both her parents worked in the pottery industry; her father was a caster with the Whieldon Sanitary Pottery Company before becoming unemployed after the First World War. Her mother worked at different periods to supplement the precarious family income.

Millie Taplin, like most of her friends, left school at thirteen to find work because, as the eldest in the family, she was expected to contribute to the family income. She first worked in a millinery shop, but soon left after being awarded a scholarship from her old Church of England school to attend evening classes at Stoke School of Art. With the help of her art teacher, she obtained a job as a liner, which involved painting gold lines on wares, at the pottery firm of Greens in Fenton. As a trainee liner she was paid 2s 6d a week. After a short time, she moved to Minton's to train as a paintress. This gave her the experience she needed to gain employment at Wedgwood in 1917. At the same time she was studying three or four nights a week at the art school where she was taught 'still-life painting, plant drawing, and pottery painting'.[13]

Most of her training at Wedgwood was undertaken in the studio established by Alfred and Louise Powell. For some nine years she gained proficiency as a paintress together with an increasing facility for design. Her working relationship with the Powells went beyond hand painting their designs in that she was frequently called upon to adapt their complex patterns to suit the skills of the paintresses. Following the success of a range of the Powells' ornamental Queensware at the 1925 Paris Exhibition, Wedgwood decided to establish a small hand craft studio. The products of this studio would offer a cheaper alternative to the elaborate hand-decorated wares. They were produced in earthenware with on-glaze enamel and lustre decoration based on stylised natural motifs.

When the studio was opened in 1928, Millie Taplin was put in charge, and was assisted by two ex-Burslem School of Arts students, Margery Hall and Mary Simpson. When the studio was merged with the hand-painting department a year later, Millie Taplin was promoted to designer and was made responsible for managing both. The products of this enlarged department included Queensware enamels and lustres, ornamental and domestic earthenware produced in the Islam-inspired Rhodian and Persian wares (introduced in 1920 and 1926 respectively) and Millie Taplin's own designs.

Promotion from paintress to designer was possible in an industry which had a long apprenticeship period for skilled workers in the artistic side of production, but it was unusual. Most women undertook apprenticeships as paintresses to develop specific decorating as opposed to design skills. These were considered to be quite distinct and less demanding than those required for design. Most designers and art directors were men who had served long apprenticeships learning the craft of modelling and design under other men. The industry was dominated by well-known male art directors who had made their reputations: Thomas Allen, Charles Noke, Louis Solon, John Goodwin and Victor Skellern. But although she worked under both Goodwin and Skellern, it was Louise Powell whom Millie Taplin emulated.[14] There were, however, important differences between the status and role of women designers, such as Louise

Powell and Daisy Makeig-Jones, and that of Millie Taplin. These ultimately limited the latter's career at Wedgwood.

Daisy Makeig-Jones, although initially learning the techniques of the paintress, did so as part of her design training. With her artistic, middle-class background, her expectation upon entering Wedgwood was to become a designer. Similarly, Louise Powell was already established as a designer before working at Wedgwood. This was not the case with Millie Taplin, who had the educational and career disadvantages typical of her class. The job of paintress was in itself a good position for a working-class woman. It offered renumerative employment with the added benefit of providing reasonably clean and safe industrial work. That it also utilised her already proven artistic abilities was an additional advantage. What is interesting about Millie Taplin was that, in a period of changing roles for women, she was able to move from the working-class job of paintress, to the middle-class profession of designer.

During the late 1920s Millie Taplin began to produce independent designs for Wedgwood. These included 'Buds and Bells', 'Papyrus', 'Spring', 'Summer', 'Autumn' and 'Sun-lit'. The last was typical of her designs at this time in that it was based on abstract and stylised natural motifs in bright orange, red, green and blue (Figure 45).

'Sun-lit' was produced in cane ware, a honey-coloured earthenware used for both ornamental and table wares. One of the chief sources for the visual appearance of these designs was the fashionable Art Deco style which became popular in Britain after the 1925 Paris Exhibition of Decorative Art. Art Deco, which was both decorative and stylish, used geometric, angular shapes combined with bright colours such as yellow, orange and red. Shiny, glossy or highly reflective surfaces were also popular. A British version of Art Deco developed towards the end of the 1920s which combined with Modernism to produce a more streamlined, and less ostentatiously lavish style known as *'moderne'*.

Taplin made regular trips to London to visit museums and art galleries in order to extend her knowledge of art and design. Her brother Eric remembers her first trip to Paris, a source of great excitement to the family who apparently did not stand in the way of her increasingly successful career, even though her lifestyle was hardly typical for a young working-class woman from the Potteries.[15]

As a member of the Wedgwood design team, Millie Taplin's role was subject to the management and policy changes that occurred in the early 1930s. When the new management team headed by Josiah Wedgwood V – a qualified economist – took over the running of the company in 1930, it was facing serious financial difficulties. The previous year's total sales had been £158,000 with a net profit of only £7000.[16] In the thirteen months from January 1930 sales had plummeted by 38 per cent and according to Josiah Wedgwood V, 'the Etruria works at that date was little changed from the time of Josiah I'.[17] The management team was made up of Hensleigh Wedgwood who joined the New York branch of the firm, Tom Wedgwood who had responsibility for buildings and plant and Norman Wilson as works manager. The team was completed in 1934 when Victor Skellern became art director.

From the outset this new team aimed to shake up the company at all levels, including the design process. First on the agenda was a programme of technological modernisation which included the introduction of an earthenware glost tunnel kiln. This oil-fired kiln was accompanied by other new developments including a flow-line rubber belt system, a quick-drying kiln, new glazes and new wares; particularly important was a translucent pink bone china. All of these changes aimed to equip the Etruria factory for the mass production of moderately priced tableware. This policy was outlined in a letter from Josiah Wedgwood V to the designer Keith Murray in 1933:

> In present conditions of trade, the demand for (expensive) goods is clearly limited. The urgent necessity at present, as I see it, is to get new 'bread and butter' tableware that can be produced in the cheapest possible manner and sold in bulk.[18]

Millie Taplin had her own role to play in this modernisation process, although it was different from the one that she had played in the company up to that time. In contrast to the previously informal, paternalistic organisation, Wedgwood became much more rationalised with a hierarchical management structure of departmental managers and supervisors. The designer was effectively removed from involvement in the decision-making process and instead designs were produced to a clearly defined brief that was determined by management policy. This was outlined in 1933 when it was decided that Wedgwood's initial strategy for combating the slump by producing more and more patterns (in fact 300 new earthenware and 200 new china patterns on average a year) was the wrong tactic. Instead, the number of patterns was to be strictly controlled, with a target of

150 earthenware patterns and 100 china patterns. It was also proposed that 'the firm should . . . pursue a definite and consistent policy as regards design, with a view to the firm's general credit in the long run'.[19] At the instigation of Skellern and the management team, a modern approach to pottery design was proposed. Keith Murray was asked to turn his attention 'to the design of new *cheap* shapes, attractive to *modern* eyes' which were to be 'the best possible for the money and reasonably attractive to that growing section of the younger public which has some taste but no money'.[20]

Millie Taplin was part of the design section which responded to these demands. As a designer of decoration she produced a range of patterns that attempted to cater for this new market. The team was headed by Victor Skellern, a local designer who had trained at the Potteries art schools before gaining a scholarship to the Royal College of Art. Skellern represented the new breed of designer who saw himself as part of a profession. The design profession, like most other professions, was eager to define itself and enhance the status of its members by demanding appropriate entry qualifications. The high profile given to design in the 1930s and the activities of bodies such as the Society of Industrial Artists encouraged this desire for professionalisation.

Millie Taplin's career progression at Wedgwood from this time onwards was dogged by her own lack of design qualifications, despite the commercial success of her designs. In 1936 a special Wedgwood exhibition was staged at the Grafton Galleries in London which was 'the first public display of the results of recent experiments at Etruria'.[21] The product of these experiments was a new body called 'Alpine Pink', a self-coloured translucent china.[21] Other wares on display were white fine china, Queensware, coloured earthenware and the moonstone and matt designs by Keith Murray. Of all the designers of domestic tableware Millie Taplin contributed the most, with eleven designs including three for the new 'Alpine Pink' body.[22]

All of Millie Taplin's designs and those by her Wedgwood colleagues were hand decorated; lithographs were not introduced until after the Second World War. Some of her china tableware designs were advertised in the pottery trade press under her own name, and this contributed to her personal profile in the industry. Most of the designs were a product of company policy: they were modern, but catered for the discerning buyer with sophisticated tastes. They were an attempt to combine contemporary Modernist interests with

Wedgwood's reputation for traditional good quality. Her designs included 'Falling Leaves', a simplified leaf pattern in shades of green highlighted by silver, and 'Winter Morn', a stylised design of natural forms in grey on a lavender ground (Figures 46 and 47). In contrast were geometric, abstract designs for china such as 'Moonlight' which had concentric bands of silver decoration, and 'Green Lattice', a diaper pattern in green with silver edge and platinum line (Figure 48). When this was shown at the British Art in Industry Exhibition at the Royal Academy in 1935, it won fulsome praise from a severe critic who had attacked ware which was more concerned with aesthetics than practicality. He described Millie Taplin as 'a talented young lady who actually operates at the factory, and of whom it has been said that she is concerned not with art *on* industry, but art *in* industry'.[23]

Wedgwood's retail outlets for these designs reveal its new marketing strategy. They included John Lewis, Peter Jones, Liberty, Harrods, Maple & Co., Waring & Gillow, Heal and Bowman Bros, all of which were known for stocking progressive design. Significantly, Wedgwood chose as its advertising slogan the phrase 'a living tradition' to emphasise both contemporaneity and tradition. Although by no means cheap, Wedgwood's new china tableware was modestly priced in comparison to its previous products. An early morning set, which comprised two cups and saucers, sugar and cream jug, teapot and one plate in the 'Winter Morn' design by Millie Taplin, cost £1 14s.

Opportunities in design at Wedgwood differed according to gender. Men such as Murray and Skellern designed shapes and pattern, whereas women such as Millie Taplin and Star Wedgwood designed only pattern. The relative cheapness of introducing new patterns, as opposed to the major investment in technology required for the introduction of new shapes, meant that there were more design opportunities in pattern than in shape. However, to many designers, the design of both shape and pattern was the ideal. This had been promoted by the contemporary design theorists, Herbert Read and Nikolaus Pevsner, as an essential feature of progressive design practice. At Wedgwood, women were unable to experience this as their roles were defined by the dominant gender stereotype. Millie Taplin apparently 'lived and dreamed Wedgwood', but during the 1930s she experienced growing disillusionment with her role in the company.[24] By this date she felt that she ought to have made greater career progress, and that she was being hampered by her poor education. Unlike Skellern and Murray she had no formal professional qualifications, and she believed this undermined her status within the design team. This was particularly acute given that Skellern officially approved her designs, and, as she thought, Murray did so unofficially.

In 1932 Millie Taplin married Joe Winfield whom she had known for some time, although she retained her own name. In addition to her job as designer, she began to teach part-time at the local art schools in 1935. This post became full-time during the Second World War, when production at Wedgwood was cut to utility and export ware and the services of designers were no longer required. With the resumption of normal production after the war, Millie Taplin continued her career at Wedgwood and became increasingly involved in designing lithographs. In 1957, 'Strawberry Hill', an over-glaze lithographic transfer designed by her and Victor Skellern for china tableware, was given a Design of the Year Award by the Council of Industrial Design. In 1962, Millie Taplin retired after some thirty-four years as a designer at Wedgwood.

Star Wedgwood

Another important designer at Wedgwood during the inter-war years was Star Wedgwood. She was the daughter of Major Frank Wedgwood, who was Chairman and Managing Director of the company between 1916 and 1930, and cousin of Josiah Wedgwood V, who took over the running of the company after her father's death. As a member of the Wedgwood family she was privileged in many ways, although as a woman her opportunities within the family company were quite different from those open to her brother Tom, who, like his male predecessors, had a managerial role.

A childhood interest in art and design was reinforced when she travelled to Florence at the age of eighteen. During the same visit she toured some local Tuscan potteries which reinforced her latent interest in pottery gained from watching the paintresses in the Etruria factory, and decided her upon a career in pottery design. Her first step in this direction was to attend art school, and to this end her father arranged for her to attend the Royal College of Art for one term in 1923. At the Royal College she was taught heraldry, lettering, general design and drawing from antique casts. She spent a lot of time in the Victoria and Albert Museum where she especially admired the Chinese ceramic collection. Next she spent a term at the Central School of Art and Design,[25] where she learned wood-engraving, drawing, general design and textile design. She did no pottery design during her year in London (her third term was spent at a private drawing school in Kensington). In fact, her pottery design skills were acquired at Burslem School of Art and at the Etruria factory. Her disjointed design education was largely determined by her father, who was not keen to have her away from home for too long.

Back in Stoke-on-Trent, she trained in the factory with Alfred and Louise Powell when they were at Etruria, but otherwise she worked independently. Along with Millie Taplin, she was one of six young women whom the Powells taught. Their methods were typical of the Arts and Crafts Movement and comprised 'learning by doing'. The paintresses were encouraged to experiment freely, although they received regular criticism from their teachers. Star Wedgwood was taught the most difficult type of free-hand painting – under-glaze rather than on-glaze. The latter could be wiped clean and a fresh start made, whereas the former was permanently fixed. Although more difficult, she always preferred under-glaze decorating because it was aesthetically more satisfactory to paint on a grained and absorbent base.[26] After her training was completed she was given her own studio.

From the late 1920s onwards she produced designs for Wedgwood, although on an informal and non-contractual basis. Indeed, her position in the company was anomalous in that she was neither employed at a set wage nor paid by the piece. Instead, she received a small fee for each pattern put into production, and was paid a 2½ per cent royalty on all ware sold; this was not enough to provide an independent livelihood. In the 1936 Grafton Galleries exhibition of new Wedgwood wares, six of her designs were featured and she was listed in the catalogue as one of Wedgwood's principal designers alongside Victor Skellern and Millie Taplin. Like Millie Taplin she designed for the new 'Alpine Pink' body, in addition to producing patterns for other china tablewares.

Her designs included 'Stars', a pattern of white stars and gold on a dark blue ground, 'Lady Jane Grey', a floral design in white and silver on a grey ground, and 'Eurydice' with a hand-painted border of silver and green on a green ground (Figures 49 and 50). Other designs included 'Fruit Box' and 'Coronation', which was designed for the coronation of King George VI and Queen Elizabeth in 1937 (Figure 51). In addition to china, she designed patterns such as

'Turkey Oak' for cane ware, and 'Play Box' for nurseryware in 1937. Most of Star Wedgwood's pottery designs were based on natural motifs and she used imaginative, though muted colour combinations such as pinks, greys and browns. Like those of Millie Taplin, they were produced as part of a clearly articulated company design strategy.

Star Wedgwood was a recognised designer at Wedgwood in the 1930s. She had her own studio and her designs were acknowledged in company advertising, yet her role and employment in the company were irregular. As a member of the Wedgwood family, she had obvious advantages in her ambition to be a pottery designer. However, her career was hampered by these family connections in that they led to an informality which undermined any plans that she might have had for a proper career. The lack of a formal contract and regular salary were evidence of this. She was serious about her job and professional in her approach to design. She was involved in the debates about design that were organised by the Society of Industrial Arts and, as we have seen, she produced a number of designs which Wedgwood manufactured and marketed in the 1930s. In Star Wedgwood's case, the combined effects of class and gender led to an acceptance of her interest in design within the ideological context of middle-class, 'feminine' leisure pursuits. To a certain extent her role as a designer at Wedgwood was marginalised because of who she was.

In 1937 she married Frederick Maitland Wright, who worked for Wedgwood and later became Joint Managing Director, and retired from design to devote herself to domestic life.

Charlotte Rhead

The role of Charlotte Rhead (1885–1947) as a designer in the pottery industry was quite different from that of the women designers at Wedgwood. As a member of an illustrious family of designers, she was introduced to pottery at an early age. Along with her two brothers, she was trained by their father, Frederick Alfred Rhead, to make a career in the pottery industry. Her father had trained as a designer at Minton under the art director, Louis Solon. Later he became art director at Wileman & Co., and then from 1913 until his death in 1933 he was art director at Wood & Sons, Burslem. His brother was the designer and educator George Wooliscroft Rhead with whom he wrote *Staffordshire Pots and Potters*.

After attending school at Longport and then Hanley, she began art classes at Fenton School of Art. At the art school, which had been established by her grandfather, also called George Wooliscroft Rhead, she learned enamelling and tube-lining.[27] Her first job in 1901 was as a tube-liner at Wardle & Co where her brother Frederick was art director. This was followed by work as a tube-liner and enameller for various companies before beginning a career as a designer at the Burslem company, T. & R. Boote, one of the leading makers of tube-lined tiles. Tube-lining, which she used to create decorative patterns, became Charlotte Rhead's hallmark. For this technique, which had been used to great effect for Art Nouveau and Art Deco tiles, thin tubes of slip were laid onto the surface of ware. The raised lines of slip hardened during firing and served as outlines for areas of colour which gave a rich, decorative effect.

Her contribution to the family income was important at that time because of the failure of her father's business partnership with F. H. Barker. Shortly after her father's appointment as art director at Wood & Sons, Charlotte Rhead joined him and began training new tube-liners. With Frederick Rhead's encouragement, Wood had established a separate hand-decorating section, Bursley Ltd, at its nearby Crown Works. This section specialised in the production of ornamental wares such as jugs, vases, bowls and plaques in a variety of sizes. It was these products that Charlotte Rhead designed and for which she used the tube-lining technique (Figure 52). In 1937 *The Pottery and Glass Record* reported: 'The introduction of this style of decoration was a revolution in the way of designing for the pottery industry and Miss Rhead has "individualised" it, putting it in a class of its own.'[28]

At the age of forty-one, and with an established reputation, she moved to the pottery firm of Burgess and Leigh, Burslem, to work as a designer and to train a small team of tube-liners. These tube-liners were responsible for carrying out the production of Charlotte Rhead's designs, while she developed new patterns. The company's announcement in the trade press read:

> We have secured the services of the accomplished lady artist CHARLOTTE RHEAD who has produced for us a number of original decorations, all pure HANDCRAFT combining grace and dignity with the most beautiful under glaze colouring.[29]

At Burgess and Leigh she designed under the trade name Burleigh using shapes already in production, and later decorating specially designed ones. These patterns included the fruit and flower designs done on dark-coloured grounds which were similar to her work at Wood. Others were 'Sylvan' and 'Garland' which consisted of black tube-lining on white grounds with blue and gold patterns (Figure 53). Other popular designs were more abstract and geometric such as 'Florentine', produced in dull green and brown on a mottled ground (Figure 54).

Charlotte Rhead was a shy woman, self-effacing and reluctant to talk about her work. The reporter for *The Pottery and Glass Record* who interviewed her in 1937, was unable to extract much information from her. The article instead became a celebration of the Rhead family. Family precedent had a strong influence on Charlotte Rhead's career, and this probably accounts for her confidence in her own designing abilities and led her to work successfully at several different companies. After five years at Burgess and Leigh, she moved in 1931 to A. G. Richardson, a company operating under the trade name Crown Ducal and based at the Gordon Pottery in Tunstall, the most northerly of the six towns. This change of job was apparently due to conflict with Harold Bennett, the other designer at Burgess and Leigh, who feared her competition for the post of art director.[30]

At Richardson's she developed many new tube-lined patterns which were marketed under the name of 'Rhodian' ware. Other designs by her included 'Byzantine' which had a stylised pattern of orange and yellow flowers within a border; 'Persian Rose' which had formalised rose heads enamelled in pink, orange and blue; and 'Manchu' and 'Golden Leaves' (Figures 55 and 56). Later she designed 'Wisteria' and 'Foxglove' using the new thick, opaque white glaze which the firm had recently developed (Figure 57). *The Pottery Gazette and Glass Trade Review* reported in 1934:

> A. G. Richardson in their new sample range, have something of everything and for everybody, besides which, . . . their wares have definite characteristics such as place them in a class which the retailer can ill afford to lose sight of.[31]

Charlotte Rhead specialised in what were called 'fancies' by the trade. These ornamental wares, which had some functional purpose, but were essentially decorative, were badly affected by the restrictions placed on pottery production during wartime. In 1943, Charlotte Rhead left Richardson's and returned to H. J. Wood as a designer. After her departure in 1926 from Wood & Sons (part of the same family company as H. J. Wood), she had maintained a working relationship with the company by supplying designs. Although the war stopped all production, she produced over 100 designs for her new employer, but the austerity measures which remained in force after the war meant that she never lived to see them in production. She died in 1947 at the age of sixty-two (Figures 58 and 59).

Charlotte Rhead made a career as a designer in the pottery industry in the same way as did her grandfather, father, uncles and brother. Within the Rhead family, she was the only woman to do so. This is attributable to a certain extent to the social context within which she worked that allowed women more flexible roles. Middle-class women like Charlotte Rhead, who had gained independence and achieved separate legal status from fathers and husbands, responded to the opportunity for a fulfilling career as an alternative to marriage. The high profile that pottery design enjoyed in Charlotte Rhead's family obviously influenced her choice of career. The designs by Charlotte Rhead for Wood & Sons, Burgess and Leigh, A. G. Richardson and H. J. Wood were primarily ornamental and decorative. Most were based on natural forms and used the tube-lining technique, although the patterns varied a great deal. Like many designers who worked in the pottery industry during the 1920s and 1930s, she produced patterns for different markets and tastes. These included those based on the decorative motifs developed within the context of Art Nouveau at the turn of the century as well as those that relied on more modern themes for their visual style.

Jessie Van Hallen

Education and training were key factors in women's access to careers as designers in the pottery industry between the wars. The Potteries art schools taught basic design skills and provided access to industrial contacts. The example of Jessie Van Hallen (1902–83) and Freda Beardmore (b. 1910) demonstrates this. Like many of her contemporaries, Jessie Van Hallen was educated at Burslem School of Art. Gordon Forsyth encouraged her successful application for a Royal College of Art scholarship which she failed to take up. Instead she married a ship's officer in 1924, and settled down to domestic life, bearing two children in 1927 and 1929. However, after she was offered a job as a modeller by the Burslem pottery manufacturer

111

George Wade in the early 1930s, she began a career as a designer. Wade produced fancies and modelled figures, and it was this latter category of goods that Jessie Van Hallen designed. Her work included figures of dancing girls, fashionably dressed women and film stars such as Norma Shearer, as well as pottery flowers, brooches and modelled animals. In 1942, when George Wade ceased production of decorative work in order to make electrical appliances for the war effort, Jessie Van Hallen left to have her third child. Her career as a designer in the pottery industry ceased at this point, although she continued to model figures in her studio at home for many years.[32]

Freda Beardmore

Burslem School of Art was the focus of the Potteries art schools and its junior art department was one of its chief innovations. It was here that Freda Beardmore began her art education at the age of 16 after leaving Hartshill Secondary School in Stoke, where she was brought up. Like her elder sisters who became teachers, it was accepted that she should undertake further training for a career, supported by the scholarship she had won.

The aim of the junior art department at Burslem School of Art, which she attended as a full-time student between 1926 and 1928, was to increase the ratio of art classes to normal academic classes for children who showed a particular aptitude for art. Usually the two or three years spent in this department were followed by another two or three years in the senior art department. Scholarships were offered to encourage children from poor families. The training was varied and covered drawing from nature and antique casts, heraldry, metalwork, calligraphy and needlework, in addition to specific skills for the local industry such as modelling and pottery decoration. Owing to family circumstances Freda Beardmore had to start work after completing only two years at Burslem although she continued to study at evening classes for four nights a week. This was supplemented with one day a week of full-time study at Burslem when she began her first job at Wedgwood's Etruria factory in 1928.

Although her parents were not wealthy, each summer the family rented a cottage in the countryside. Stoke-on-Trent was dirty and unhealthy but only a few miles south was the rural village of Barlaston. It was during these holidays that Freda Beardmore met Major Frank Wedgwood's daughters, who lived at Barlaston. This contact led Freda Beardmore to her first job as a trainee designer in Wedgwood's hand-painting department in 1928, where she was trained by Millie Taplin and stayed for two years. To be trained at a prestigious company such as Wedgwood was an excellent start to her career as a designer.

After a brief spell at the firm of Maddox in Burslem, in 1930 Freda Beardmore joined E. Brain & Co., which owned Foley China at Fenton, as company designer. She now had a salary of £2 per week and her brief was to organise a small hand-painting department on similar lines to the one at Wedgwood. Her arrival at Brain's coincided with that of Bill Brain, son of the Managing Director. His appointment marked an attempt to revitalise the company, which had fallen into serious financial difficulties largely due to the impact of the First World War, the loss of markets in the 1920s and the serious economic problems of the early 1930s. Design was to play an important role in the revitalisation process. Until her marriage in 1946, Freda Beardmore along with Bill Brain and the other 200 employees worked to establish the company's reputation for progressive design. Hand-painted wares with fresh, brightly coloured floral patterns formed the basis of Freda Beardmore's designs, although she was also responsible for some modern abstract designs and for one new shape named 'Savoy'. These new patterns, which included 'Harebell' and 'Oakleaf', were hand painted by the team of twelve paintresses trained by Freda Beardmore (Figure 60).[33]

In 1933 she was involved in an unusual enterprise to promote better quality design in industry. This was initiated by Thomas Acland Fennemore, one of Brain's directors, who invited several well-known British artists to submit designs for pottery and glass. Harrods, the department store, planned to exhibit the wares, and one glass and two pottery companies agreed to manufacture the artists' designs. E. Brain & Co and A. J. Wilkinson were responsible for producing the designs in bone china and earthenware respectively with Freda Beardmore and Clarice Cliff co-ordinating the adaptation of the designs to mass production. The list of artists involved was long and prestigious; it included Vanessa Bell, Duncan Grant, Paul Nash, Graham Sutherland, Laura Knight, Frank Brangwyn, Ben Nicholson and Barbara Hepworth.[34] In addition, there were several designers with specific knowledge of the pottery industry such as Gordon Forsyth, his daughter Moira and Freda Beardmore.[35]

This liaison between art and industry aimed to improve the standing of British pottery through better design. Various reports were published which tackled the issue of improved industrial design including the report by Lord Gorell on *The Production and Exhibition of Articles of Good Design and Everyday Use*, 1932, and a report by the Pottery Committee of the Council for Art and Industry on *Design in the Pottery Industry*, 1937.[36] Both reports highlighted the potential of education to produce better designers for industry and to teach the public to appreciate and buy good quality designs. Some pottery manufacturers claimed that they were already producing what the public wanted, whereas companies like E. Brain & Co. responded more positively.

At both Brain and Wilkinson, costs had to be kept low because the intention was to show that good design did not necessarily mean high prices. The marketing of the designs emphasised the role of the artist/designer by stamping their names on the bottom and designating the first twelve sets 'First Editions'. The style of the designs varied enormously, although all those for bone china were applied to Brain's standard shapes. In adapting their designs to the shapes, Freda Beardmore had to liaise with the artists and to negotiate changes which were required to make a two-dimensional pattern compatible with a three-dimensional shape. Although some of the artists (including Graham Sutherland) visited the factory to learn the production processes and gain a better understanding of the medium, many did not and their designs were heavily dependent on Freda Beardmore's skills. In fact, several were very unsuitable as pottery decoration and were adapted only with difficulty to Brain's shapes. Freda Beardmore's own designs, which included 'Feathers', 'Sherwood', 'Shah' and 'Carillon', were based on either stylised natural forms or linear abstract ones (Figure 61). Although she is less well known than the other contributors to the project, her designs successfully demonstrated her ability as a designer. Unlike some of the other designs, hers showed an understanding of the relationship between form and flat pattern.

Ambitious plans to take the project a stage further by asking the designers to produce new shapes were never carried out. Of the patterns produced for the Harrods exhibition only a few remained in production after the event. The exhibition was well reviewed as 'a unique experiment', but the production process was plagued by technical difficulties which led to some modifications. Unfortunately, the wares were commercially unsuccessful. Clarice Cliff later recalled that 'it was so disappointing that it was the closest thing to a flop that, I am glad to say, I have ever been associated with'.[37]

Fennemore apparently promised Bill Brain a 20 per cent increase in turnover as a result of the experiment, and although this was over-optimistic, it did mark an upturn in Brain's fortunes.[38] By the end of the 1930s, Foley China was noted for modern, well-designed tableware. As with other pottery firms, the Second World War brought changes in organisation and production. Freda Beardmore worked as an aeronautical inspector at the motor company Alvis which had moved to Stone in Staffordshire after being bombed in Coventry. She returned to Brain's in 1945 after undertaking a refresher course for designers in London. Before the war she had become engaged to a farmer in Barlaston and in 1946 was married. With the birth of her first child in 1947 she gave up her career and for the next ten years devoted herself to bringing up three children. In the late 1950s she began teaching pottery on a part-time basis and this she continued until her retirement in 1977.

Like Jessie Van Hallen, the key to Freda Beardmore's successful career in design was her art school training. This was combined with a supportive middle-class background, and the active encouragement of Gordon Forsyth who often provided introductions for students to the various companies with which he was personally connected. Many of his former students entered companies with a keen interest in design, such as Wedgwood, E. Brain & Co and A. E. Gray.

A. E. Gray had been founded by Albert Edward Gray in 1912. Gray began his career as a salesman with special responsibility for pottery and glass in a Manchester wholesale firm. As his sales confidence grew, he came to the view that much of the pottery he sold was lacking in artistic quality and was failing to meet the needs of the consumer. He saw a gap in the market and with the financial support of two friends established his own pottery decorating company in Stoke-on-Trent. From 1913, the company developed decorative pattern designs for white earthenware which had been bought in from local producers. At the same time Gray became involved in the local debates about pottery design. He was a member of the Ceramic Society which provided a forum for the exchange of information and research, organised visits to other potteries – both at home and abroad – and generally offered an information service to manufacturers and those associated with the pottery industry. In 1917 he urged the Society to establish a separate art section. This was achieved the following year and aimed to improve the decorative side of the business.[39]

During the 1920s and 1930s, A. E. Gray made design a priority. The company became well known for highly stylised, hand-painted patterns in bright colours which related to the fashionable 'moderne' and Art Deco styles. In order to find the staff to decorate these wares, Gray recruited directly from secondary schools and the local art schools, and then trained the apprentices in specific hand-decorating techniques such as banding or free-hand painting. In his search for a replacement designer in 1922, he accepted Gordon Forsyth's recommendation and appointed Susie Cooper, a woman determined to work as a designer in the pottery industry.

Susie Cooper

Susan Vera Cooper (b. 1902) came from a moderately wealthy family which owned a small oil refining business and farm in the village of Milton on the rural outskirts of Stoke-on-Trent. Her grandparents ran a small pottery in Hanley. She was the youngest of seven sisters and was brought up on the farm by her mother (her father had died when she was eleven). Her mother supported her keen interest in art by encouraging her to attend evening classes at Burslem School of Art, and by suggesting that she could make a living from this.

At first Susie Cooper took both art and cookery classes, but on the advice of Gordon Forsyth, she successfully applied for a scholarship to pursue her art studies in a more systematic fashion. She began day-time studies at Burslem School of Art, probably in 1919. For three years she trained in the newly organised art school before applying to the Royal College of Art in 1922. Without industrial experience she was rejected, so she decided to acquire this by taking a job in the pottery industry. To this end Forsyth introduced her to his old friend and colleague, A. E. Gray.

In 1922, when Susie Cooper started at A. E. Gray as a trainee designer, she found herself in a company which had established a distinctive style of decoration. A year after her arrival, a new range of lustre, Gloria Lustre, designed by Forsyth, was introduced. This particular ware, which was both ornamental and practical, was brightly coloured and hand-painted. Before achieving the position of designer, Susie Cooper learned the paintress's skills by decorating this ware. Within two years, she was promoted to designer, and to coincide with this a special named backstamp was produced for all ware which she designed. Her designs for A. E. Gray were colourful, abstract and floral patterns for the free-hand paintresses (Figure 62).

On her twenty-seventh birthday in 1929 Susie Cooper left Gray's, determined to set up her own company. Edward Gray warned her that it would be hard going and that she would last eight months at the most. As she said more recently, 'It was of course taboo for women to go into industry in those days. But I knew what I wanted to do.'[40] Her decision to leave A. E. Gray was influenced by her desire for a new challenge in her career, an ambition she could not fulfil by staying at A. E. Gray. She was dissatisfied with designing decoration in isolation from shape, and wanted to develop both aspects of pottery design together.

The finance for her company came largely from her family, and with her brother-in-law, Jack Beeson, as partner, space was rented in a small factory in Tunstall in the autumn of 1929. On one of the painting floors of the George Street pottery, Susie Cooper established the facilities needed to hand-decorate blank ware. This modest enterprise was jeopardised three weeks after the Wall Street crash, when the creditors of the pottery from which she rented space foreclosed on the loan which had kept the business solvent. She was without premises until the spring of 1930 when she was once again ready to start production in the Chelsea Works in Moorland Road, Burslem, in space rented from Doulton's, one of her suppliers of blank pottery. *The Pottery Gazette and Glass Trade Review* reported in April 1930; 'it is only rarely . . . that one comes across an instance of a pottery artist – and particularly a lady – who has the confidence and courage to attempt to carve out a career by laying down a special plant and staff on what must be admitted to be something suggestive of a commercial scale.'[41]

From the outset, the Susie Cooper Pottery was noted for its modern design. Early examples were fairly simple using over-glaze enamel colours. These included 'Polka Dot' and 'Exclamation Mark', both of which were produced in a single colour on cream-coloured earthenware (Figure 63). Other typical patterns at this time were based on concentric shaded and washed bands of colour (Figure 64). More complicated patterns based on floral motifs included 'Briar Rose'. She has since said that many of these designs resulted from her need to produce designs which could be reproduced perfectly by her paintresses.[42]

Paintresses started working for Susie Cooper at the age of fourteen and were initially trained to grind colour and apply it to blank ware. Gradually they acquired skills that could then be passed on to new trainees. Florence May Hancock went to work for Susie Cooper as a bander in January 1938 at the age of fifteen. As a trainee bander she earned about 5 shillings a week, then after two years of training she went on to piece-work and earned about 17 shillings a week.[43] Banding was one of the decorative techniques that Susie Cooper employed in her designs. It could take various forms including shaded, solid, narrow, flat and wash banding, and it could be combined with other decorative techniques such as lithographs.

Following the considerable interest which her designs generated at the 1931 British Industries Fair, Wood & Sons, another of her blank ware suppliers, offered her new premises in its factory, the Crown Works on Newcastle Street, Burslem. Susie Cooper was keen to take up this offer as she preferred Wood's blank shapes to those of all her other suppliers. She was keen to develop a close relationship with a manufacturer, in the hope that eventually she would be able to have her own shapes produced.

Confirmation of Susie Cooper's early success came in 1932 when the Queen ordered a breakfast-in-bed set and a jug from her display at the British Industries Fair. In the same year, Harry Wood agreed to manufacture shapes to her own designs; these were to be produced in an ivory-bodied earthenware. They were named Kestrel and Curlew and had streamlined outlines reminiscent of bird forms (Figures 65 and 66). Their shapes were clearly related to the smooth, undecorated forms found in the Modernist-inspired architecture and design of the 1930s in which form was emphasised in preference to applied decoration. These were followed in 1937 by two more designs – Falcon and Spiral. With the introduction of Kestrel and Curlew, Susie Cooper began to fulfil her ambition which was described in *The Pottery Gazette and Glass Trade Review* in August 1935:

> Form, decoration and even texture in the Susie Cooper ware are part of a considered scheme; it is not merely a case of sticking a decoration on to pot regardless of context . . . [44]

With her new shapes in production, Susie Cooper developed suitable surface decoration. She introduced under-glaze patterns such as 'Crayon Lines' in 1933 which was created by the use of thin crayon sticks. Other new hand-painted patterns included 'Spirals' and 'Beechwood', although with increased production, the demands on the paintresses' time were becoming too great. It was in response to this problem that Susie Cooper turned her attention to lithographs.

In April 1933, she had attended and contributed to a debate organised by the North Staffordshire branch of the Society of Industrial Artists on 'Lithographs as a Means of Pottery Decoration'. During this debate it was claimed that 'most of the time of the lithographic transfer printers had been taken up in the past in producing cheap, gaudy imitations . . . '[45] Susie Cooper contributed to the debate by arguing for co-operation between the pottery and lithograph manufacturers, and proposing 'that it was no use the lithographer bringing out lithographs produced by an artist who knew nothing at all about the manufacturing processes'.[46] Her own approach to the use of lithographs was constructive in that she was prepared to work closely with the lithograph manufacturer to develop a better product. She produced her own watercolour designs to demonstrate the required effects to the lithograph manufacturer. By this method she established satisfactory sources for her lithographs which she combined with hand-painted dots, shaded bands and stripes to produce designs such as 'Endon Border', 'Dresden Spray', 'Iris' and 'Clematis' (Figure 67). All these designs had both hand-painted and lithographed decoration of such high quality that it is almost impossible to distinguish them from fine hand-painted designs.[47]

Susie Cooper's involvement in the debate about lithographs highlights her increasing confidence as a pottery manufacturer. In September 1932, she was elected to the Council of the Society of Industrial Artists' North Staffordshire branch, and she became an active participant in its debates and those organised under the auspices of the Ceramic Society and Design and Industries Association. As an employer she was fair, although exacting.[48] Her workforce numbered 70–100 in the late 1930s, including free-hand paintresses, lithographers, aerographers, biscuit-workers, kiln-loaders. There was also a small printing shop. Even though the enterprise was begun in what *The Pottery Gazette and Glass Trade Review* described as an 'unpropitious period', it made 'steady progress from the start'.[49] By the mid 1930s she was exporting ware to Europe, Scandinavia, South Africa, Australia, Canada and the United States. Her company thrived even during the worst years of the Depression and by the financial year 1930–40 it had a turnover of £250,000. Susie Cooper was involved with the company at every level. She produced about 200 new pattern designs a year, but in the meantime she was involved in the day-to-day running of the company which included recruitment, work organisation, promotion and marketing.[50]

Within the framework of the British pottery industry in the 1930s, Susie Cooper's company was an undoubted success, although a puzzle to the trade press. A writer in 1931 advised the pottery trade 'to steel yourself against them if you will, but they persist in attracting. . . By some quality which is difficult to analyse, Miss Susie Cooper's work confounds her critics – and makes them her customers.'[51] From the outset, she identified a distinct market which she believed to be professional, with little money, but plenty of taste. The trade press recognised that 'the designs of this artist are, per-haps, not intended to appeal to the surging multitude, but rather to the relative few – those to whom tradition counts for much less than originality and the desire to explore the possibilities of new fields and methods'.[52] Moreover, it was thought at the time that 'she has found, if not actually created, a market for her productions'.[53]

Susie Cooper placed great emphasis on marketing and retailing. She had a London outlet in her own showroom at Audrey House, Holborn; she advertised regularly in the pottery trade journals and exhibited at the annual British Industries Fairs and most of the major exhibitions in the 1930s (Figure 68). These included the Dor-land Hall Exhibition of 1933, the British Art in Industry Exhibition at the Royal Academy of 1935, and the 1937 Paris Exhibition. For all these exhibitions she designed display stands which were described as 'totally unlike anything else' due to their striking modern design.[54]

One of her marketing successes was to identify the demand for smaller sets of pottery rather than the enormous dinner sets of the preceding decades. She thought that 'the drastic changes that have come over the domestic life of many people warrant the provision of smaller and better balanced services'.[55] To this end, she introduced new combinations of ware such as a fifteen-piece dinner set, a break-fast-in-bed set and an early morning set.[56] In the mid 1930s, the cheapest early morning set, which had banded decoration, retailed at five shillings in stores such as Peter Jones, Selfridges, John Lewis, Waring & Gillow, Harrods and Heals. The appeal of her ware was consistently attributed by a variety of writers to its modernity, simplicity and audacity. She was described in 1931 as being 'a gifted, creative artist of the modern school of thought, one who reveals in her work a lively imagination combined with a unique capacity to achieve the maximum degree of effectiveness in pottery decoration by recourse to the simplest modes of expression'.[57]

In manufacturing terms, the Susie Cooper Pottery was a small to medium-scale unit, the production of which was closely tied to the design abilities of its owner. In turn, any new designs were introduced with the paintresses' skills in mind, and as a consequence new decorating developments were accommodated with relative ease within the flexible factory organisation. Susie Cooper found the business arrangement which she had made with Harry Wood ideal. He agreed to produce blank ware to her own design leaving her free to concentrate on the decoration of ware and the business organisation of her company. In return, she designed shapes specifically for her supplier such as Wren, Jay and Rex which were well reviewed when they were exhibited in 1935.

The concept of good design, which was central to her aims, was formulated within the context of the debates organised by the SIA, the DIA and Ceramic Society which she had attended. As the 1930s progressed, these debates were increasingly shaped by the theories of continental Modernism, articulated by visiting speakers such as Serge Chermayeff and Paul Nash. Her own views about design represented a confirmation of these theories. She emphasised the importance of modern design for contemporary needs. She was committed to new production techniques and she pioneered the development of modern decorating methods such as lithography. She wanted to combine 'low cost with good design', and argued that 'the pottery manufacturer should cost his products to cover production costs not design'. She believed that 'the difference cost-wise in producing very poor design and very good design in the pottery industry is negligible – therefore it is the duty of manufacturers to produce the best they can'.[58] Evidence of modernity, which was a characteristic of her design method, could be seen in the streamlined shapes and the innovative lithographic decoration.

The reporters for the two major trade journals of the pottery industry, *The Pottery Gazette and Glass Trade Review* and *The Pottery and Glass Record* discerned in Susie Cooper's designs a 'feminine' style. In their reporting of the various trade fairs where she had exhibited, they made much of this, claiming 'Miss Cooper is a lady who designs from the standpoint of the lady.'[59] In this article the writer stressed the importance of the female consumer to the pottery industry and emphasised Susie Cooper's special insight into this market as a woman designer. There was also grudging acceptance in other articles that 'the woman's point of view . . . counts for a good deal – in domestic pottery design at all events'.[60]

Several features distinguished the designs of Susie Cooper from most of her competitors in the 1930s and in these we can find the basis of this so-called 'femininity'. There was a subtle range of colours, delicacy and lightness of decoration, simplicity and modernity in shape, and practicality in terms of shape and material (hard-wearing earthenware). An excellent example of these qualities can be seen in the 'Iris' soup cup (Figure 69). Within the context of 1930s design, this had a modern shape with a shallow bowl and slightly angular handles. Susie Cooper's innovative use of decoration was apparent in the way that it was applied to the inside of the bowl, and in the combination of lithographic and hand-painted decoration. The 'Iris' lithograph was stylised, though based on clear observation of nature. The colours were a dull grey-blue and deep yellow with touches of black. These were combined with a thin, solid band of the same grey-blue around the inside rim which merged into a washed band shaded towards the bottom of the bowl. The decoration was restrained and elegant, and incorporated onto a hard-wearing, though fine earthenware. This was designed in practical and easy-to-clean shapes which were none the less contemporary in style. It seems, then, that the so-called 'femininity' of Susie Cooper's designs was determined by the soft colours, the lightness and delicacy of decoration and the practicality of a product designed for a domestic purpose. It is significant that although in many ways she challenged the dominant stereotype by working as a businesswoman, independent designer and manufacturer, her products were analysed within the same framework of conventional gender attributes as the work of Vanessa Bell and Marion Dorn. It is even more interesting that the work of male contemporaries such as Keith Murray at Wedgwood was not discussed in gender-specific terms even if in retrospect it can be seen to be just as delicate and subtle.

This 'feminine' analysis of Susie Cooper's products, which was mainly the invention of the trade journals, was superseded by a Modernist analysis which began to appear in national art journals such as *The Studio*, and in publications by Modernist writers such as Nikolaus Pevsner, Herbert Read and Gordon Forsyth. In Pevsner's *An Enquiry into Industrial Art in England* special mention was made of Susie Cooper's innovative use of lithographs, while other writers emphasised the modernity, functionalism and progressive quality of her work.[61] Due to the attention of this small but powerful group of writers who were responsible for the vigorous promotion of Modernism in Britain in the 1930s, Susie Cooper had a high profile. Her work was praised and reviewed as a pioneering example of the very latest in design, and as a result of this group's approval, her company and career were given a boost. For this reason, and because she owned and managed her own business and clearly stamped her products with her own name, she did not suffer in her career from the lack of recognition experienced by her female contemporaries. The most important fact of Susie Cooper's role in the pottery industry in the 1930s was her decisive control over her own career potential. In this she was unique.

Clarice Cliff

Only one other woman designer achieved anything like the same sort of prominence in the pottery industry in this period as Susie Cooper; this was Clarice Cliff (1899–1972). She gained a certain notoriety, not just for her striking designs, but through her love affair with Colley Shorter, the managing director of the company for which she worked, A. J. Wilkinson of Middleport, Stoke-on-Trent. This personal relationship has been used to account for Clarice Cliff's success, disregarding her undoubted ability as a designer and promoter.

Clarice Cliff was born into a working-class family of eight; her father was an iron moulder. She attended the High Street Elementary School in Tunstall until the age of 10, and then continued her education at the nearby Summerback Road School. In 1912 she began a seven-year apprenticeship as an enameller at the Tunstall firm of Lingard, Webster & Co., a manufacturer of domestic tableware. She earned one shilling for a five-and-a-quarter-day week while learning free-hand painting. After three years she moved to Hollingshead & Kirkham, another local pottery, to learn the techniques of lithography. At the same time she attended first Tunstall and then, from the mid 1920s, Burslem School of Art for two evenings a week. Within another year she had moved on to work as a lithographer at the earthenware manufacturer, A. J. Wilkinson.

A. J. Wilkinson was owned and managed by Arthur Shorter (who had purchased the company from his partner in 1894), and his two sons Colley and Guy. During the first decade of the twentieth century, the company established regular customers and consolidated its position with the introduction of a new ware in 1911. Tibetan ware, which was designed by John Butler, won a diploma at a major exhibition in Ghent. This was a decorative design in rich golds and purples, which built on the company's reputation for tableware and fancies in traditional, ornate patterns. The period 1915–25 was one of expansion, with Colley and Guy Shorter becoming joint directors, and the company changing its traditional working practices and product range to cater for the larger market for inexpensive, practical earthenware. A. J. Wilkinson increased both its output and market share, and when the opportunity arose in 1920, the factory was expanded by the purchase of the adjoining Newport pottery.

With the completion of her lithographic training in 1920, Clarice Cliff's design ability was recognised by Wilkinson's decorating manager, Jack Walker. It was agreed that she should be given an opportunity to develop her talent for drawing, and to facilitate this she was moved from the general decorating shop and put in the studio shared by the two company designers, John Butler and Fred Ridgway. Here she worked as a gilder, in addition to modelling small figures of Indians and Arabs which were then hand painted in bright colours. These were some of the first wares which she signed. During the 1920s A. J. Wilkinson was producing a range of different designs which catered for all tastes. But the company's growth had slowed down because of a series of trade slumps, and the development of the Newport pottery took longer than had been anticipated.[62]

In 1926 Clarice Cliff was given her own studio in the Newport factory. Along with her growing confidence as a designer her relationship with Colley Shorter was changing. This generated a great deal of gossip and disapproval as he was married with two daughters. Shorter encouraged her ambitions to be a designer and in 1927 sent her on a short course at the Royal College of Art. Here she studied under Gilbert Ledward, learning modelling, figure composition and life drawing, in addition to enjoying the London art galleries and museums. After her return to Stoke-on-Trent, she worked closely with Colley Shorter on a project to develop new designs. A small studio was established in a corner of the Newport Pottery showroom where she developed a range of decorative patterns with the aid of the paintress Gladys Scarlett. These were first tried out on old warehouse stock and then adapted to the company's regular wares. The market testing of these bold new patterns took place in 1928, and although it came as a surprise to some of the company's sales staff, it was an immediate success. The new range was launched with its own backstamp – 'Hand Painted Bizarre by Clarice Cliff' – to distinguish it from the company's other wares.

'Bizarre' was a geometric, boldly patterned design which at first utilised shapes already in production (Figure 70), but from 1929 used new geometric shapes specially produced to complement the patterns. These included 'Conical' introduced in 1929, and 'Biarritz' and 'Le Bon Jour' in 1933. Most of Clarice Cliff's new shapes were unusual and severely geometric with their triangular handles, circular sides and conical bodies (Figure 71). They were well suited to the abstract, brightly coloured patterns which were developed in rapid sequence following the success of 'Bizarre'. One of the most popular and best selling of these was 'Crocus', introduced in 1928 and still in production in 1963 (Figure 72). Although based on a hand-painted flower motif, 'Crocus' was a stylised design in bright orange, blue, purple and green. Other popular patterns included 'Latona', 'Lodore', 'Delicia' and 'Appliqué', and like 'Crocus' these were produced in vivid colour combinations.

Designs for domestic tableware were Clarice Cliff's main concern, although like other companies Wilkinson manufactured a range of fancies. These included vases, covered pots, candlesticks, table centrepieces, book-ends and teapots. It was in these latter two categories that Clarice Cliff produced some of her most outrageous designs, including book-ends in the form of parrots and extravagantly modelled teapots (Figure 73). At the same time, she was designing wall masks and jazz-age figures such as dancing couples, pianists, banjo players, drummers and trumpeters which were modelled by Peggy Davies (Figure 74).

Between 1929 and 1935, Clarice Cliff's designs for A. J. Wilkinson enjoyed great popularity through effective advertising and promotion both to the retailer and the public. The company exhibited at the yearly British Industries Fairs, the *Daily Mail* Ideal Home exhibitions, the British Industrial Art in Relation to the Home Exhibition held at Dorland Hall in 1933, and the 1935 British Art in Industry Exhibition at the Royal Academy. Small exhibitions and promotional demonstrations of hand-decorating techniques by the 'Bizarre' ware paintresses were organised in conjunction with retailers such as Barkers, Harrods, Liberty, Waring & Gillow, Selfridges and Lawley's. As usual the pottery trade press was quick to respond:

Never before had such powerful and intensive colourings been
applied en masse in flat brushwork effects. At first . . . the
designs and colourings struck one as being so unlike anything
previously attempted, and so revolutionary in character as to
be likely to prove short-lived.[63]

The writer for the *Pottery Gazette* was undoubtedly surprised that
this had not been the case,

but experience has proved that any such fears were
unfounded . . . although many retailers . . . who when they saw
'Bizarre' ware for the first time, said that it was too far advanced
for their particular market . . . were quick to change their
minds when they saw how the bold colourings and whimsical
decorations were finding a market in the shops of their more
courageous competitors.[64]

The tableware was made in earthenware and consequently moderately priced; in 1931 an early morning set cost eight shillings and a
13-inch wall plaque cost 7s. 9d. Like Susie Cooper, A. J. Wilkinson
recognised the market for progressive design at reasonable prices.

After one year of trading, the whole of the Newport factory was
given over to the production of the new range of wares. Even so
the enterprise remained quite a small part of A. J. Wilkinson's total
manufacturing output. In 1931, the number of paintresses required
for the 'Bizarre' wares was increased from the modest twenty-five
who had been hired in 1928 to 150, many of whom were boys and
girls who required training. With the success of her designs, she was
appointed art director in 1931. At the same time, Colley Shorter
joined the Society of Industrial Artists and began to develop a keen
interest in the debates about good design and Modernism. Most of
the reviews of A. J. Wilkinson's new wares enthusiastically commented on their modernity and the important role of Clarice Cliff:
'undoubtedly this lady has a versatility that is quite exceptional, and
she is continuing to produce a mass of new designs, the majority of
these are ultra-modernistic in spirit'.[65]

Support for Clarice Cliff's designs was not forthcoming from the
promoters of Modernism who discerned a superficial interpretation
of its theories. Gordon Forsyth believed that her geometric patterns
revealed a lack of any real understanding of the principles of modern
design and that the triangular-handled cups and teapots were
impractical and unsuited to regular use. More recently, the popu-

larity of her work with collectors has brought about a revival of interest in her activities, but she is still poorly regarded by historians of pottery who consciously or unconsciously adopt the values of Modernism. Isabelle Anscombe reflected this in her account of women's role in design in *A Woman's Touch*. In this book, Clarice Cliff is dismissed not only for her attitude to Modernism, but because Anscombe claims that the driving force behind the whole 'Bizarre' ware enterprise was Colley Shorter. Anscombe then asserts, with little justification, that 'the part she played in promoting her tableware did little to establish her as a person to be taken seriously in the design world'.[66] This is an extraordinary comment from a writer whose aim was to account for the important role which women played in the history of design.

Clarice Cliff provoked strong feelings in the pottery industry because of her publicity-seeking and self-promotion. Among her designer contemporaries she was not widely admired because of her apparent lack of design skills.[67] However, most recognised her immense ability in marketing and advertising her products. In this she paralleled Susie Cooper, although, unlike her contemporary, Clarice Cliff was interested in the fashionable and witty. Her jazzy angular designs in brash primary colours were a product of the vibrant Art Deco style of the 1920s, whereas Susie Cooper's designs originated in the sophisticated Modernism of the 1930s. In the final analysis, whether historians like or do not like Clarice Cliff and her designs is not really the issue. What matters is that an account is made of Clarice Cliff's major role in pottery design at A. J. Wilkinson in the 1920s and 1930s. Like Millie Taplin, Clarice Cliff was one of the few women to become a successful designer without the advantages of a privileged class background. As such she is representative of the women designers in the inter-war years who had 'new opportunities'.

In part because of the precarious economy, some pottery manufacturers were responsive to the issue of design in the 1920s and 1930s. A. E. Gray, E. Brain & Co., A. J. Wilkinson, as well as established companies such as Wedgwood, began to promote their products on the basis of quality and modernity. At the same time they began to develop new marketing and advertising skills in order to sell their wares in the increasingly lucrative home market. Within this context women had a role as designers and as consumers.

Numerous women designers gained employment in these companies, while others challenged the dominant female stereotypes to work as independent producers and art directors. The success of this group of women depended on several factors which were specific to the inter-war period. The high profile given to design encouraged manufacturers to employ designers; in the Potteries these tended to be those educated at the local art schools which were accessible and supportive of local manufacturers. The vogue for hand-painted wares offered job opportunities for paintresses and those trained in surface design, and because of the sexual division in pottery design, reinforced by the industry and allied art schools, qualified designers of surface pattern tended to be women.

As women gained greater legislative independence from men, a design career in the local potteries had many advantages. Traditionally, a large number of women had worked in the industry, and within the still dominant sexual division of labour, there was a clear place for skilled women in the decorating side of production. A career route in pottery design was mapped through the art schools with their flexible system of day and evening classes, scholarships and industrial contacts. Class background was a critical determining factor affecting access to art school and design jobs, although internal job ladders and cheap evening classes enabled working-class women, Clarice Cliff and Millie Taplin, to become designers. However, the professionalisation of design which began to take place in the 1930s, ultimately restricted these two working-class women; one suspects that class played no small part in the patronising attitudes of upper-middle-class design theorists to Clarice Cliff's work.

For middle-class women, Susie Cooper and Charlotte Rhead, pottery design provided an excellent career. Both worked in an independent way; the latter searching for job satisfaction by moving from company to company, the former playing a substantial part in redefining women designers' roles by producing both shape and decoration, and running a successful business.

Marketing was an activity in which Clarice Cliff and Susie Cooper excelled; both recognised the importance of creating and stimulating a market for their strikingly modern products. These skills were acknowledged at the time and gender was used as an apparent explanation for these. It was argued that as a woman, Susie Cooper had a special insight into the needs of the female consumer and that her designs were 'feminine'. This interpretation enabled contemporary commentators to account for her extraordinary success by ultimately reducing it to biology. It also served to undermine and diminish Cooper's achievement by implying that women's needs as consumers were unified (irrespective of class, profession and educational background) because of gender, and that merely by virtue of being of the same sex, Cooper was able to satisfy the demands of the female consumer. The considerable skills which she had acquired at art school, at A. E. Gray's and in her own company were put aside in favour of a simplistic form of biological determinism.

The notion of 'intrinsic femininity' provided the key for analysing the work of many women artists and designers in the 1920s and 1930s when dominant gender stereotypes permeated art, design and society. Women were generally supposed to have a biologically determined facility for colour co-ordination, the arrangement of interior and domestic spaces, and the design of products for these. The painter Vanessa Bell was noted for her 'feminine' approach in the use of domestic subject matter, decorative ability and subtle colour range, whereas the same qualities in male artists such as Bonnard, Vuillard and Matisse were conveniently ignored or interpreted within the framework of Modernism.

Modernist methods of analysis enabled critics to emphasise the formal, technical and innovatory aspects of art and design; thus minimising social and cultural meanings. Whereas Susie Cooper's work had been interpreted within the narrow framework of gender stereotypes by some writers, others discerned the signs of a Modernist pioneer. Much was made, by 1930s Modernist critics such as Pevsner, of the technical innovations in her lithographs, the formal simplicity of her shapes and patterns, and her commitment to modernity and functionalism. As an independent manufacturer, Susie Cooper retained control over design, marketing and advertising, and presented herself as a serious person engaged in the debates of the day. This, combined with her friendship with Gordon Forsyth, brought her into contact with progressive Modernist theorists who began to illustrate her designs in their didactic texts. At this stage a different interpretation of her work became apparent which, to some extent, guaranteed her status in the Modernist history of twentieth-century pottery design in Britain.

In this history, Susie Cooper is the only woman pottery designer to find a place. She fits into the picture as one of the contributors – alongside men like Keith Murray, Eric Ravilious, and Victor Skellern – to the development of a technically and formally innovative type of ware. Significantly there was no place in this history for Cooper's contemporaries, whose designs did not fit the bill; Clarice Cliff was thought to be too superficial in her modernity, while

Charlotte Rhead and Millie Taplin were not sufficiently progressive. Most importantly none, except for Cooper and Cliff, was able to overcome the sexual divisions in pottery production and to design both shape and decoration as a whole: one of the central tenets of Modernism.

With hindsight, we can see that neither the 'feminine' nor the Modernist analysis adequately explains the roles and work of these women pottery designers between the wars: one ties women to a patriarchal interpretation of biology, the other celebrates only one as a pioneer.

Notes

1. G. M. Forsyth, 'The Pottery Designer. What the Industry Needs', *The Pottery Gazette and Glass Trade Review*, 1 April 1932, p. 514.
2. S. Rowbotham, *Hidden From History*, Pluto Press, 1980, p. 124.
3. ibid., p. 130. Between 1921 and 1931 the numbers of women in domestic service went up by 200,000.
4. 'Female Labour in the Pottery Industry', *The Pottery Gazette and Glass Trade Review*, 1 May 1919, p. 478.
5. 'Notes From the Potteries', *The Pottery Gazette and Glass Trade Review*, 1 April 1924, p. 683.
6. Rowbotham, op. cit., p. 129.
7. 'Buyers' Notes', *The Pottery Gazette and Glass Trade Review*, 1 October 1932, p. 1249.
8. 'Potteries M.P.s and the Tariffs', *The Pottery Gazette and Glass Trade Review*, 1 June 1932, pp. 750–1. 'Japanese Competition', *The Pottery Gazette and Glass Trade Review*, 1 January 1934, pp. 85–6.
9. 'British Institute of Industrial Art', *The Pottery Gazette and Glass Trade Review*, 1 December 1923, p. 1976.
10. Forsyth, op. cit.
11. G. M. Forsyth, 'Modern Art in Pottery Manufacture', *The Pottery Gazette and Glass Trade Review*, 1 November 1932, p. 1389.
12. See the Wedgwood advertisment in the *Pottery Gazette and Glass Trade Review*, 2 April 1934, p. 438.
13. J. Lodey, 'A flower was picked and a famous pottery design was born', *Six Towns Magazine*, September 1963.

14. Star Wedgwood in conversation with author, October 1983.

15. Eric Taplin in conversation with author, April 1985.

16. J. Wedgwood, *A Personal Life of the Fifth Josiah Wedgwood 1899–1968*, Josiah Wedgwood & Sons Ltd., Barlaston, 1979, p. 10.

17. ibid., Sales figures from the documents at the Wedgwood Museum, Barlaston.

18. Letter dated 10 August 1933, the Wedgwood Museum, Barlaston.

19. 'Future arrangements with regard to New Designs', December 1933. The Wedgwood Museum, Barlaston.

20. Letter from Josiah Wedgwood to Murray, dated 10 August 1933 in the Wedgwood Museum, Barlaston.

21. Grafton Galleries, *Wedgwood*, 1936, p. 1.

22. Grafton Galleries, *Wedgwood*, 1936.

23. 'Report on the British Art in Industry Exhibition at the Royal Academy', *The Pottery Gazette and Glass Trade Review*, 1 February 1935, p. 216.

24. Eric Taplin in conversation with author, April 1985.

25. Star Wedgwood in conversation with author, October 1983.

26. Star Wedgwood in conversation with author, October 1983.

27. B. Bumpus, *Charlotte Rhead. Potter & Designer*, Kevin Francis Publishing, 1987.

28. 'Miss Charlotte Rhead. Pottery Artist and Designer', *The Pottery and Glass Record*, 1937, vol. 19, p. 220.

29. From B. Bumpus, 'Pottery designed by Charlotte Rhead', *Antique Collector*, January 1983, pp. 60–2.

30. ibid., p. 42.

31. 'Buyers' Notes', *The Pottery Gazette and Glass Trade Review*, 1 February 1934, p. 185.

32. 'Jessie Van Hallen, Pottery Artist', *Cheshire Life*, February 1979, p. 70.

33. Freda Beardmore in conversation with author, March 1988.

34. Brain's Foley China pattern books are now held at the Wedgwood Museum, Barlaston, Staffordshire. In these there are some 51 designs by the various artists who contributed to the Harrods experiment.

35. For further information see A. Eatwell, 'A Bold Experiment in Tableware', in *Antique Collecting*, November 1984, pp. 32–5; and R. Pelik, 'The Harrods Experiment', in *Ceramics*, August 1987, pp. 33–41.

36. Report of the committee appointed by the Board of Trade under the chairmanship of Lord Gorell on *The Production and Exhibition of Articles of Good Design and Everyday Use*, 1932; and Report by the Pottery Committee of the Council for Art and Industry on *Design in the Pottery Industry*, 1937.

37. F. Hannah, *Ceramics*, Bell & Hyman, 1986, p. 54.

38. Freda Beardmore in conversation with author, March 1988.

39. The most comprehensive account of the A. E. Gray company is the City Museum and Art Gallery exhibition catalogue, *Hand-painted Gray's Pottery*, Stoke-on-Trent, 1982, p. 14.

40. Susie Cooper in conversation with author, March 1983.

41. 'Buyer's Notes', *The Pottery Gazette and Glass Trade Review*, April 1930, p. 593.

42. Susie Cooper in conversation with author, March 1983.

43. Florence May Hancock in conversation with author, September 1986.

44. 'Buyers' Notes', *The Pottery Gazette and Glass Trade Review*, 1 August 1935, p. 975.

45. 'Lithographs as a Means of Pottery Decoration', *The Pottery Gazette and Glass Trade Review*, 1 June 1933, p. 701.

46. ibid., p. 713.

47. For detailed descriptions of the patterns, processes and shapes of Susie Cooper's pottery see A. Eatwell, *Susie Cooper Productions*, Victoria and Albert Museum, 1987.

48. Florence May Hancock in conversation with author, September 1986.

49. 'Buyers' Notes', *The Pottery Gazette and Glass Trade Review*, 1 June 1931, p. 817.

50. S. Snodin, 'Susie Cooper: Diverse Designer', *The Antique Collector*, August 1982, pp. 52–5.

51. 'Buyers' Notes', *The Pottery Gazette and Glass Trade Review*, June 1931, p. 819.

52. 'Report on the British Industries Fair', *The Pottery Gazette and Glass Trade Review*, 1 February 1934, p. 225.

53. 'Buyers' Notes', *The Pottery Gazette and Glass Trade Review*, 2 April 1934, pp. 467–8.

54. 'Report on the British Industries Fair', *The Pottery Gazette and Glass Trade Review*, 1 April 1932, p. 489.

55. 'Buyers' Notes', *The Pottery Gazette and Glass Trade Review*, 1 October 1932, p. 1251.

56. A breakfast-in-bed set included tea cup and saucer, sugar bowl,

creamer, teapot, covered muffin dish, cruet, toast rack, egg-
cup, marmalade and butter pots. An early morning set included
two cups and saucers, sugar bowl and creamer, teapot and two
biscuit plates.

57. 'Buyers' Notes', *The Pottery Gazette and Glass Trade Review*,
    June 1931, p. 817.
58. Susie Cooper in conversation with author, March 1983.
59. 'Buyers' Notes', *The Pottery Gazette and Glass Trade Review*,
    1 October 1932, p. 1249.
60. ibid., 1 August 1935, p. 975.
61. N. Pevsner, *An Enquiry into Industrial Art in England*,
    Cambridge University Press, 1937, p. 80.
62. See L. Griffin, L. K. and S. P. Meisel, *Clarice Cliff, The Bizarre
    Affair*, Abrams, New York, 1988.
63. 'Buyers' Notes', *The Pottery Gazette and Glass Trade Review*,
    2 June 1930, p. 941.
64. ibid., p. 943.
65. ibid., 1 April 1933, p. 479.
66. I. Anscombe, *A Woman's Touch. Women in Design from
    1860 to the Present Day*, Virago, 1984, p. 183.
67. Peggy Davies in conversation with author, March 1988.

Chapter 5

.

A Studio of One's Own
Craft workshops and mass production

By the end of the 1930s the pottery industry saw the introduction of several new ideas about design which were to change the roles of some women designers and paintresses. The work of studio potters such as Bernard Leach (1887–1979) and Katherine Pleydell-Bouverie (1895–1985) provided a further incentive to those women who were keen to design both pottery shape and surface decoration. This was reinforced by knowledge of the Scandinavian pottery industry which served as a model for those committed to high quality pottery designed within a modern mass-production context, but with respect for craft processes. Within two years of the outbreak of war, most of the industry had been turned over to essential manufactures, and what remained produced a severely limited product. The end of war brought hopes of a modernised, prosperous industry. For Arthur Hollins, the General Secretary of the National Society of Pottery Workers, this meant 'better wages and working conditions, including better lighted and ventilated workshops, and the provision of protective clothing'.[1]

Women designers worked in the industry in different capacities during this period. Agnete Hoy adopted the Scandinavian method in the craft studio formed by Bullers, the electrical porcelain manufacturer in 1934. This was a practice which she continued at Doulton's Lambeth pottery from 1952 until 1956. In this she maintained the tradition established in the nineteenth century by Henry Doulton and carried on by designers such as Vera Huggins (d. 1975) and Joan Cowper (b. 1912). From the mid 1930s until its closure in 1956, Doulton's Lambeth studio offered opportunities for women designers who were interested in combining the theories of the studio potters with the practice of a large manufacturer. At their Burslem factory, Doulton employed Peggy Davies (née Gibbons) as a table-ware designer and modeller. Grete Marks worked as a freelance designer for Wedgwood, Minton, Ridgways, Foley China and John-son Brothers, before forming her own company, Grete Pottery, in 1938. Meanwhile, the post-war enthusiasm for design led Susie Cooper in her own company, and Jessie Tait at Midwinter, to pursue the goal of mass-produced, well-designed pottery. This desire to improve design standards was highlighted by the 1946 Britain Can Make It and the 1951 Festival of Britain exhibitions. At the same time, technological changes which followed the Second World War resulted in the increased use of lithographs by most manufacturers, and the decrease in popularity of hand-painted wares. This led to a modification in the paintresses' role with an emphasis on mechanical and repetitive skills rather than the artistic, free-hand skills of the inter-war period.

Grete Marks

Grete Marks (born Marguerite Heymann in 1901) came to Britain in 1936 after her company, the Haël Werkstätten, was taken over by the Nazis in July 1934. By moving to Britain, she followed the example of her contemporaries Walter Gropius, the ex-director of the Bauhaus, who arrived in October 1934, Marcel Breuer and László Moholy-Nagy, both ex-Bauhaus teachers, who joined Gro-pius within a few months. The Bauhaus School of Design, which Gropius had headed from 1919 when it was first established in Weimar, and which he had seen through its move to Dessau in 1925, was closed by the Nazis in October 1932.[2] Gropius had resigned his post in 1928 to be followed shortly by Breuer and Moholy-Nagy, and had been replaced by the Swiss architect Hannes Meyer.

During its brief existence (1919–33) the Bauhaus proposed a Modernist approach to design, using bold shapes and minimum decoration, which celebrated modern technology, mass-production methods and materials.[3] Importantly, it outlined a radical method of design education which was to prove influential for the next forty years, especially in Britain and the United States. 'The Bauhaus method', as it was called, was initially based on an examination of craft methods of production. Eventually, these were rejected in favour of a commitment to design for industrial production involving practical training in the workshop. This led to liaisons with nearby manufacturers which earned some revenue for the Bauhaus. An involvement with industry was more apparent when the school moved to Dessau, an industrial town two hours from Berlin by train.

Grete, born in Cologne into an artistic family, was trained at the Cologne and Berlin Schools of Art as well as at the Weimar Bauhaus. She enrolled at Weimar in 1919 at the age of 18, and undertook the six-month preliminary course taught by the Swiss painter Johannes Itten. The aim of the course was threefold; to free the students' creative powers from 'dead conventions'; to allow students to experiment in different materials thereby aiding their choice of career; and to teach the students the fundamental principles of design.[4] When the course ended she chose to specialise in pottery design. The pottery workshop was run by Gerhard Marcks, an artist who had also worked in ceramic sculpture. The workshop operated outside Weimar at Dornberg in a pottery run by Max Krehan, who provided both the facilities and space for throwing and firing. Krehan was a skilled potter who worked in a traditional manner producing simple craft products for the local market. At Dornberg, Marcks, together with the potters Theo Bogler and Otto Lindig, developed a distinctive type of ware based on vernacular designs, but which at the same time utilised geometric forms to provide prototypes for mass production. To contemporary observers and subsequent writers the success of the pottery workshop 'demonstrated the feasibility of the Bauhaus ideal'.[5]

During her three years at the Bauhaus, Grete was taught both the formal and practical aspects of pottery design, although she disagreed with Marcks over design matters. She thought that Marcks was too concerned with the 'classic', purely formal aspects of pottery design.[6] In 1923, she started work as a designer at the Haël Werkstätten for Artistic Ceramics Co. Ltd at Velten, in the stoneware producing region of Marwitz. The company was owned by Gustav Loebenstein whom she married in 1924. After his death in 1927 she managed the company and its ninety employees. She designed stoneware vases, bowls and domestic tableware which were noted for their modernity in form, pattern and colour. She used vivid glazes combined with unusual patterns inspired by the work of Bauhaus teacher and artist Wassily Kandinsky.[7] As a member of the German Werkbund, the Haël Werkstätten was committed to progressive design and its concept of this was clearly informed by Bauhaus theory and practice. The economic crisis in Germany in the early 1930s, which affected other local stoneware producers also, caused the company to cease production in 1932. It was eventually seized by the Nazis in 1934. Fearful for her future in an atmosphere of increasing anti-Semitism, Grete headed for London with the help of Ambrose Heal, the head of the retailing shop, and Harry Trethowan, the company's pottery buyer both of whom she knew through their association with the Haël company.

It was through Heal's contacts that she was put in touch with Gordon Forsyth in Stoke-on-Trent who offered to help her to find work in the pottery industry. Like the other German émigrés who came to Britain at this time, she was initially given a one-month passport stamp by the Home Office which was extended when she had demonstrated that her skills were useful to British industry by finding work. She stayed in London for a short time before going to Stoke-on-Trent to arrange a small exhibition of her work at Burslem School of Art. It was here that she found her first job teaching for one term in 1937. She was employed by Forsyth, who apparently thought that she was 'strenuous to work with'.[8] By her own admission, she was an independent and confident woman who would not play a submissive role. No doubt the male-dominated hierarchy in the north Staffordshire pottery industry was taken aback by this. Forsyth, however, acknowledged her ability as a designer and made great efforts to help her find employment. Within a short time of her arrival in Stoke-on-Trent, she was offered a post as designer at Minton.

At Minton, largely through Forsyth's and Heal's encouragement, a separate modern design department was established to be headed by Grete. A special backstamp was produced for all ware which she designed, which read 'Grete Pottery at Minton'. At Minton her designs were thought to be outrageous and wild, although the company gave her a great deal of assistance. She was shocked by the slackness of the management, and at her insistence she was put on the board of directors – an exception for any designer, especially a woman. The conditions at Minton were primitive, with gas lighting and cramped spaces, quite unlike the modern German factories with which she was familiar.

The tablewares that she produced at Minton, like most of her subsequent designs, were extremely striking, combining stark geometric forms with vivid colours and minimal surface decoration. She left Minton in 1938 because of conflicts with the art director John Wadsworth, who refused to market her designs alongside the other Minton products. As a result she had to find her own sales outlets, but, undaunted, she persuaded Heal and Fortnum and Mason to stock her work.

To find work she visited numerous potteries in Stoke-on-Trent, and eventually gained several freelance design commissions. These were at Ridgway, where again she had her own mark 'Grete Pottery at Ridgway, Shelton', and at E. Brain's Foley China. At Brain & Co. she worked with Freda Beardmore, designing, as well as some children's ware, white porcelain tableware which won the approval of the design theorist and writer Nikolaus Pevsner (Figure 75).[9] She was also briefly employed by the Johnson Brothers at a fee of £2 10s. for each design. From these various freelance jobs she managed to make a living, but with her undoubted ability and experience this role was hardly fulfilling. With this in mind and with the aid of Harold Marks, an extra-mural tutor for Oxford University whom she had married in 1938, she decided to launch her own company.

The Grete Pottery was formed on 10 January 1938 at Summer Street, Stoke. It was a small-scale company started on a low budget. Biscuit ware was bought in from different suppliers including Gosse and Wedgwood, to be decorated and then fired by the six part-time workers (Figure 76). Grete Marks was responsible for the surface design which consisted of matt glazes painted directly onto the biscuit ware and then fired. The use of matt glazes in strong colours, especially yellow, with dot and small flower motifs painted onto the surface, was characteristic of her work. Having her own company gave her more artistic freedom and the resulting designs were clearly based on Modernist principles, whereas her work at Brain's had had to fit in with that company's image. The wares from the Grete Pottery were retailed through a number of shops with a reputation in the 1930s for stocking modern design including Heals, John Lewis, Dunn's of Bromley, Bowman Bros of Camden, Peter Jones, Dunbar Hay and P. E. Gane of Bristol.

When war was declared, the Grete Pottery like many other small-scale potteries was forced to close. In 1946, Grete Marks and her husband left Stoke-on-Trent and moved to London where she set up a studio at her home and began teaching at Camberwell School of Art. The domestic conditions of production meant that her work after this date consisted of craft wares thrown and decorated by hand. At the time, and subsequently, she believed that the north Staffordshire pottery industry was conservative and unconducive to women designers who were treated as exceptions and oddities.[10] As

138

an established businesswoman who had run her own profitable pottery in Germany, Grete Marks was not prepared to tolerate the paternalism and prejudice of many pottery manufacturers.

Royal Doulton (as it was designated by Edward VII in 1901) continued to employ women designers mainly at its Lambeth rather than at its Burslem pottery between 1920 and 1956. Several new designers joined the company, including Vera Huggins, Joan Cowper and Agnete Hoy who worked for Doulton between 1923–50, 1936–39 and 1952–56, respectively. Under the art director, James H. Mott, the much reduced studio with its staff of under thirty developed restrained forms of decoration for the salt-glazed stoneware. These included loose, free-hand brushwork on white and coloured slips, simple slip-trailing patterns, and incised and carved decoration. Mott, who was an excellent glaze chemist, broadened the range of colours for the stoneware bodies. He was especially inspired by oriental glaze effects and experimented with new glazes such as '*sang de boeuf*', 'hare's fur' and 'oilspot', in addition to the matt and semi-matt speckled glazes such as 'thrush's egg' and 'buff crackle' which were very fashionable in the 1930s. As well as the hand-thrown vases and bowls which were decorated by the designers, a range of cast and moulded shapes such as book-ends, dressing-table trays and ashtrays were produced in some quantity.[11] Both the hand-thrown shapes and the cast and moulded products were designed by Vera Huggins and her colleagues.

Vera Huggins

Vera Huggins was noted for her versatility as a designer and her excellent throwing. For surface decoration, she utilised several decorative techniques, including sgraffito, intaglio, under-glaze painting, tube-lining, modelling and splashed glaze effects (Figure 77). The simple outlines of the hand-thrown vases, bowls and dishes provided an ideal medium for her subtle decorative effects which were intended to harmonise with contemporary interiors. Her colour range was based on soft blues, greens, beiges and yellows which were combined with either linear, incised patterns based on natural forms, or abstract effects created by the fusion of different glazes in the kiln (Figure 78). A writer in *The Studio* magazine in 1929 claimed that Lambeth was 'still producing decorative, artistic stoneware of highest excellence'.[12]

Her designs were first shown at the 1925 Paris Exhibition of Decorative Arts where critics discerned a 'primitive' quality in the wares; this probably referred to the linear patterns and glazes (Figure 79). By the 1930s she had become one of Doulton's best known designers and her work was shown at the British Art in Industry Exhibition at the Royal Academy in 1935, and at various other exhibitions abroad, including Paris in 1937. The market for her work was an international one and she achieved particular success in the United States, Australia and New Zealand.

Joan Cowper

Doulton's in-house magazine *Ceramics in Art and Industry* made much of the company's reputation for employing women designers. In 1936 Vera Huggins had been joined by another woman designer, Joan Cowper, who, Doulton claimed, was 'one of the comparatively few women potters in England'.[13] Unusually for women designers at the time, Joan Cowper designed, threw and decorated her wares, and so was responsible for introducing some of the ideas of the studio pottery movement into the pottery industry.

Joan Cowper was born into a middle-class professional family, the daughter of a doctor. Her mother was awarded an MBE for her services during the First World War in organising hospital supplies for the front, and was a keen amateur artist. Joan Cowper attended Wycombe Abbey public school where she received a solid education which included science and, unusually, pottery. After school her mother sent her to Berridge House, Hampstead to learn domestic economy, apparently so that she could be self-sufficient.[14] Between 1931 and 1934, she attended the Central School of Arts and Crafts where she was taught pottery by Dora Billington, and design by Bernard Adeney.

Adeney had trained as a painter at the Royal Academy and at the Académie Julian in Paris. He was associated with the writer and artist Roger Fry, and participated in the various exhibitions of progressive painting and design which were organised by Fry. These included the second Post-Impressionist Exhibition of 1912–13, and those at the Omega Workshops between 1913 and 1919. From Adeney, Joan Cowper learned general principles of design, and from Dora Billington she acquired specific knowledge of pottery design and making. Billington was apparently an excellent teacher who had an extensive knowledge of the different approaches to pottery design and production.[15] Her background and training in Stoke-on-Trent had equipped her with an understanding of industrial pottery manufacture which was coupled with direct knowledge of the alternative production methods found in a small art pottery. In the 1930s as the influence of the studio pottery movement grew, this was invaluable experience for a teacher.

The studio pottery movement formed part of the general revival of craft which occurred in Britain in the inter-war years. To some extent this marked a continuation of the craft theories which had been developed within the context of the Arts and Crafts Movement, but this tradition was invigorated by the influx of new ideas originating in the Far East. Studio pottery was dominated by the theory and practice of several potters; most notable were Bernard Leach (1887–1979) who established a pottery at St Ives in Cornwall in 1920, William Staite-Murray (1881–1961) whose pottery at Rotherhithe was founded in 1919, and Leach's apprentices, Michael Cardew (b. 1901) who revived English slipware in his Winchcombe pottery in Gloucestershire, and Katherine Pleydell-Bouverie and Norah Braden (b. 1901) who worked together at the Coleshill pottery, Wiltshire, developing wood and vegetable ash glazes.

Studio pottery was the major influence on the young Joan Cowper. Most important was the emphasis laid on the potter's complete responsibility for all stages of production. This led to the total creative involvement of the craftsperson with the mixing and forming of the clay, the firing, glazing and decorating. For many, the appeal of studio pottery was the integration of technique and final object, and of shape and decoration. This was particularly important for women potters. To studio potters, the divisions of skills and labour in the pottery industry were anathema as they destroyed the overall creative process. In contrast, the irregular hand quality of the studio pottery was unacceptable to the industrial pottery manufacturer who strove for a precision-formed and glazed pot. In her art school education, Joan Cowper was exposed to both approaches to pottery design.

During the 1930s Dora Billington taught mainly the techniques of hand production. However, the Central School like several other art schools in Britain had begun to establish design courses which were firmly linked to the needs of industry. In 1926, *The Studio* encouraged the school's efforts 'to establish effective contact with every industrial output and enterprise'.[16] Two years later the same journal noted that 'the record of the pottery section at the Central

School is distinguished, and its equipment has recently been increased by the installation of high temperature kilns which make possible the production of stoneware'.[17] The pottery section trained several women designers whose work was regularly illustrated in *The Studio*. These included Sybil Finnemore and Dora Lunn who designed and threw their own pots. *The Studio* reported on numerous women designers who worked in a variety of materials and it provided vital information for other women interested in career opportunities in the visual and applied arts. It also illustrated contemporary work from Europe and America, and in the late 1920s and 1930s it was a useful source for new ideas about design which originated in France, Scandinavia and Germany.

After leaving the Central School, Joan Cowper established a small pottery in the family home at Leighton Buzzard; in this she was clearly inspired by the example of the studio potters. In 1936 she was offered a job as a designer at Doulton's Lambeth studio after the company's chairman, Lewis J. E. Hooper, saw a display of her work at Olympia. Her career at Doulton's began in 1937, but was cut short by wartime uncertainties and marriage in 1939. However, during those two years she established herself as an able designer who brought some of the principles of studio pottery to the Lambeth art pottery. Due to the methods of production and its commitment to artistic products, the Lambeth pottery was an ideal venue for her experimentation with studio pottery. She designed, threw, glazed and decorated each piece of ware individually (Figure 80). In some of her work, she used salt-glazed stoneware in the traditional way, whereas other designs were noted for their unusual qualities. She frequently left the coarse stoneware body unglazed or undecorated, and in the manner of her contemporaries, she achieved artistic effects through the texture of the materials, the subtle colours of the wood ash glazes and the shape of the body (Figure 81). In the development of suitable glazes, she had a fortunate ally in the young Doulton chemist Edward Lawrence, who helped her achieve the right glaze effects.

In the late 1930s her work was admired for its simplicity and modernity. Nikolaus Pevsner advised her to examine Scandinavian design which he suggested might offer a solution to the dilemma of producing craft objects within an industrial context. Her designs were sold through various progressive retailers including Peter Jones and Heal's, the latter staging an exhibition of her work.

After her marriage, Joan Cowper deliberately cut herself off from the world of pottery and craft, and spent her time bringing up her two children. Her interest in craft reasserted itself in the 1960s when she and her husband separated. From this date until her retirement in 1986, she worked extensively in the promotion and exhibition of craft, although never again as a practitioner. In 1983, following in her mother's footsteps, she was awarded an MBE for her services to the arts.

Joan Cowper's gender played an important part in the way in which Doulton marketed her designs. She was presented as something of an exception because she threw her own pots; in this she represented a challenge to the gender divisions which dominated the pottery industry.[18] The precedent for this had been established in a practical way by the women studio potters, Katherine Pleydell-Bouverie and Norah Braden. For both, the involvement of the craftsperson in all the stages of production was critical. In this they provided a theoretical justification for the rejection of the division of shape and decoration which underpinned industrial pottery manufacture.

Agnete Hoy

The introduction of new ideas into the Lambeth art pottery continued with the appointment of the Danish designer Agnete Hoy in 1952. She brought with her a distinctly Scandinavian approach to design which marked the pottery's first post-war initiative. As a result of war, most of the Lambeth art pottery was turned over to the essential production of laboratory and technical equipment with only a tiny amount of decorated salt-glazed stoneware being produced for export. Until 1952 the pottery barely survived, but following the positive attitude to design evident at the Festival of Britain in 1952, Doulton decided on a policy of revitalisation.

Agnete Hoy was born in Britain in 1914. Her family, which had moved from Denmark to London in 1910, were from the professional classes and comfortably off: her father had trained as a pharmacist and worked as a bacteriologist. She was educated in Denmark and, because of her passion for art, enrolled at the Central School of Art and Crafts in Copenhagen instead of going to university. From the age of 17 to 20, she was taught drawing and design in the art school by the sculptor W. Staehr Nielsen as well as following several months of industrial placement in the local Royal Copenhagen Porcelain Company. At the art school she learned craft techniques of production which were supplemented with specific industrial training at the Royal Copenhagen factory. During this period she learned throwing, modelling, firing, painting and glaze-making. After receiving her diploma in pottery design she became a designer at Gerhard Nielsen's Holbaek Stoneware in 1937–38 and a year later at Natalie Krebs of Saxbo.[19] In these two companies she acquired experience of designing in stoneware and high temperature porcelain, the two materials on which her career in pottery in Britain was to be based.

Her arrival in Stoke-on-Trent in 1939 was unplanned; she had gone to England to visit her family, but because of the outbreak of war she was unable to return to Denmark. Exiled in England, she went to stay with her brother in Stoke. It was at the suggestion of someone at Wedgwood, to whom she had unsuccessfully applied for a job, that she arranged to see Gordon Forsyth at Burslem School of Art. With her knowledge and experience in using hard-paste porcelain in Denmark, Forsyth immediately recommended her to Guy Harris, one of the directors of Bullers, a company that manufactured electrical porcelain.

In 1934, Bullers opened a small studio in its factory at Milton on the outskirts of the Potteries for the production of art wares. In charge was Anne Potts, a sixteen-year-old ex-student of Burslem School of Art and protégé of the superintendent of the Stoke-on-Trent art schools, Gordon Forsyth. It was through Forsyth's initiative that such an unlikely combination of art wares and electrical porcelain came about. As Principal of Burslem School of Art, Forsyth was keen for his students to gain experience of designing with hard-paste porcelain, the material used by Bullers for the production of insulators and switch-gear for the electrical industry. Hard-paste porcelain was not a material used extensively in the north Staffordshire pottery industry, and Forsyth began to buy from Bullers. The material posed specific design problems for the students in that it was fired at very high temperatures.

The results of these early experiments were exhibited at the Dorland Hall Exhibition of Industrial Art in Relation to the Home in 1933, and their modest success encouraged Bullers to establish a permanent studio. From the outset, Guy Harris was closely involved with the enterprise. He was an excellent glaze chemist who was keen to reproduce the glaze effects of oriental ceramics. At Bullers he had the advantages of a fully equipped laboratory which enabled him to expand the range of glazes available to the designer, and to perfect Japanese and Chinese glazes such as celadons, chun, crackle, aventurine and *flambés*. From 1935 until she left to marry in 1939, Anne Potts was responsible for designing figures, ornamental and table wares which attracted a great deal of critical acclaim when they were exhibited at the British Art in Industry Exhibition at the Royal Academy in 1935, and at the Paris International Exhibition of 1937. Anne Potts had excellent craft skills as a modeller, and her figures exploited the particular qualities of hard-paste porcelain with its fine close body. In addition to these ornamental figures, the studio produced a range of vases, dishes and bowls usually with sparse decoration on the unusual glazes. With Anne Pott's departure and the onset of war, the studio was closed for a short time.[20]

Agnete Hoy's arrival was a timely one. Initially, Bullers had turned their attention to war work, but it was soon apparent that the studio could stay in production as long as it manufactured goods for export. Following six months of experimentation with their hard-paste porcelain at Burslem School of Art, Agnete Hoy was appointed Bullers' designer at a wage of £6 a week and asked to reopen the studio.[21] Her first task was to design a range of oven-to-tableware for which the heat-resisting hard-paste porcelain was perfectly suited. This was followed by coffee sets, cooking-ware and tea sets, and then later by decorative wares which included vases, bowls, covered pots and dishes. Agnete Hoy experimented with iron, cobalt and other oxide brushwork in different thicknesses. Other forms of decoration included carving with bamboo at the leather-hard stage which she learned from Gordon Forsyth, and painting in slip which had been applied to the body of the ware. Generally though, decoration and shape were kept simple to show off and enhance the spectacular glazes.[22] According to the *Pottery and Glass Record*, these had 'the quality of jade, soap-stone or polished ivory. The palette has a wide range of subdued and harmonious tones. Soft brown, buffs, grey and stone colours, celadon greens, ivory and honey colours predominate.'[23]

By 1950 a team of ten had been established at Bullers; these included Harold Thomas, whom Agnete Hoy considered one of the best throwers in Stoke-on-Trent, Fred Hanley, the dipper, a fireman, turner, and several young designers and decorators including James Rushton, Elsie Forrester, Hilda Hine, Leslie West and Derek Wilshaw. At various points this team was joined by other designers including Denise Wren. Work organisation was based on the Scandinavian model whereby the studio provided prototypes for mass production in the main factory. However, because the factory manufactured electrical porcelain, the studio operated as a distinct unit and approved prototypes were hand-thrown, turned and numbered to produce a series of each design. In this, it paralleled the Doulton Lambeth art pottery. The prototype was designed and initially thrown by Agnete Hoy who also produced a set of working drawings. Once thrown, the wares were hand decorated by the team of designers who signed their work.

Scandinavia proved to be a strong influence on British industrial design throughout the inter-war years. To some extent it represented the acceptable face of Modernism in that craft and industrial processes were combined to produce designs which bore more relation to traditional design values than those inspired by the harsh modernity of the Bauhaus. Journals such as *The Studio* reported on the Scandinavian approach to design for industry, and in 1935 *The Pottery Gazette and Glass Trade Review* reported the visit by the Stoke-on-Trent Ceramic Society to the Gustavsberg Pottery in Sweden and the Royal Copenhagen and Bing and Grondahl factories in Denmark.[24] The modernisation of machinery, the emphasis on research into new bodies and glazes, the hygienic work conditions and the respect for skilled workers such as throwers, casters, decorators and designers was especially noted and contrasted with most north Staffordshire manufacturers.

Bullers' studio was an unusual enterprise because of its small scale and the willingness of the company's directors to subsidise its operation. The lack of financial constraints allowed time-consuming production methods which were based mainly on craft techniques. During its second phase from 1940 to 1952, the Bullers' studio gained a reputation for high quality products that rivalled that of hard-paste porcelain producers in France and Germany.[25] The marketing and retailing of the wares was done, apparently not very efficiently, by Heal's of Tottenham Court Road. Although these attracted favourable reviews at both the Britain Can Make It Exhibition of 1946, and the Festival of Britain of 1951, the company decided to close the studio in 1952 in order to consolidate its production of insulators.[26]

At Bullers, Agnete Hoy enjoyed a rare degree of independence as a woman designer. Due to the relative isolation of the studio, the organisation of work was free of the usual constraints experienced by women designers in the north Staffordshire pottery industry. Like Joan Cowper at Doulton, she was able to design both shape and decoration, and although knowledgeable about the studio pottery movement in Britain, it was largely her experience in Denmark that enabled her to overcome the gender divisions dominating pottery production in Britain.

With the closure of Bullers, Agnete Hoy made a permanent home in London with her husband and began a new career as a designer at Doulton's Lambeth studio. Salt-glazed stoneware represented a new challenge, although she was well aware of the studio's reputation in the nineteenth century for high quality art wares. By examining the wares produced by Hannah Barlow and the other women designers, she planned to build on the traditional decorative techniques established at Lambeth, and at the same time to develop some new ones. As at Bullers, she designed and threw prototype shapes, which were decorated by incising, slip-trailing, carving and coloured slips (Figure 82). These were then produced in either hand-thrown series or were cast.

Salt-glazed stoneware was a material she enjoyed working with. The element of chance involved in the firing was especially appealing, and by using her knowledge of glazes, she was able to create some unusual effects (Figure 83). At the same time, she designed a range of stoneware with a natural cream-coloured glaze that was particularly suitable for free-hand painted decoration (Figure 84). Characteristically, her approach to decoration was understated and recalled the calligraphic effects of oriental pottery. Although most of her wares were vessels of one form or another, she modelled some pieces, including a stoneware cat with incised and painted decoration (Figure 85).

In the company's magazine in 1953, it was remarked that 'these decorative pots [serve] as prototypes for a new range of Doulton ware, distinct from the rest of the firm's production, yet equal to it in significance and standing'.[27] However by 1956, in a changing and competitive market, Doulton decided to close its Lambeth works and consolidate its production in Burslem. After Doulton, Agnete Hoy established a wheel and kiln in her West London home and for the next twenty-five years became preoccupied with teaching at both Richmond and West Surrey Colleges of Art.

At the time of its closure the studio was operating on a similar basis to its nineteenth-century predecessor. Although it was much reduced in size, it still specialised in ornamental wares which were hand-decorated by a skilled craftsperson. Throughout its existence, it had provided opportunities for many women pottery designers, including Vera Huggins, Joan Cowper and Agnete Hoy. In contrast, at Doulton's Burslem factory, women worked in traditional roles as paintresses and few became designers. Indeed, the only woman designer in this period was Margaret May (Peggy) Davies who was born in Burslem in 1920. She was appointed in 1939 by the art director Charles Noke, who had seen her work at an annual Burslem School of Art exhibition.

Peggy Davies

Peggy Davies was brought up by her grandfather, as he had the financial resources to care for her. In 1932 she won a scholarship to attend the junior art department of Burslem School of Art where she was taught by several well-known designers and modellers including Victor Skellern and William Ruscoe. Within two years family circumstances caused her to leave in order to earn some money. In 1935 she started work at A. J. Wilkinson as assistant designer to Clarice Cliff and stayed for three years. She managed to keep her scholarship by attending four evening classes and one full day at art school each week – an arrangement made with the employers' agreement.[29]

At Wilkinson's she designed tableware and developed her skills as a modeller of face masks and figures. Although she learned a great deal working under Clarice Cliff, she was shocked by Cliff's approach to design which was the antithesis of her training at Burslem School of Art. At Burslem, Gordon Forsyth had introduced design principles which had their origin in the German Bauhaus and emphasised the need for rational designs for modern industrial production techniques. To create her aptly named 'Bizarre' wares, Clarice Cliff's methods were contrary to those of Bauhaus Modernism because they required substantial hand work to form the angular shapes. To Peggy Davies, there seemed little relationship between Clarice Cliff's rapid sketches and the reality of production. After the end of her three-year contract, she left Wilkinson's and joined Midwinter where she worked with another designer, Nancy Greatorex. At Midwinter she designed a range of nurseryware but left within the year to take up the job at Doulton.

Doulton at Burslem was apparently Edwardian in outlook when Peggy Davies joined.[30] After beginning as a tableware designer, she quickly found a niche as a modeller. Initially she produced small birds and animals which were decorated in *flambé* glazes. Before she was properly established at Doulton, war intervened and she

148

played her part in the war effort as a nurse. It was during the war that she met and married her husband who took a year off from teaching to undertake a pottery management course in order to help her career. When she returned to Doulton after the war she worked as an independent artist on contract rather than as an in-house designer (Figure 86). Her association with Doulton lasted almost fifty years during which time she modelled over 250 figures beginning with 'Minuet' designed straight after the war. The production of her modelled figures was heavily dependent on traditional Staffordshire figure-making techniques, particularly those of the mould-maker. Without the craft skills of a mould-maker, it was impossible to recreate the quality of the original model.

Doulton at Lambeth was one of many potteries which did not survive the harsh conditions of wartime and post-war reconstruction in the industry. During the war manufacturers were restricted in their output, and only undecorated wares could be made for the home market, although even these were governed by quotas. The concentration of the pottery industry into nucleus companies brought about enforced rationalisation. Many small companies which closed or merged in response to these regulations never reopened, while other parts of the industry were caught between the conflicting demands made by government for the release of labour into essential industries, which did not include pottery, and its desire for increased exports. Because of its independence from imported raw materials, the pottery industry was strategically placed to increase exports, if it could solve its labour shortage problems. However, with a labour force reduced from 65,000 in 1938 to 31,000 in 1945, this was almost impossible.[31] For pottery workers, wages did not keep up with increases in the cost of living, and differentials between skilled and unskilled work were eroded.

Pottery design during the war was governed by the Utility scheme, which was introduced to regulate the number of different designs and types of ware being manufactured. Shapes had to be registered, numbered and stamped, and only designs that were thought to be of high quality were approved. This government intervention in production and design resulted in rationalisation and an emphasis on multi-purpose uncluttered shapes that were easy to mass produce. Until 1952, when regulations were relaxed, all wares for the home market were undecorated. With the exception of a few manufacturers such as Wedgwood, which had already streamlined methods of production, design processes and product ranges in the late 1930s, the imposition of design and manufacturing restrictions was anathema. Most producers attributed the demise of craft skills and loss of variety in design to government control.

The National Society of Pottery Workers had hoped that wartime controls would lead to the closure of old, inefficient and unhealthy factories, but this was not to be. In its proposals for post-war reconstruction, the union argued:

> It has to be emphasised and often reiterated that slum factories, like slum houses, are a menace to health and must be eliminated
> ... The object should be to modernise the factories, either by building new factories or by reconstructing factories where this is possible; and to bring them up to the highest standard of efficiency in layout, labour-saving devices, dust prevention, and management.[32]

At the end of the war, the union wanted to see a planned policy for the pottery industry which would avoid a return to the free market uncertainties of the 1920s and 1930s. Not surprisingly, the manufacturers opposed any form of continuing government control on the industry. The Board of Trade Working Party Report on the Pottery Industry of 1946 proposed a compromise. It recommended that controls should remain as a short-term measure in order to encourage the industry to rationalise its production and modernise its buildings and plant. It suggested that manufacturers should examine the flow-production methods in the factories of other industries and it proposed increased automation to overcome labour shortages. It made specific comments on design and encouraged the manufacturers to look outside of the region for designers who had a fresh approach, and who were not encumbered with the traditional attitudes of the industry.[33]

Susie Cooper after the War

It was within this context of post-war reconstruction that Susie Cooper resumed production at her factory, and that Jessie Tait worked as chief designer at Midwinter. By 1940 Susie Cooper's success was consolidated when she was made Royal Designer for Industry, becoming the first woman designer in the Potteries to be acknowledged in this way. The war brought particular problems for such a small company, but she managed to continue production for export until 1942 when a factory fire halted manufacture. At this point she became preoccupied with domestic matters. In 1938 she had married the architect Cecil Barker, and in 1943 she gave birth to a son. However, in 1945, with her husband as a partner, she re-started her business as a producer of decorated wares for export. Her key role in promoting good design was acknowledged in 1946 when she was asked to join the selection committee for the Britain Can Make It Exhibition which was to be held at the Victoria and Albert Museum. Three of her own designs were shown in this exhi-bition, and a year later she showed a new range of designs at the British Industries Fair, including 'Tree of Life'.

Initially, she faced many difficulties as a producer of decorated ware; most pressing was the lack of a regular supplier of plain white earthenware. In order to overcome this, she bought the Jason China Co. of Longton in 1950 and began to manufacture her own fine china wares after her husband had 'transformed the factory, its production methods and body recipes until Jason Works was a model establishment'.[34]

Susie Cooper was keen to produce modern designs to a high standard in both china and earthenware. Some of her patterns were applied to both types of body, and others were specially designed for the new china wares. Usually earthenware was used for dinner-ware, and china for tea and coffee sets and fancies. For some time, hand-painted designs for under-glaze or in-glaze decoration domi-nated, until lithograph supplies, which had been destroyed in the fire, were built up again. In 1951 she designed a new shape for bone china which made its first appearance in the Royal Pavilion at the Festival of Britain held in London on the South Bank. It was named 'Quail' and had a smooth curvilinear outline which suggested some knowledge of new design trends (Figure 87). Later in the 1950s two more new shapes were introduced: one was fluted and the other was a geometric design called 'Can'. Although popular patterns from the 1930s such as 'Wedding Ring' and 'Spirals' were continued, newer ones were introduced which had the fluid, slightly quirky appearance of the 1950s Contemporary Style. Susie Cooper's interpretation of this was very restrained in comparison to some of her contemporaries, including Jessie Tait. As in her pre-war work, her designs were characterised by a tastefulness and subtlety that made her popular with the promoters of 'good' design. The source for most of her patterns was nature, and new designs included 'Teazle', 'Whispering Grass', 'Sea Anemone', and 'Wild Strawberry' (Figure 88). During the 1950s, she combined solid areas of aerographed colour with sgraffito patterns to reveal the white china body (Figure 89).

Wares continued to be decorated at the Crown Works in Burslem, but by the mid-1950s only a small part of this was done by hand. (Figure 90). Lithographs were used for complex patterns such as 'Azalea' and 'Blue Orchid', and also for simple ones such as 'Blue Star' and 'Astral'. Marketing and retailing were increasingly important to Susie Cooper as she strove to maintain her reputation at home and abroad. Boxed gift sets in combinations of different ware were sold in addition to single boxed plates, candlesticks, and covered boxes. Unlike many of her competitors, Susie Cooper was alert to changing market demands, and rather than merely reworking traditional themes, she kept abreast of new ideas. As a result, her designs were still popular in North America when the taste for modern designs had led to reduced export opportunities for many British manufacturers who stuck to the traditional lines.[35] However, the company's success was short-lived as disaster struck again in 1957 when a fire badly damaged the Crown Works and halted production for almost a year.

In 1961 in order to increase production of bone china she merged with R. H. & S. L. Plant, and in 1966 the joint company was taken over by the Wedgwood group. At first this seemed to offer an excellent opportunity, although as she later said, 'It's very ... masculine. There is no eminence for an individual, or for individual ideas. I produce designs, but they feel they can't afford to take the risk, so they are not put into production.'[36]

Susie Cooper's experiences with Wedgwood were fairly typical of other designers working in large companies, although Wedgwood had been moving in that direction since early in the 1930s when it had been reorganised. Disappointment with Wedgwood did not completely dampen Susie Cooper's desire to design, and in the early 1980s the Tesco supermarket and Boots the Chemist chains launched two of her designs, but not under her name. Ironically, Wedgwood have belatedly recognised the interest in Susie Cooper and in 1988 reintroduced the Kestrel shapes with three surface designs from the 1930s. Although Susie Cooper would probably prefer the company to put one of her contemporary designs into production, this is an acknowledgment of her reputation and status as one of Britain's foremost designers.

The role of the designer in industry and the potential benefits of design for the manufacturer were as fiercely debated in post-war

Britain as they had been in the preceding century. Reticence about design continued to dominate the British pottery industry, although a more progressive approach had been urged on manufacturers in the Board of Trade Report of 1946.[37] Whereas the report encouraged standardisation and modernisation in production and design, many manufacturers believed the strength of their product was in its craft basis, its individualism and its variety. The test of the product was to be in the export field, especially in the early 1950s when North American, German and Japanese manufacturers resumed full production.

Midwinter and Jessie Tait

Historically, North America had provided a substantial market for the British pottery industry, but export sales to America were generally poor in the early 1950s. Buyers were told that the American public wanted a modern product, whereas many British manufacturers believed that the Americans wanted eighteenth-century 'English' styles. The Midwinter company, established in 1910, became aware of these problems when its trade tour to North America and Canada in 1953 met with little success. Roy Midwinter, the son of the company's founder, was told by a Canadian buyer that he should travel to California to see the sort of products that were in demand by the North American consumer. The buyer particularly recommended the products of firms such as Hallcraft and Metlox and the work of designers such as Eva Zeisal and Raymond Loewy.

Streamlining was the key feature of the Californian designs seen by Roy Midwinter. Eva Zeisal's designs for Hallcraft, including 'Tomorrow's Classic', were characterised by a sweeping, curving line which drew attention to the horizontality and low centre of gravity of the shapes. The use of streamlining as a visual motif was popular in the design of a range of different products in the United States in the 1950s. These included not only things that moved, such as motor-cars, locomotives, airplanes, but also radios, kitchen appliances and other products. Streamlining symbolised the dynamism and modernity of post-war American life, as well as its increased affluence. Roy Midwinter was quick to see the potential for such positive symbolism in a recently deregulated and ration-free Britain.

Back in Stoke-on-Trent, Midwinter set to work on an equally modern design; one which was to attract new sales both at home and abroad. Stylecraft, which was launched in February 1953, was based on the American 'coupe'-shaped flatware (Figure 91). The forty newly modelled designs for earthenware dinner, tea, coffee and breakfast services included several features which demonstrated the Californian influence, but they were more restrained and had a more compact cubic appearance to appeal to the home market.

Stylecraft was followed in 1955 by the Fashion shape which was much more obviously influenced by progressive American design (Figure 92). Fashion was curvilinear and organic; its fifty shapes included novel combinations of wares such as the television set which comprised a cup and tray and a 12-inch chop plate for those American-style steaks. Particularly striking were the combinations of single-coloured dishes and bowls with patterned, but co-ordinated lids, plates and saucers. Midwinter's designer at this time with responsibility for the production of appropriate patterns for the surface decoration of the new wares was Jessie Tait (b. 1928).

Like many of her predecessors, Jessie Tait was trained at Burslem School of Art. She started in 1940 at the age of twelve when she passed the entrance exams for the junior art department. After this she progressed to the senior art department where she had three years of art training. Pottery design featured as part of this course, and she was taught throwing and decorating. In addition to this she attended evening classes at the art school, sometimes as many as five in a week, to learn engraving and life drawing. During these three years her fees were paid by her oldest brother who was working at the time. Without this financial support, a full-time course would have been most unlikely given Jessie Tait's working-class background. She was fortunate in that she was the youngest of three children, and her brother had won a scholarship to London University and as a result obtained a good job.[38]

Jessie Tait's ambition as a student was to go to the Royal College of Art, and although she took the entrance exams when she was seventeen years old and had a grant arranged, the war and family responsibilities intervened. Her father retired from his job with the gas board and her earnings were required to maintain the family. As a result she decided to make a career in the pottery industry. She began in 1945 at H. J. Wood's Burslem pottery as assistant designer to Charlotte Rhead who taught her the tube-lining technique. She continued her evening classes, however, because she was determined to work as an independent designer and not just as a decorator. In

1946, the Principal of Burslem School of Art recommended her for a job at W. R. Midwinter which she started in August of that year.

For the first five years at Midwinter she designed under-glaze crayon decoration for fancies in addition to traditional patterns. From the early 1950s, she began to work closely with Roy Midwinter in order to up-date the company's product range. He tended to forecast general trends in terms of colour and style, but he then gave Jessie Tait an open design brief. Her designs for the Stylecraft and Fashion shapes are typical of the Contemporary Style in design which influenced furniture, interiors and textiles in the 1950s. Patterns such as Hollywood, Festival, Capri, Primavera and Pierrot combined bright yellows, reds, blues, subdued pinks and greys, black dots, dashes, asterisks, wavy lines and loosely drawn natural forms (Figures 93 and 94) which were often intentionally unregistered with the infill colours. Many of these 'Contemporary' designs, for example 'Homeweave', were inspired by the textiles and wallpapers of the period, and were distinctively linear and two-dimensional. Early patterns were designed to be hand-painted under-glaze in order to keep the paintresses in work. Eventually, lithographs became more widely used as they were less time-consuming.

These new patterns were marketed to 'blend perfectly with modern decoration'.[39] The Fashion range of tableware was an ideal accessory to the modern interior with its spindly, metal-framed or plywood furniture, gaily printed textiles and rubber plant. A sales leaflet advertising the Pierrot design for the Fashion range advised the potential buyer that 'a very smart effect could be obtained by using bright coloured table cloths or mats'.[40] This contemporary image was reinforced by packaging and advertising, which from the outset played an important role in promoting this unusual tableware. The twenty-piece ready-packed starter set contained the essentials which 'were inexpensive . . . to meet your family's immediate requirements'.[41] Advertisements aimed at the female consumer appeared in magazines such as *Woman*, as well as in the trade press. Like many other manufacturers, W. R. Midwinter realised the importance of women's role in determining family expenditure. Prices of the Stylecraft and Fashion ranges were moderate at £3 9s. 6d. for the starter set in the 'Homeweave' pattern which was aimed at the young middle-class couple.[42]

As a company devoted to modern design, W. R. Midwinter employed young freelance designers such as Hugh Casson, Colin Melbourne, David Queensberry and Terence Conran. Conran designed several patterns including 'Nature Study' and 'Salad Ware' which were adapted to the capabilities of the Midwinter production system by Jessie Tait.

Jessie Tait was committed to her work at W. R. Midwinter, and enjoyed a fruitful working relationship with Roy Midwinter. Like many professional women, she carefully balanced career and family; she married at the age of forty-three after caring for her father and aunt. She was influenced as a young woman by the example of Susie Cooper and Charlotte Rhead who had established successful careers in the pottery industry and demonstrated that it was possible to succeed in the male-dominated profession of pottery design.

Opportunities for women designers prior to and just after the Second World War were informed by the attitudes and practices established during the preceding hundred years. Some worked in a conventional way as designers of surface decoration, but the introduction of new ideas from the Studio Pottery Movement and the influence of Scandinavian design enabled others to design both shape and decoration.

Without exception, the women designers at Royal Doulton adopted less orthodox roles than their nineteenth-century predecessors. In fact, the company celebrated these new roles by showing photographs of Vera Huggins, Jean Cowper and Agnete Hoy at the potter's wheel. These images were clearly legitimised by the practice of the studio potters which sanctioned the designer's involvement in all stages of production in much the same way as the Arts and Crafts Movement had done between 1890 and 1914. The photographs also functioned as powerful challenges to the traditional gender division in the pottery industry. By mixing clay, making glazes, tending kilns, as well as throwing and decorating, women such as Katherine Pleydell-Bouverie demonstrated the ideological nature of the conventions that had confined women designers to the separate sphere of decoration.

At the same time the Scandinavian example illustrated that craft and industrial methods of production were not mutually exclusive, and could be combined in an innovative way in the pottery industry. In the art studios of Bullers and Royal Doulton the rigid separation of pottery shape and decoration design was transformed; especially since fashionable taste, influenced by Oriental ceramics, demanded more simplicity with subtle glaze effects and minimal surface decoration.

Within the streamlined post-war pottery industry, women designers had their place, although, with the exception of Susie Cooper, it was one still shaped by traditional notions of feminine artistic skills. This stereotype, based on the proposition that biology made women intrinsically suited to decoration, detailed work and certain types of subject matter such as flowers, proved immensely resilient. Although maintaining the stereotype, the post of designer in a pottery offered women such as Jessie Tait an alternative to domestic roles.

Since then numerous women have worked both inside and outside the patriarchal structure of the pottery industry. Design studios in the pottery factories are filled with young women graduates designing pottery decoration, while outside the industry some women produce their own wares in small studios inspired by the example of the 1930s studio potters. At the other end of the spectrum, women such as Alison Britton undermine the hierarchical and gender-specific divisions in the arts by producing work which can be labelled neither craft (women's) nor art (men's).

Notes

1. National Society of Pottery Workers, *Reconstruction in the Pottery Industry*, Manchester, Co-operative Printing Society, 1945, foreword.

2. Although it was moved to Berlin by the architect Mies Van der Rohe, it was subsequently closed permanently in July 1933.

3. See G. Naylor, *The Bauhaus Reassessed*, Herbert Press, 1985.

4. Fully quoted in Naylor, op. cit., p. 76.

5. ibid., p. 72.

6. Grete and Harold Marks in conversation with the author, February 1987.

7. K. H. Bröhan, *Sammlung Bröhan. Kunst der 20er und 30er Jahre: Gemalde, Skulpturen, Kunsthandwerk, Industrie Design*, vol. III, Berlin, 1985.

8. Grete and Harold Marks in conversation with the author, February 1987.

9. ibid.

10. ibid.

11. 'Modern British Manufacturers. The Royal Doulton Pottery', *The Studio*, vol. 97, April 1929, pp. 263–8.

12. ibid.

13. 'Throwing a Vase', *Ceramics in Art and Industry*, no. 2, 1939, p. 12.
14. Joan Cowper in conversation with author, 5 February 1988.
15. ibid. See D. Billington, *The Art of the Potter*, Oxford University Press, 1937.
16. *The Studio*, vol. 92, August 1926, p. 90.
17. 'Miss Sybil Finnemore's Pottery', *The Studio*, vol. 95, January 1928, p. 33.
18. See short article on Joan Cowper in *Ceramics in Art and Industry*, no. 2, 1939, pp. 12–13.
19. Agnete Hoy in conversation with author, April and July 1987.
20. For further information see P. Atterbury, 'Art Among the Insulators', in *Antique Collector*, February 1977, pp. 32–5; also 'An Adventure in Porcelain', in *Pottery and Glass Record*, August 1947, pp. 29–31.
21. Agnete Hoy in conversation with author, April and July 1987.
22. A. Hoy, 'Art Among the Insulators', *Ceramic Review*, no. 69, May/June 1981, p. 10.
23. *Pottery and Glass Record*, August 1947, p. 31.
24. E. J. Biggs, 'Art and Mass Production in Sweden', *The Studio*, vol. 106, November 1933, pp. 305–8; and 'Visit to the Scandinavian Potteries', *The Pottery Gazette and Glass Trade Review*, 1 November 1935, pp. 1402–3.
25. W. B. Honey, *The Art of the Potter*, 1949, quoted by A. Hoy in op. cit. p. 11.
26. Atterbury, op. cit, p. 32.
27. 'New Stoneware from Lambeth', *The Royal Doulton Magazine*, no. 4, June 1953, p. 17.
28. See brochure edited by P. & J. Wain, *Peggy Davies*, Royal Doulton Tableware and Wain Antiques, 1983.
29. Peggy Davies in conversation with author, March 1988.
30. ibid.
31. F. Burchill and R. Ross, *A History of the Potter's Union*, Stoke-on-Trent: Ceramic and Allied Trades Union, 1977, pp. 203, 213.
32. *Reconstruction in the Pottery Industry*, 1945.
33. Board of Trade Working Party Report on the Pottery Industry, 1946, HMSO.
34. 'Susie Cooper OBE, RDI', leaflet written by Kathy Niblett to accompany the 80th Birthday Tribute to Susie Cooper at City of Stoke-on-Trent Museum, 29 October 1982.

35. A. Eatwell, *Susie Cooper Productions*, Victoria and Albert Museum, 1987, p. 72.

36. Susie Cooper in conversation with author, April 1982.

37. op. cit., pp. 15–17.

38. Jessie Tait in conversation with author, May 1985 and September 1986.

39. Sales leaflet, Festival pattern for Fashion range.

40. Sales leaflet, Pierrot pattern for Fashion range.

41. Sales leaflet, 'Stylecraft Contempary Tableware'.

42. A. Eatwell, 'Streamlined Ceramics', *The Antique Dealer and Collectors' Guide*, May 1986, pp. 58–61.

Conclusion

■

Women Pottery Designers, Femininity and Feminism

Design, work organisation and the activities of women were inextricably linked in the British pottery industry between 1870 and 1955. Women designers played an important part in the development of pottery design, while skilled and unskilled women made a major contribution to the manufacture of pottery in a variety of roles. Most confronted the patriarchal conventions of British industry and society in their everyday lives as they attempted to obtain better pay, conditions of service, education and jobs. Some women were able to effect real change, while others remained trapped in poorly paid, physically demanding and mundane work. Within a framework of changing social conventions, trade union practice, and political and economic uncertainty, opportunities widened for specific groups of women pottery workers including designers, paintresses and semi-skilled machine operators.

Throughout this analysis of the roles of women pottery designers there have been several recurring themes: first, the precise historical shape of the sexual division of labour in the pottery industry and the design process; second, the issue of femininity and the separate sphere which shaped women's roles, defined the sort of designs they could make, the type of subject matter they used and the market at which their designs were aimed; and finally the important issue of attribution – what they designed and who signed it.

Underpinning work organisation in the pottery industry was gender. Women's jobs were defined by one of the cornerstones of patriarchy: the sexual division of labour. Although women worked at all stages of the manufacturing process, their access to the best-paid skilled jobs was dependent on an *ideological* interpretation of

160

gender difference masquerading as *natural*. Men and women, it was widely believed, had biologically-determined skills. Not surprisingly, men's 'biological inheritance' gave them access to the most prestigious work both in the industry at large and in pottery design in particular. Men threw the pots and designed the shapes; the former was at the apex of the craft skill hierarchy and the latter was considered one of the crucial factors for the economic viability of a pottery. With effective trade union organisation, men maintained a stranglehold on the best jobs until, in the latter half of the nineteenth century, manufacturers' quest for increased efficiency and profits undermined the role of the crafts*man* through the introduction of machinery.

In patriarchal theory, women's 'biological inheritance' equipped them for skilled work which was separate and distinct from men's; that which utilised apparently 'intrinsic' skills such as those of the decorating shops. In practice most jobs for women were unskilled until the end of the nineteenth century and beginning of the twentieth, when they took skilled or semi-skilled jobs from men; first as operators of the new machines and second as 'substitutes' for men during the First World War. The disparity between the patriarchal model of the weaker sex in a separate sphere and capitalist demands for cheap female labour in industries such as pottery was never seriously called into question. Well into the twentieth century, women worked wherever they were required, undertaking heavy, physical jobs such as carrying clay and pots. Because these were considered inappropriate roles within patriarchy they faced middle-class disapproval as well as antagonism from men of their own class who feared for their jobs.

In only one sector of work in the pottery industry did the separate sphere and the idea that women had biologically determined skills allow them access to good jobs. This was in decorating, which offered women decent pay, relatively clean work conditions and the satisfaction of skilled work. As 'women's work', including skills thought to be inherently female, competition with men was avoided and a space was found for skilled women. Dominance in the decorating shops established a precedent for women's intervention in pottery design, although the separation of skilled men's work in the potting shops from skilled women's work in the decorating shops, meant that opportunities for women were mainly as surface pattern designers.

Patriarchal ideology identified women with certain types of art –

161

the lesser or applied arts – and specific artistic abilities – subtlety in the use of colour, a fascination for complex patterns and a love of subject matter drawn from nature or domestic life such as flowers, children and home. Within this framework, women could work with some success as designers.

As pottery designers, women produced diverse designs that were shaped by changing social, economic and cultural factors. Unifying their lives and their opportunities in the industry was their gender, although as we have seen, the effectiveness of patriarchy to fix women in particular types of design work was greater in the nine-teenth than in the twentieth century. For Hannah Barlow, designing surface pattern at Doulton's Lambeth art pottery offered her a way out of the impasse which faced a substantial number of middle-class women who had to earn a living. China painting and design pro-vided a socially acceptable method of earning money: it took place outside the main manufacturing process and separated women from the corrupting influence of men. Although the precedent for women's involvement in this type of design was set in the eighteenth century, it was the success of the Lambeth venture which firmly established this as a suitable occupation for women.

By the early decades of the twentieth century, the basic tenets of Victorian patriarchy were being challenged. In society at large, women demanded more control over their lives and greater job opportunities. Encouraged by their contribution to the war effort and political changes after 1918, women began to work in ways quite alien to their nineteenth-century precursors. Middle-class women in particular attended art school, studied in Paris and planned their lives around careers rather than men. Susie Cooper, Charlotte Rhead and Millie Taplin are all evidence of this. In Stoke-on-Trent, the Potteries art schools offered a viable career route to working-class as well as middle-class women, and the close relation-ship of these to the local pottery industry and the improved job prospects which such training brought, encouraged numerous women.

New theories of design, some informed by the socialist beliefs of Morris and his circle, criticised labour divisions between skilled and unskilled workers, and designer and executant. An insistence on the designers' involvement in all stages of production and the import-ance of unity in form and decoration applied to women as well as to men, and as a result there existed the theoretical justification for women's participation in the design of pottery shape and decoration within the Arts and Crafts, Art Pottery and Studio Pottery Movements. Women such as Louise Powell and Truda Adams responded positively to this. At the same time the vogue for hand-painted wares between 1900 and 1940 offered enhanced opportunities for women within the ideologically sanctioned arena of surface pattern design: Freda Beardmore and Star Wedgwood came to prominence as a result of these changes in taste.

The majority of women designers who have been discussed in this book signed their pottery. Without this physical record of their work, knowledge of their existence would be more difficult. Attribution of designs to specific women demonstrates their undeniable role in the development of different ranges of products. For some such as Susie Cooper, Ruth Bare, Hannah Barlow and Agnete Hoy their backstamp or signature has guaranteed a place in one type of history or another; for others such as Millie Taplin and Star Wedgwood a place has yet to be achieved. For Louise Powell who worked alongside her husband and jointly signed wares, her own independent role needs to be asserted. However unsatisfactory it may be to produce a history which dwells on lists of names, it is a useful exercise given that so few of these women pottery designers are widely known. At the same time, we need to keep in mind that these designs were produced as art-wares, special designer-products or high quality design-conscious ranges by relatively prestigious companies such as Wedgwood and Doulton, and small, well-respected manufacturers such as A. E. Gray. Almost all of these companies were well known for design and were well documented in the trade press. Clearly then, this is a partial history which examines only the designers of self-consciously designed and artistic wares.

In conclusion, women such as Hannah Barlow and Susie Cooper deserve in-depth investigation by design historians, in addition to the attention that they have already received from pottery collectors and museum curators, because they demonstrate that women have worked in specific aspects of design as a result of *ideology*, not *biology*. For the feminist, these women potters are yet another example of how women have struggled and how some have succeeded in finding an outlet for their creative talents in a society which undermined them. The work which they produced between 1870 and 1955 stands as an answer to those who still argue that women's role in design has been negligible.

To date, an uncritical acceptance of patriarchal values and a failure to address the key issues has led some design historians largely to ignore the contribution of women to pottery design. Both historically and contemporarily women's relationship to design has not been properly considered. Instead, design historians have distorted their discipline by celebrating male designers, male clients and male values.

Obviously it is important to find a place in history for a major designer such as Susie Cooper, but what value is a history that denies the roles of all those other women? Extraordinary as she may have been (as a designer of shape and decoration and as a manufacturer), her role was clearly dependent on the example of women pottery workers and designers prior to the 1930s, and her commercial success was contingent on numerous factors beyond her direct control.

Today, design history is taught as part of practical art and design courses which recruit large numbers of women students. But as a discipline it does little for these women; in fact, it legitimises and maintains the patriarchal prejudices of design theory and practice. It allows students and tutors to conflate women with nature to produce a biologically-determined notion of femininity. This still locks women into a separate sphere of design which accords with a narrow definition of gender. Women students are still more likely to choose textiles and fashion rather than industrial design and architecture. They and their designs are presented as being intuitive, delicate and subtle; merely a result of their femininity and their physical dexterity, rather than as a consequence of lively and intelligent minds. Analysed within a patriarchal framework, they and their designs come a poor second to men.

For those who are interested in women's past and present interventions in design, feminism provides a critical tool for exposing the patriarchal basis of the discipline. It reveals the ideological framework within which terms such as 'feminine', 'delicate' and 'decorative' are constructed. In particular, this account of women designers in the British pottery industry between 1870 and 1955 illustrates the changing shape of these patriarchal values. It highlights their power to restrict women's opportunities, but at the same time it shows that they can be challenged and transformed. The case studies of the careers of Clarice Cliff, Charlotte Rhead and Susie Cooper are clear indicators of this. Although a stereotypical notion of women's artistic abilities dominated the pottery industry, we have seen how some women designers worked in ways which were quite different from their predecessors. They had more control over their career opportunities, they were employed in innovative and creative roles, they managed design studios and some ran their own businesses. They cut across the dominant gender divide in design by producing both pottery shape and decoration. They are an effective demonstration that patriarchy is not a fixed universal concept with total power over our lives, but something that we can confront and change both as designers and as historians.

Select Bibliography

Unless stated otherwise, books listed are published in London.

Atterbury, P. and Irvine, L., *The Doulton Story*, Stoke-on-Trent: Royal Doulton Tableware, 1979.

Attfield, J. and Kirkham, P., *A View From the Interior. Feminism, Women and Design*, The Women's Press, 1989.

Batkin, M., *Wedgwood Ceramics 1846–1959*, Richard Dennis, 1982.

Billington, D. M., *The Art of The Potter*, Oxford University, 1937.

Blacker, J. F., *The ABC of English Salt-glaze Stoneware from Dwight to Doulton*, Stanley Paul & Co, 1922.

Board of Trade, *Report of the Committee Appointed by the Board of Trade under the Chairmanship of Lord Gorell on the Production and Exhibition of Articles of Good Design and Everyday Use*, HMSO, 1932.

Board of Trade Working Party Report, *Pottery*, 1946, HMSO.

Boone, G., *The Women's Trade Union Leagues in Great Britain and the United States of America*, New York: AMS Press, 1968.

Bumpus, B., *Charlotte Rhead. Potter & Designer*, Kevin Francis Publishing, 1987.

Burchill, F. and Ross, R., *A History of the Potters' Union*, Stoke-on-Trent: Ceramic and Allied Trades Union, 1977.

Callen, A., *Angel in the Studio. Women in the Arts and Crafts Movement 1870–1914*, Astragal, 1979.

Catalogue of an Exhibition of Doulton Stoneware and Terracotta, 1870–1925, Richard Dennis, 1971.

Catalogue of an Exhibition on Doulton Pottery From the Lambeth & Burslem Studios, 1873–1939, The Fine Art Society, 1975.

166

Collins, J., *The Omega Workshops*, Secker & Warburg, 1983.

Council for Art and Industry, *Report on Design and the Designer in Industry*, HMSO, 1937.

Council for Art and Industry, *Report on Design in the Pottery Industry*, HMSO, 1937.

Coysh, A. W., *British Art Pottery*, David & Charles, 1976.

Crafts Council, *Omega*, exhibition catalogue, 1984.

Drake, B., *Women in Trade Unions*, Virago, 1984.

Eatwell, A., *Susie Cooper Productions*, Victoria and Albert Museum, 1987.

Elinor, G. et al. (eds) *Women and Craft*, Virago, 1987.

Eyles, D., *The Doulton Lambeth Wares*, Hutchinson, 1975.

Eyles, D., *The Doulton Burslem Wares*, Barrie & Jenkins, 1980.

Fontaines, U. des, *Wedgwood Fairyland Lustre*, Sotheby Parke Bernet, 1975.

Forsyth, G. M., *The Art and Craft of the Potter*, Chapman and Hall, 1934.

Forsyth, G. M., *20th Century Ceramics*, The Studio, 1936.

Gosse, E., *Sir Henry Doulton. The Man of Business as a Man of Imagination*, Hutchinson, 1970.

Griffin, L., Meisel, L. K. and S. P., *Clarice Cliff. The Bizarre Affair*, New York: Abrams, 1988.

Haggar, R., *A Century of Art Education in the Potteries*, pamphlet, Stoke-on-Trent, 1953.

Haggar, R. G., Mountford, A. R. and Thomas, J., 'The Staffordshire Pottery Industry', in *The Victoria History of the County of Stafford*, 2 volumes ed by M. W. Greenslade and J. G. Jenkins, University of London, Institute of Historical Research, 1967.

Hannah, F., *Ceramics*, Bell & Hyman, 1986.

Haslam, M., *English Art Pottery, 1865–1915*, Antique Collectors' Club, 1975.

Hawkins, J., *The Poole Pottery*, Barrie & Jenkins, 1980.

Hewitt, M., *Wives and Mothers in Victorian Industry: A Study of the effects of employment of married women in Victorian Industry*, Rockliff, 1958.

Lane, P., *Studio Ceramics*, Collins, 1983.

Lomax, A., *Royal Lancastrian Pottery 1900–1938*, Brighton: Lomax, 1957.

Machin, D. J. and Smyth, R. L., *The Changing Structure of the*

British Pottery Industry 1935–1968, Department of
Economics, University of Keele, 1969.

McCarthy, F., *A History of British Design, 1830–1970*, Allen &
Unwin, 1979.

Meteyard, E., *The Life of Josiah Wedgwood*, 2 vols, Hurst &
Blackett, 1865–6.

Niblett, K. (ed.), *Wedgwood of Etruria & Barlaston*, exhibition
catalogue, City Museum and Art Gallery, Stoke-on-Trent, 1980.

Niblett, K., *Hand-painted Gray's Pottery*, exhibition catalogue,
City Museum and Art Gallery, Stoke-on-Trent, 1982.

Pankhurst, R., *Sylvia Pankhurst. Artist and Crusader*, Paddington
Press, 1979.

Parker, R. and Pollock, G., *Old Mistresses: Women, Art and
Ideology*, Routledge & Kegan Paul, 1981.

Rhead, G. W. and Rhead, F. R., *Staffordshire Pots and Potters*,
E. R. Publishing, 1977.

Rose, P., *Hannah Barlow, A Pioneer Doulton Artist*, Richard
Dennis, 1985.

Royal Commission on Labour, *The Employment of Women.
Conditions of Work in Various Industries in England, Wales,
Scotland and Ireland*, HMSO, 1893.

Sarsby, J., *Missuses & Mouldrunners. An Oral History of Women
Pottery Workers at Work and at Home*, Open University Press,
1988.

Shaw, C., *When I Was A Child. By an Old Potter*, David and
Charles Reprint, 1969.

Thomas, J. H., *The Rise of the Staffordshire Potteries*, Adams &
Dart, 1971.

Warburton, W. H., *The History of Trade Union Organisation in
the North Staffordshire Potteries*, Allen & Unwin, 1939.

War Cabinet Committee, *Report on Women in Industry*, HMSO,
1919.

Watkins, C., Harvey, W. and Senft, R., *Shelley Potteries. The
History and Production of a Staffordshire Family of Potters*,
Barrie & Jenkins, 1980.

Weatherill, L., *The Pottery Trade and North Staffordshire,
1660–1760*, Manchester University Press, 1971.

Wentworth-Shields, P., and Johnson, K., *Clarice Cliff*, L'Odeon,
1976.

Woodhouse, A., *Elegance and Utility, 1924–1978. The Work of
Susie Cooper R.D.I.*, Arthur Sanderson & Sons, 1978.

Glossary

Aerographing   Colour is applied using a spraygun or airbrush.

Alpine Pink   A tinted bone china from Wedgwood.

Argenta   Majolica tableware – white earthenware body and glaze with relief decoration and painting with majolica colours.

Ash glaze   Ashes from plant materials such as wood contain useful glaze ingredients and are combined with other materials to make very fluid glazes.

Aventurine   Crystalline glaze. Usually brightly coloured crystals can be seen in the glaze.

Banding   Concentric bands of colour are applied evenly by centring the pot on the wheel, holding the brush still, and allowing the pot to rotate past it.

Bas-relief   The decoration protrudes only very slightly from the surface.

Biscuit or bisque   Unglazed ware that has been fired once so that it is still porous. This makes the ware less fragile so that glaze may be applied more easily.

Blank ware   Biscuit ware which is to be decorated.

Bleu soufflé   Transfer-printed ware with a special underglaze blue decoration which blurs during firing.

Body   Any clay or mixture of clays used to make a pot. Few clays are used just as they are found; most bodies are blends of several clays to give certain characteristics.

Bone china   A European attempt at formulating true oriental porcelain. The recipe includes a high proportion of animal bone ash. This gives high translucency, but is not easy to throw, so is usually moulded.

Boss   Moulded clay dot added to the surface.

Bottle kiln   Huge coal-fired, bottle-shaped industrial kiln used extensively in the Potteries until the 1950s.

Carrara porcelain   A fine white stoneware resembling marble, often with a matt translucent glaze.

Casting   A hollow plaster mould is filled with slip. The porous plaster draws out water from the slip. The excess slip is poured off, leaving a shell of clay stuck to the plaster.

Celadon   A semi translucent, jade-like glaze used mainly on porcelain.

Ceramic   A term used to denote anything made permanent by heat. When clay is heated the particles are converted to a glassy state, causing sintering or fusing.

China   In Britain this usually refers to bone china, but can refer to any vitreous domestic whiteware. The official definition equates it with porcelain.

Chinoiserie   The imitation of Chinese motifs.

Chun   A milky-blue opalescent glaze with bubbles suspended in the glaze.

Cobalt   A metal oxide used to create blues. It is very stable even at high temperatures, and is the characteristic blue of most blue and white china.

Crackle   A glaze with intentional decorative cracks in it.

Diaper pattern   Diamond pattern.

Dipping   Method of applying glaze by submersing the pot in a bucket of liquid glaze for a few seconds. The porous pot draws out the water, leaving the powdered glaze evenly attached to the surface.

Earthenware   Pottery made of sedimentary clays (clays which have been moved by weathering, usually picking up impurities on the way). Earthenware clay usually has a high proportion of iron in it, giving a red or buff colour. It will not fire to a high temperature, and is usually porous.

Enamel   Colours applied to pots already glazed. They are then fired a third time, at a lower temperature, just enough to melt the surface of the glaze and make the enamels adhere. This method provides a broader range of colours, and can be crisper and cleaner, but they will eventually wear off.

Engraving   Designs are gouged out of plastic clay rather than scratched, using a wooden, bamboo or metal tool. The harder the clay the sharper the line.

Faience Once-fired, tin-glazed decorated ware from eighteenth-century France. Later used to mean any glazed earthenware.

Fettling Trimming and smoothing of a green pot, especially smoothing the hard edges left by moulds.

Firing Heating clay causes it to become permanent. The particles fuse. A pot can be once-fired (raw clay is coated with glaze and then the whole is fired) or it can be biscuit-fired and then glost-fired. A third, low temperature enamel or lustre firing can also be made.

Flambé A glaze streaked with copper reds and purples (flame-like), formed in a reduction atmosphere.

Flat ware Industrial name for plates, saucers, etc. These need special care in drying.

Gilding Liquid gold or other metals are melted into the fired glaze in a third, low-temperature firing.

Glaze A decorative glass coating fused on to a pot to ensure the pot is watertight and easy to clean. Usually applied as a powder suspended in water.

Glost firing The second firing, in which the glaze is fused to the body of the pot.

Granite ware A hard white body resembling porcelain but not translucent.

Green ware Unfired pottery. While a pot is still green it is very fragile and can be reclaimed as clay by adding water.

Groundlaying Applying an even layer of colour by dusting powdered pigment on to a layer of tacky oil previously applied to the pot.

Hard paste 'True' high-firing European porcelain made of china clay and china stone or feldspar. It is difficult to throw so is more usually moulded.

Hare's fur glaze Range of mottled or streaked dark brown glazes.

Hollow ware Any pot enclosing a space, e.g. cup, vase. In industry these require more complex moulds than flat ware.

Impasto Thickly painted in coloured slips, usually on raw clay, making a pattern in slight relief.

Incising Patterns scratched into soft clay before firing.

In-glaze Pigments are applied to the raw glaze and then fired together.

Intaglio Design carved into raw clay, see 'engraving'.

Ironstone A hard iron ore which makes a dark, vitrified body.

Jasperware   Fine-grained, unglazed, vitreous stoneware, often coloured, developed by Wedgwood.

Jigger and jolley   Machinery used to 'throw' a lump of clay in a mould using a template.

Lapis ware   Green, misty glaze with trapped bubbles.

Lead glaze   Lead melts at a low temperature so is very useful for earthenware glazes and was widely used. Lead oxide in its raw state is very poisonous, and is permitted in glazes today only if it is first 'fritted', bonded chemically with silica, and then only on decorative wares, not on food utensils.

Lithographic transfer   A design is etched on to the surface of stone or aluminium with the use of acid. For every colour used in the design a different stone is required. This is then printed on to specially prepared paper called duplex, a thin printing tissue with a detachable backing to enable easy positioning on the ware. The ware has to be coated in size and then the lithograph applied. When dry, the tissue is sponged away and the design remains. During firing, the heat softens the glaze on the ware, and allows the colour to soak in and become permanent.

Lustre   A thin metallic coating on glaze. Metallic salts are fired on to an already fired glaze until the glaze softens and the metal adheres to the surface of the glaze.

Maiolica   Italian decoration on earthenware. An opaque white glaze was applied, to which colouring oxides could be added.

Majolica   A British development from Italian Renaissance maiolica; glazed earthenware modelled with relief decoration and painted in brightly coloured glazes developed by Arnoux at Minton.

Marqueterie   A mosaic body of coloured clays sliced thinly built up in moulds to make very light vases, dishes and teasets.

Modelling   The building up of a form from small lumps of clay.

Moulding   Plaster moulds are widely used industrially as they give a consistent quality and speed up production. They can be used with slip as casting moulds, with sheets of clay as press moulds, or with a jigger and jolley.

Neo-classicism   Restrained, formal style based on themes and motifs from ancient Greek and Roman art.

Oilspot   An iridescent, lustrous glaze effect, usually caused by colouring oxide precipitating out on to the surface of the glaze.

On-glaze   Enamel colour applied to an already glazed and fired pot, usually copied from detailed pattern books.

Oxides Powdered metal oxides are the basic colouring pigments for bodies, slip and glazes.

Parian porcelain A matt, white porcelain body, slightly translucent, often smear-glazed, resembling marble or ivory, used for statuary.

Pâte-sur-pâte A method of decorating one body by painting on to it with layers of slip of a different tint. Light and shade could be built up in the decoration by this method.

Placer One who sets the pots in the kiln. Positioning of pots in the kiln is crucial to the evenness of firing and is a skilled job.

Porcelain Any fine, white primary clay (one which has not been moved from its original position) which will fire to vitrification at a high temperature.

Potting shop Area where throwing is done.

Pressing A sheet of clay is pressed into a plaster mould, rather than slip.

Pug mill Machine to mix clay, expel air and consolidate clays, giving an even working consistency.

Reduction Colour changes brought about by starving the glaze of oxygen during firing, e.g. copper blues and greens change to reds in a reducing atmosphere.

Relief Any form of decoration where clay stands out from the surface of the pot.

Rococo Style characterised by delicate, curving asymmetrical motifs of rock, shell, floral and leaf forms from eighteenth-century France.

Saggar A box in which pottery is fired to protect the ware from flames, falling grit and ash.

Salt glaze When common salt is added to the kiln at 1200°C poisonous chlorine gas is given off and the sodium reacts with the clay to form droplets of glaze, giving an orange peel effect which is very strong.

Sang de boeuf A deep copper red glaze formed in a reducing atmosphere.

Sgraffito A coating of slip or glaze is applied to a pot and decoration is scratched through the coating to reveal the original, contrasting clay underneath.

Silicon ware A smooth, light reddish-brown or occasionally off-white stoneware with fine texture and smear glaze.

Slip A smooth mixture of clay and water of a creamy consistency, used for casting or for decoration.

Slip trailing Slip is applied as decoration using a nozzle to trail across the surface, similar to cake icing, but runnier.

Slip-house Place where slip casting was done.

Soft paste Low firing European experiments to produce an equivalent of oriental porcelain – bone china is the most successful of these.

Sponging The smoothing of sharp or rough edges, especially on moulded ware.

Sprigging Low relief clay decoration added to the surface of ware, often made in a mould and then stuck on.

Stain A prepared pigment for colouring bodies, slips or glazes.

Stoneware Clay bodies fired to above 1250°C to vitrification. They usually have some impurities making them light buff, cream or grey.

Studio potter An artist–craftsperson who takes part in all ceramic processes, not just one as in industrial factories.

Terracotta Unglazed earthenware fired at low temperature.

Throwing Using a wheel to help produce virtually symmetrical hollow forms.

Towing The industrial term for smoothing plate rims.

Tube-lining Thin clay coils or stiff slip is poured or trailed on to the surface, leaving raised fine tubes. Used to prevent the different coloured slips or glazes from running into each other.

Tunnel kiln A continuous firing process in which ware is wheeled slowly through a tunnel. As one trolley comes out at one end, another is going in at the other.

Turning The trimming of a thrown pot on a wheel, or forming of a plaster blank on a lathe, from which a mould will be made.

Under-glaze Colouring pigments applied to raw or biscuited clay, which are then covered with a glaze and fired.

Vitreous pigments Colours which will not burn out during high firings. Many oxides become unstable at high temperatures and disappear.

Vitrified Heated to the point of fusion. A clay body will be porous unless it is fired high enough for the glassy compounds to melt and fuse together. Earthenware clay is rarely vitrified, needing a glaze to make it waterproof; stoneware and porcelain are usually vitrified, and glaze is added more for decoration.

Wedging The process of mixing clays to form a body, to expel air and to even out the consistency of the clay, making it easier to work with and less prone to cracking during firing.

Index

175

Index

Index

Sickert, Walter 77, 81
signed work 45, 64, 65, 163
silicon ware 59, 60
Simmance, Eliza 6, 57, 60
Simpson, Mary 101
Skellern, Victor 39n, 100, 101, 104–7, 129, 148
Slade School of Art 80
slip 85, 109, 147
slip-houses 22, 23
slip-trailing 17, 38n, 139, 147
slipware 141
Smallfield, Katie Blake 59
Smiles, Samuel 45
Smith, Rachel 87
Society of Arts 55
Society of Industrial Artists (SIA) 20, 99, 104, 108, 119, 121, 126
Society of Scribes and Illuminators 77
Solon, Louis 39n, 101, 108
Somerset House 46, 47
South Kensington Museum 50, 54, 72
Sparkes, Catherine 61
Sparkes, John 53, 54, 55, 57, 59–62
Special Rules (1894) 27
specialisation, and increased levels of demand 16
'Spirals' (Cooper) 118, 151
sponging 23
sprigging 17, 38n, 60
'Spring' (Taplin) 102
stability, women's alleged lack of 29, 30
Stabler, Harold and Phoebe 86–7
Staffordshire Pots and Potters 63, 108
Staffordshire Sentinel 78
staining 83
Staite-Murray, William 141
'Stars' (Star Wedgwood) 107
steam-power 23
steel industry 34
stippling 83
Stock Market crash (1929) 83
Stoke-on-Trent 6, 13, 19, 22, 26, 35, 37, 50, 51, 55, 56, 71, 77, 87, 89, 90, 98, 112, 115, 116, 123, 124, 137, 141, 144, 153, 162
Stoke School of Art 90, 91, 100
stoneware 85, 139
  salt-glazed 6, 18, 52–5, 61, 139, 142, 143, 147
  acid-resisting 52
  Rhenish 53
  German 54
  Flemish 54
  silicon ware 59, 60
  designing in 144
'Strawberry Hill' (Taplin and Skellern) 106
'Streamline' tableware 86
streamlining 100, 153
strength, women's alleged lack of 29, 32
strikes 15, 97
Stubbs, George 19, 44, 65
Studio, The 90, 122, 139–40, 141–2, 146
Studio Pottery Movement 141, 146–7, 156, 163
'Stylecraft' (Midwinter) 154, 155
sub-employment system 23–4, 25, 28
'Summer' (Taplin) 102
'Sun-lit' (Taplin) 102
Susie Cooper Pottery, The 98, 117, 121
Sutherland, Graham 113, 114
'Sylvan' (Rhead) 110

tableware, domestic 86, 103, 104, 105, 114, 123–4, 135, 137, 145, 148
  and women designers 3, 5, 88, 98
  market 100, 120
  and Clarice Cliff 125, 126, 127
  and Jessie Tait 155
Tait, Jessie 7, 135, 150, 151, 153–7
Talbot, Sam 36
Taplin, Millicent Jane 6, 36, 79, 96, 97, 100–108, 113, 127, 128, 130, 162, 163
'Teazle' (Cooper) 151
technology, new
  and trade unions 5
  developments in 5, 16
  introduction of 15–16
  and increased profitability/production 15
  and design 21
  and craft skill hierarchy 22
  and women employees 24
Templetown, Lady Elizabeth 19, 44–5, 64–5, 66
terracotta wares 85
Tesco supermarket chain 152
textiles 3, 11n, 76, 164
Thomas, Harold 145
throwing 20, 21, 23, 24, 55, 57, 75, 84, 85, 87, 99, 136, 143, 146, 147, 154, 156, 161
Thumbelina nurseryware 82
Tibetan ware 124
Tinworth, George 39n, 53, 54, 57, 75
'Tomorrow's Classic' (Zeisal) 153
Tooth, Florence 71
Torquay School of Art 81
towing 23
trade press 12n, 98, 104, 109, 120, 122, 125, 155, 163
trade unions 160, 161
  and new technology 5
  increase in membership 14
  failure to amalgamate 15
  new combined 15, 21, 27
  craft 15, 21, 24–5
  and skilled work 23
  subscriptions 25
  and Factory Act (1891) 26
  and First World War 15, 27
  agreement with Manufacturers' Association 27–8
  and wage rates 32
  women's lack of involvement in 33, 40n
  statistics 40n, 41n
  power reduction 97
traditional processes 6
  patterns 6, 79, 124
  designs 21
training
  art school 5, 6, 19, 20, 111
  restrictions for women 22–3, 29, 30
  designing for industrial production 135
transfer-printing 16, 18, 21, 73
  and unions 27, 39n
  wages 33, 56
Tremblay 71
Trethowan, Harry 137
tube-lining 5, 17, 20, 38n, 60, 87, 109, 110, 111, 139, 154
Tuckwell, Gertrude 27, 41n
Tunstall 13, 110, 117, 123
  School of Art 89
Turin 90
'Turkey Oak' (Star Wedgwood) 108

183

Index